Tribal Identity and the Modern World

The United Nations University's Programme on Peace and Global Transformation was a major worldwide project whose purpose was to develop new insights about the interlinkages between questions of peace, conflict resolution, and the process of transformation. The research in this project, under six major themes, was coordinated by a 12-member core group in different regions of the world: East Asia, South-East Asia (including the Pacific), South Asia, the Arab region, Africa, Western Europe, Eastern Europe, North America, and Latin America. The themes covered were: Conflicts over Natural Resources; Security, Vulnerability and Violence; Human Rights and Cultural Survival in a Changing Pluralistic World; The Role of Science and Technology in Peace and Transformation; The Role of the State in Peace and Global Transformation; and Global Economic Crisis. The project also included a special project on Peace and Regional Security.

Tribal Identity and the Modern World

SURESH SHARMA

United Nations
University Press

TOKYO • NEW YORK • PARIS

Sage Publications
New Delhi/Thousand Oaks/London

First published in 1994 by

Sage Publications India Pvt Ltd
M-32 Greater Kailash Market, I
New Delhi 110 048

Sage Publications Inc
2455 Teller Road
Thousand Oaks, California 91320

and

Sage Publications Ltd
6 Bonhill Street
London EC2A 4PU

United Nations University Press

TOKYO • NEW YORK • PARIS

The United Nations University
53-70, Jingumae 5-chome
Shibuya-ku, Tokyo 150, Japan

Published by Tejeshwar Singh for Sage Publications India Pvt Ltd, phototypeset by Pagewell Photosetters, Pondicherry, and printed at Chaman Enterprises.

Library of Congress Cataloging-in-Publications Data

Sharma, Suresh, 1945–
    Tribal identity and the modern world / Suresh Sharma.
        p.   cm.
    Includes bibliographical references and index.
    1. Indigenous peoples—India. 2. India—Scheduled tribes. 3. Ethnicity—India. 4. India-Ethnic relations. I. Title.
    GN635.I4S4495   1994   305.8'00954—dc20   93–50134

ISBN: 0–8039–9155-X (US)
        81–7036–383–7 (India)

        92-808-0687-4   (United Nations University Press)

To My Father

To My Father

Contents

Contents

Preface

Words like 'tribe' and 'tribals' have come to acquire an impassioned salience in our discourse on social science and social change. Such words denote both an anthropological category in its classical sense as it has historically been in the Americas, Australia and Africa, and a metaphor for the most victimised segments of our society.

Two paradoxical facts are characteristic of the tribal situation in India. One, the absence of neat impermeable demarcations of tribal identity. Two, the significant magnitude of the tribal reality in India. Hence the provision in the Indian Constitution for the notification of certain communities as 'tribes', and the prevalence of the usage 'scheduled tribes'.

It would indeed be exceedingly difficult for anyone to state that all the varied communities listed as tribes in the schedule fully conform to the notion of a tribal community in its classical sense. Conversely, it would be as difficult for anyone to claim that all the communities which could be regarded as primarily tribal are included in the schedule of tribal communities. And yet, for all practical as also theoretical purposes, be that legislation, social or political intervention, collection of data or social theory, the 'schedule of tribes' notified by the government remains the crucial referent.

Until quite recently, the comforting certainty implicit in our political and social science discourse has been that the tribal formation represents an early form of human organisation in the universal though often complicated scheme of human evolution.

Inevitably therefore, the expectation has been that in the march of progress the tribal form would gradually weaken and give way to more advanced modern forms of social cohesion.

The sheer persistence and resilience of tribal identities in India raises certain issues of immense intellectual and social significance.

1. Does the survival and resilience of tribal cohesions signify the continuing power of an archaic social substance?
2. Should the conceptual ground upon which the prevalent categorisation and understanding of the nature of the tribal identity is predicated be re-examined?
3. What constitutes the distinctive substance in the historical texture of relationships and sensibilities, in relation to tribal identity in India?
4. What is the nature of the reassertion of tribal identity in the modern context? And what kind of possibilities does this reassertion make available for a serious reconsideration of the problem of ecology and human survival, as also the nature and role of the modern state and modern development?

Meaningful consideration of these questions requires reappraisal of the awful grim details that touch upon the past and present of the struggle for livelihood and survival of tribal cohesions in a perspective wherein the tribal reality could be grasped not merely as a complicating detail in the problematique of modern transformation. In other words, such consideration has to seek beyond the strategy for a reasonable political bargain. Such reappraisal would perhaps help clarify the cultural and institutional possibilities that could in some measure modulate the suicidal edge inherent in the modern predicament.

It is important at this point to spell out certain basic difficulties that confront any attempt to conceive and represent the tribal reality in terms that would remain almost untouched by the evolutionist premise so very basic to the idea of progress. This refers not so much to the practical and technical difficulty, enormous as it may be; but to theoretical difficulties inherent in such an enterprise.

In focusing upon the inherent theoretical difficulties, the intent is not to provide for safe ground for retreat and self-justification in the event of failure; or to suggest that an attempt so worthwhile and audacious be muted or given up. Rather, it is the clear sense that such an attempt could acquire substance only if one begins with a firm recognition of certain impediments that are basic to the discourse and method of historical representation and understanding.

The first formative difficulty concerns the fact that the 'departure' and freedom from the 'evolutionary premise' has so largely to be sought through cognitive forms whose anchor of ultimate repose lie in the idea of the museum. It is an idea conceived and elaborated as the definitive in-depth marker for the grand march of progress. To grasp something of what this fact entails, consider the paradox: even those fiercely vigilant against the taint of evolutionism and passionately committed to the truth of cultures smothered under the modern onslaught to near extinction, concede Evolution as the Fact in Nature.

The making and origins of the museum are marked by: (*a*) decimation and disappearance of diverse cultures and; (*b*) the desire to preserve surviving fragments of vanquished cultures. Notions of significance that determine placement of artifacts and cultural sensibilities in the museum reflect these seemingly contrary impulses. An awful certainty haunts even the most impassioned commitment to cultures which the museum seeks to place within the reach of modern cognition. That certainty is that such cultures are devoid of significant historical possibility in the future. And precisely for that reason, artifacts and sensibilities that sustained cultures now extinct or pushed to the brink of extinction, acquire value.

The ground from whence arises recognition of what is of value and significance is constituted by a core of definitive certainty that tends, perhaps ineluctably, to shade off into an ambiguous terrain. This core is constituted by the certainty that surviving fragments of vanquished cultures demarcate the hesitant initial steps in the grand journey of progress. And its ambiguous circumfusion is constituted by the intuition that fragments of a discarded past may yield something that still retains, or could acquire significance for the modern world. It is this intuition that has kept alive, albeit on the thin margins of modern discourse, the possibility for pre-modern cultures to be of significance beyond their ordained function as enunciators of the superseded human past. Hence the attempts in recent years from within anthropological discourse, towards an understanding that seeks in some basic sense to negate the placement of pre-modern cultures as essentially archaic stratum.

To clarify the principal difficulty that confronts attempts at elaborating placement and representation that rejects or subverts the reading of the human past as the grand highway of Evolution, consider the following propositions:

1. Theoretically, one could reject or simply be unaware of the specific social–cultural context of, say, Plato or Hegel. And yet, recognise in what survives of their thoughts significance and relevance for the modern world.

Implications

Recognition of universalist inherence that goes beyond the specificities of artifacts, institutions and events. Hence the categorical insistence that meaningful consideration of the human possibility can only proceed in reference to certain formulations, which even in moments of severe rejection, can never be really superseded.

2. In instructive contrast, recognition and understanding of cultures variously designated as primitive, folk or pre-modern proceeds entirely in terms of their specificities: artifacts, institutions, and events. Significance in reference to pre-modern facts is seen to subsist in organic fusion with the specific details within which it unfolds.

Implications

Absence of a mode of recognition and placement that would provide for universalist inherence in pre-modern facts. Hence the complete fusion of fact and value in relation to pre-modern facts.

Negation of the evolutionist premise in any substantial sense requires a sustained move towards a different kind of cognitive ground. The foremost need is to clarify certain basic considerations from which recognition of universalist inherence in pre-modern facts could proceed. Such considerations would have to be sought in terms that go beyond the notion of instrumental use value of pre-modern facts. What could such considerations be?

The cognitive salience of two large facts merits careful notice in this context.

1. The deepening awareness in recent years of the fragility of the earth's ecology and its grave implications for human survival has made possible from within modern discourse a qualitatively different kind of attention to the nature and significance of pre-modern facts. Survival of the human species as an ineliminable concern basic to the human condition, has reacquired something of its immemorial relevance.
2. The sheer resilience and magnitude of diversity in India posits a cognitive terrain for enunciating boundaries (both as geographical and cognitive demarcations) and relationships in terms that negate centre–periphery as the definitive referent. Implicit in this situation are rhythms of living and imagination that attenuate the truth of monogenic metaphors as sovereign explanatory referents.

Reading historical and contemporary evidence pertaining to the survival and resilience of tribal cohesions, like all acts of knowing and understanding, happens in intimate if not always discernible reference to categories and deep dispositions. Social analysis, even of the most profound kind, is perhaps just at a remove from ordinary perception. Its illuminating quality and incisive power derives from a reflective act of self-placement.

The first part of the study, Problem of Method, outlines the conceptual difficulties, possible self-placements and their implications, and the conceptual referents in terms of which I have attempted to indicate the texture of tribal–non-tribal interaction in India. It is intended as a statement of certain basic considerations of theoretical significance.

The second part, Pre-modern Proximity and Tribal Social Cohesions, seeks to delineate the pre-colonial pattern of inter-action worked out in the tribal regions of India. It examines the implications of the modern onslaught for the pre-colonial equations between social cohesions and political authority. The intent is to analyse the relationships between legitimate spaces of existence and redefinition, as also that between political authority, modern institutions and technology. The attempt is to formulate the prob-lematique of survival of distinct and autonomous cultural entities informed by possibilities suggested by what Gandhi perceived as the everyday rhythm of Indian civilisation.

I like to believe that the fieldwork serves to demarcate what persist as deep continuities, and also as a reference to read written records in terms of tribal perception. Fieldwork for the study, spread over three years (1983–86), was confined primarily to two tribal communities in central India. I was assisted by two sensitive researchers, Narendra and Madhu Ramnath. Narendra worked among the Madias living in the relatively untouched Abujhamad hills of Bastar in Madhya Pradesh. Abujhamad is one of the rare areas that has not been surveyed by either the Forest Department or the Department of Land Revenue. Direct intrusions of the modern world were few and fragile until barely thirty years ago. Hence the salient cognitive distance between Madia sensibility and the world outside.

Madhu Ramnath's work has been among the Durwa community of the Tulsi hills near the river Kolab in Orissa. Relatively, Durwas have been through a much longer interaction with impulses recognised as Hindu. Unlike the Madias, they rigorously refrain from killing cows and eating beef. But very like the Madias of Abujhamad, Durwas passionately cling to the immemorial rhythm of Man–Nature interaction implicit in their slopes of shifting cultivation.

The intent is to formulate a critique of what appears to be definitive to modern discourse: the instrumental mode of validation. The concern is to focus on the requirements for and possibilities of authentic survival of distinct cultural sensibilities that have somehow managed a fragile survival on the margins of the modern world. And that is sought not as an expression of belated remorse or generosity, but in the belief that their presence is an assurance of human sanity.

Acknowledgements

I am extremely grateful to the United Nations University (Tokyo) for the two year research grant which made it possible for me to begin work on this study. I owe special gratitude to Professors Rajni Kothari and Giri Deshingkar, Directors of the UNU Programme on Peace and Global Transformation, for their encouragement and understanding in an undertaking that often involved tampering with entrenched notions concerning discipline boundaries and research methods.

In my work among the Madias of Abujhamad (Bastar), I was assisted by Narendra. Even after the research grant came to an end he continued to help in my work in Abujhamad. His keen sensitivity to Madia life and love of the resilient wilderness of Abujhamad helped me to see and know much that I would have otherwise missed. It gives me great satisfaction to be able to record my appreciation and gratitude to Narendra for his help in the fieldwork. I am most thankful to Madhu Ramnath for helping me to understand something of the life rhythms of the Tulsi hills Durwas in Orissa. I am also grateful to P. Girija for her diligent work in locating research materials in the libraries of Delhi.

I owe an inexpressible debt to Sudhir and Geetanjali for almost compelling me to sit down and rewrite the manuscript I had submitted to the UNU, in the quiet and warmth of their lovely home in Surat. I feel I would never have thought through the basics of the argument of this study but for their entirely unmerited concern and encouragement. I also remember with gratitude the courtesy and consideration shown to me during my stay at Surat by the Librarian and the Director of the Centre for Social Studies, Surat.

I am grateful for stimulating and intense conversations to Vijai Pillai, Bhikhubhai Parekh, Dhirubhai Sheth and Gopal Krishna. To Ramashray Roy and B.K. Roy Burman I am most grateful for exceedingly helpful discussions. I am particularly thankful to Harsh Sethi for his quiet encouragement. Conversations with Shiv Visvanathan on the salience of modern technology helped towards clarity. To know something of the sheer intellectual energy and zest for truth of Jyotirmaya Sharma and Tridip Suhrud has been a source of joy and unfailing sustenance. Sujit Deb has been most kind and resourceful in locating books and papers. I have been fortunate in being able to use the exceptional skills of Bhuwan Chandra and Shankar for typing and retyping the manuscript. I am thankful to them for their patience and diligent labour.

To Bharat Bhavan (Bhopal) and its creators, Ashok Vajpeyi and J. Swaminathan, I owe a special debt. I am particularly grateful to Ashok Vajpeyi for helping me find my way in the MP State Records. To J. Swaminathan I owe many insights into tribal sensibility and immense gratitude for allowing me to use his magnificent painting on the cover of my book. My deep appreciation and gratitude is due to Nirmal Verma and C. Badrinath for insightful and always grand conversations.

Deepa is responsible in a quiet and invisible way for the completion of this work.

Primila Lewis has been most indulgent in coping with my delays and revisions. I am very grateful for that. I also owe profuse thanks to Ms Ritu Vajpeyi-Mohan for editing the final draft.

SURESH SHARMA

PART I

PROBLEM OF METHOD

1. CULTURAL DIVERSITY IN THE AGE OF PROGRESS

For the past 200 years, the world has been changing at a pace unthinkable at any time in previous human history. Change has been grasped, as perhaps never in the past, as the self-conscious and continual unfoldment of creative human effort. Change is seen as the quest towards an ultimate universal human destiny with Man at the centre, as the only true measure of worth. This process of change began with what is recognised as the 'industrial revolution' on the fringes of Europe in the British Isles.[1]

Braudel discerns the first glimmer of that irresistible dynamic of change associated with the 'industrial revolution' in the Mediterranean of the 'long sixteenth century' (1450–1650).[2] It demarcates the duration of decisive shifts. After nearly a millennium, the fierce nomadic warriors from the steppes and deserts deep in the hinterland of Asia virtually disappear from Europe. 'The ancient biological regime' marked by the inflexible parity between births and deaths began to loosen. Population gradually increased.[3] Europe, after the unexpected success of Christian arms against the Turks in the sea battles at Lepanto (1571), emerged with a sense of new vigour and self-confidence. It shed completely the fearful 'depression' and 'sense of inferiority' of preceding centuries.[4] Henceforth, the 'Christian Mediterranean' was to be the fount of power and civilisation. From within this new Mediterranean was set in motion an irreversible movement of Man and things that extended Mediterranean frontiers all around and across the globe.

The Mediterranean, in this context, signifies both a geographic–historic space and a metaphor for the quest of Modern Europe to measure and master what in the sixteenth century was experienced as the forbidding expanse of elements that enclosed man.[5]

The so recent emergence of the modern world and the historical progression it implies confronts us, in the words of Levi-Strauss, with the 'Neolithic Paradox'. Like a level plain between ascents, several thousand years separate the 'neolithic revolution and modern science'. The stupendous crafts of pottery, weaving, agriculture and domestication of animals that nurtured civilisations came to be firmly established during neolithic times. These 'enormous advances', Levi-Strauss is clear, could never be the result of 'fortuitous accumulation of a series of chance discoveries'. Each of these crafts 'assumes centuries of active and methodical observation, of bold hypothesis tested by means of endlessly repeated experiments'. Hypotheses, however confined their possibilities, presuppose the conscious presence of a 'long scientific tradition'. And yet, thousands of years of 'stagnation', a seemingly ascentless even flow of non-progression 'intervened' between the awesome acquisitions of neolithic times and the modern breakthrough.[6]

For Drekmeir the element of surprise and gnawing perplexity lies, as it were, in the opposite direction. During the long sixth century BC—to transpose onto the Ancient World the rubric of Braudel—Greece, Persia, India and China emerged as centres of ancient civilisation.[7] Their emergence was preceded in each instance by a long process of arduous cultural elaboration. And true, their sense of themselves as distinct entities would never have been what it came to be in the absence of these stupendous acquisitions first crafted during neolithic times. But cultural visions that nurtured the distinctive accents of these ancient civilisations, never sought validation in terms of their not inconsiderable achievements in what is seen as the realm of material culture. The near simultaneity of their emergence as distinct civilisational textures suggests perhaps the historical working out of a mode of being and becoming sharply distinct from that of the modern civilisation.[8]

The Modern Universal and the Instrumental Mode of Validation

Modern transformation, unlike pre-modern transforming impulses—Buddhism, Confucian Ethic, Christianity and Islam—assumes as its starting point, not Man, but the physical material world. This signifies a fundamental shift of attention: reshaping Man through reshaping Nature. The comforting expectation of being able to ultimately replace 'governance of Man' by the 'administration of things' is not the passing fancy of naively optimistic minds.⁹ Both the starting point and the ultimate expectation are rooted in a complex ensemble of beliefs, human dispositions and social forces which in the first instance precipitated that protean force: the industrial revolution and modern discourse.

The entirety of existence—Nature and Man—acquires significance and meaning in modern discourse as an expression of the universal project of evolution and progress. Like distinct stages of development in 'individual time'—childhood, adolescence, adulthood— the stages in 'historical time'—primitive, feudal–medieval, modern—signify the inexorable law of growth and progress. 'Backward' and 'primitive' societies are seen to mirror the dim distant past of progress and advanced societies. Hence the certainty that comprehension of the human 'past' and 'future' can proceed only on the basis of categories predicated by the matrix of progress and history. Significance in the 'past' is sought in terms of what it can yield as the 'future'.

Mircea Eliade perceives a certain metaphysical valorisation of human existence as ingrained in the metaphors of progress and history.¹⁰ The concept of progress is a definitive statement concerning the nature of the human presence and its ultimate possibility on our planet and in the universe. This statement is instinct with concerns that in the past have been comprehended as profoundly spiritual: the meaning and purpose of Man and life on earth.

Modern discourse is sustained by a deep axiomatic faith in the inherently liberating power of Man's continually enchanced ability to reshape the material world. Progress is the sovereign form of modern civilisation as also its cardinal referent for significance and validation. Unification of the world is seen as co-extensive with universalism. Modern discourse is pivoted on the certainty that Man has at last been able to shatter the cosmic fetters that had set limits, virtually inflexible, to human freedom.¹¹ Power to reshape material reality has linked the farthest corners of the earth. And that is seen to provide as never before an objective, rational basis for constituting truly universal categories for defining the total existence of Mankind: past, present and future. Hence the sense in modern discourse, of clear and qualitative distance from that ancient impulse of empires and religions in the past, to extend their sway and conquer the world.

The claim to universal validity for definitions and values of the modern industrial civilisation would have been of little consequence were it not for the stark fact that the world has, indeed, been recast in a substantial sense according to its requirements. Against its universal there is no other universal. And no particular in a situation so defined can for long hope to survive even as a particular. A particular beyond the ambit of modern validation, can at best seek toleration as archaic survival, harmless and amusing. To secure a legitimate presence in modern discourse, it is under constant compulsion to either posit another universal (an alternative), or yield to be moulded by the universal already posited. Hence the ineliminable centrality of the notion of 'centre and periphery' in the discourse of progress.

Modern universalism, in significant contrast to pre-modern faiths, seeks acceptance and validation in its demonstrable ability to transform and control the phenomenal world. It is rooted in the perception of Man as the primum mobile. The belief is that unlike all other forms of life, Man is imbued with a unique and ineradicable impulse to live in freedom. Emergence of the human species is seen as the leitmotif of evolution. Man as a self-conscious force signifies an embodied locus for what is grasped as a progressive occurrence in evolution towards ever higher and more complex forms of life. Hence the belief in the exceptional character of Man's relationship to evolution.[12]

Evolution in Nature is seen to be marked by recurrent ambivalence. It tends frequently to meander and fragment. The modern belief is that to Man—a product of evolution—it is given to vitalise and intensify what subsists in evolution as fragmented progressive occurrence. Man alone among the varied forms of life on earth can step beyond the confines of 'evolutionary time'. The capacity for self-conscious intervention vouchsafes to Man the possibility to master and completely overcome the recurrent uncertainties and the wayward somnolence of 'evolutionary time'. For Man to realise in full measure this possibility, Nature has to be reconstituted as an immense technological grid of infinite possibilities. Man's relationship to the progressive happenings in evolution thus comes to be perceived as akin to a powerful lens that intensifies blazing bright a dim diffused ray of light. The modern certainty is that Man in his quest for freedom would chisel the meandering somnolence of 'evolutionary time' into the sharp and vibrant clarity of 'historical time'. To extend Trotsky's strident metaphor: just as revolution is the locomotive of history, Man is the locomotive of evolution. Hence the ineffable resonance of Man as his own maker and the sovereign of all that is on earth and beyond.[13]

Nature in this vision is perceived as a forbidding constraint on Man's yearning to live in freedom. It is seen as an immense hostile presence to be tamed and mastered. The belief is that Nature untouched by man is devoid of worth and purpose. For it is the human gaze which imparts value and purpose to Nature.[14] It is the primal realm to be worked upon and remade by Man. In the working upon and remaking of Nature, Man affirms the power and purpose of human reason, and thereby the true worth of his being. Structures of mediation—techniques, instruments and concepts— between Man and Nature embody, as it were, the objectified measure of the extent to which Man has realised his innate quest for freedom. Technology as reified reason signifies the emergence of Man into a world growing ever more plentiful and unified. Hence a framework of validation that could be characterised as the 'instrumental mode of validation'. Its final referent flows from the assumption that the demonstrable effectiveness of mediating instrumentalities between Man and Nature furnishes the only possible criterion for validation.

Change as Discontinuity and Progress

Change has been defined both as 'organic process' and as 'progress'. But social theory in the developed world—the fount of change and definition—has been dominated by the notion of progress. Notions of change as organic process dwell in modern discourse somewhat like a residual refrain; as reiteration and restatement in modern European culture of what is deemed as worthwhile and of universal significance in Europe's past. Change, so far as it concerns the underdeveloped world beyond Europe, has come to acquire a severely constricted meaning. Social substance of the world beyond Europe is seen as demonstrably devoid of that quality which engendered dynamic self-movement in Europe. Thus, change in the world beyond Europe is seen exclusively as progress, which necessarily entails discontinuity and sharp breaks. Hence also the perception of 'tradition' and 'modernity' as dichotomous, polar categories.[15]

Critique of industrial society began quite appropriately by invoking social criteria accepted as valid in modern discourse. The definitive concern was to measure the implications of progress for different social segments of an industrial society. Social critics, some of them profoundly sensitive, were quick to point out that in the very process of producing wealth the producers themselves were reduced to utter misery. Karl Marx gave to this critique its most forceful and decisive formulation.

Marx's critique, rich in creative possibilities and inspired by a deep humanist concern for the fate of Man, remained nevertheless blindly segmented. Even such a radical critique, which sought to reach out towards conditions for entire humanity to emerge in freedom and realise in full measure all its innate possibilities, failed to truly reflect in its conception the condition of mankind outside the privileged confines of European civilisation. Social and human justice for the world beyond Europe was of little immediate relevance. For a social substance incapable of self-transformation had first to be restructured in accordance with the requirements of progress. Expectations of justice in the midst of social facts so consistently impervious to the dynamic stimulus of progress could have no historical significance. Life situations structured by a social substance whose very existence and vitality is predicated upon an impermeable distance from the dynamic flux of History, are perceived to negate, as it were, the unique stature and protean possibilities vouchsafed to Man. The plaintive cry for justice by those vanquished or about to be vanquished by the relentless logic of progress, awful and tragic as it was, remained nevertheless devoid of historical reason. The process of incorporating a world powerless on its own of historical progression into the dynamic realm of progress and history had unfortunately to be brutal and violent. Marx felt profoundly sad that it had to be so. But the inexorable logic of progress was seen to offer no choice. Hence the characterisation of British rule in India as the 'unconscious tool of history'.[16]

The shift in attention—so far as it concerns the immobile world of non-progression—from 'freedom' to 'progress', signifies a definitional shift of cardinal significance. The prime concern is not with freedom but with consolidating the resource for sustaining continual progress. Appropriation of surplus—its magnitude and complex forms—has been seen to constitute the primal hub around which historical progression unfolds.[17] It is the referent of dialectical possibilities in relation to which the human subject may extend and enrich the progressive reach of the historical process: within stern limits (as stages of development), and infinite possibilities (as revolution and movement towards perfection).

Just as heresy seeks to recover and affirm the original ground of belief and ultimate hope, scientific social critique seeks to unshackle the rationale inherent in the protean origins of progress. Theological heresy and scientific social critique alike arise from a deeper abiding concern with first principles, the formative ground of faith and hope. Both seek to clarify the truth and reality of their vision in a fierce uncompromising spirit quite above the lure of petty temptations. Precisely as heresy of the grim puritanical kind aspired to bring about the dissolution of the established church— the first to embody the original Christian promise—as a necessary step towards fulfilment of the original promise; Marx's scientific critique aspired to bring about the dissolution of capitalism so as to unfetter and accelerate the grand mechanism of progress, which had been first harnessed and embodied as capitalism.

Alikeness in the cognitive morphology of heresy and modern radical critique merits careful consideration. First, a clarification. Apperception in modern discourse is accented squarely in terms of discontinuity and definitive leap. This alikeness does not negate the reality of sharp break and discontinuity that the working-out of the idea of progress has entailed. It is significant in that it seeks to clarify the meaning and specific forms of historical reason, or what could be characterised as the telos latent in History. Heresy and scientific social critique in their impassioned insistence on laying bare the telos which a contaminated praxis tends almost always to diffuse and veil indicate as it were the lines of cognitive closure beyond which thought and thinking cease to be legitimate.[18]

Acquisition of Things as the Quest for Freedom

The definitional shift from 'freedom' to 'progress' is not an instance of an intellectual lapse, induced by inadequate and flawed information concerning the world of 'non-progression' beyond Europe.

Rather, it consolidates what inheres as a prime impulse within the modern cognitive mode. Scientific social critique imparted to this shift an all the more severe accent. And this shift of referents—from freedom to progress— has come to be decisive in orienting the structure of attention in modern cognition.

Concern for justice is seen to acquire scientific relevance and reality only with the advance of progress. The endeavour has been—as indeed it had to be given the modern mode of validation— to pivot that abiding human expectation for justice as the prime function of progress. The modern faith has been that to our age of progress is given the singular privilege of pursuing acquisition of things as a quest for freedom. It arises in the certainty that the grand mechanism of progress could only work out its ultimate possibility in continual change towards perfection if it were grounded in social relations of equity and justice. Should that grand mechanism continue unimpeded to sharpen and enchance its awesome reach in flagrant disregard of equity and justice, the epistemic space for moral concern in the humanist vision of progress as universal freedom simply dissolves. Modern discourse does not provide firm cognitive space for a non-negotiable ethical referent in terms of which one could judge and validate progress. Technological mediation constitutes the only firm anchor and definitive referent for human life.[19]

Technological mediation as the definitive fact and referent has come to demarcate a sense of righteous distance from all pre-modern impulses towards expansion and conquest. Modern technological mediation in its capacity for limitless self-generation is seen to represent a new terrain of infinite promise for human living. The belief is that in time this terrain would provide for all alike. Its inexhaustible dynamic quality would prise apart the 'control of things' from the 'control of Man'. So long as human effort was confined by the grim realm of necessity, there was no choice but to seek control over other human beings to realise the desire for things. Hence the significant contrast: whereas pre-modern conquest sought mastery over Man, modern conquest seeks mastery over things.

Moral anguish within modern discourse, voiced with passion and daring in radical social critiques, has essentially been in relation to the grave uncertainty as to the nature and duration of the turbulent process of transition. As a historical phenomenon, the dynamic of progress had to have a point of beginning in time and space. Its universalist promise inhered in the possibility unique to this dynamic: universal reach and applicability. The foremost concern of modern critiques of progress has been with the long and uncertain duration of transition. For in that difficult duration of transition, the modern quest for mastery of things remains entangled with mastery over Man. Until the mechanism of progress in full bloom has created the basis of that decisive separation—mastery of things disentangled from mastery of Man—moral choice which simultaneously resists injustice and quickens the march of progress, is seen as difficult and at times impossible. And, therefore, as age old ways of living and thought unwilling and incapable of grasping the promise of progress as universal freedom are relentlessly smothered, the only relevant moral question could be: what is the threshold of the 'necessary price' in a particular situation?[20]

Cognitive Closures in Modern Discourse

Persistent inattention in the otherwise sensitive and incisive critiques of capitalist development to the spatial–regional dimensions of progress is indicative of the actual limits that condition perceptions and theories in modern discourse. Modern social theory until very recently failed to recognise the significance of the spatial–regional dimension of the problematique of surplus appropriation. The colossal concentration of resources and power in developed regions was seen as evidence of an effective working out of the mechanism of progress. Any suggestion of an intrinsic connection between development in one part of the world and its near absence in another part—postulated in the very recent theories of 'underdevelopment'—for a very long time seemed no more than an expression of rage. The duration of this inattention—more than a century—merits close attention.

Unlike 'ecology' and 'gender', issues that have acquired sharp salience during recent decades, recognition of the inherent spatial–regional dimension of progress was available to modern social theory quite within its definitive categories. But such recognition would have entailed having to contend with a sense of searing uncertainty. The very basis of epistemic clarity in modern discourse would have shrivelled well before progress had become an irreversible reality. Neat projections of a future as it ought to be, and categorical faith in the certainty of an ultimate universal human destiny would have perhaps been impossible to sustain. Modern social theory, as perhaps any theory that seeks to explain and orient all facts and life has to be, is an expression of faith. Categorical certainty regarding the future signifies its point of teleological repose. Universality in the Marxist vision, as also in the capitalist vision of progress, is founded on a deceptive certainty: unification of the world provides an ascertainable rational ground for formulating truly universal categories.[21]

In the past few centuries the entire planet has indeed been swept into a common destiny. But it is a destiny in which different segments—identifiable both in terms of social–cultural formations within nation-states and political–economic entities at the global level—participate on unequal terms. The process of world unification, in its very inception, fragmented the world into unequal segments. Unification has meant the inexorable binding of progressively unequal segments to a single unified grid of production and validation. To invoke a parable, it is akin to the experience of a *Chandala* outcaste sharing a common destiny with a Brahmin. Universal theories of modern discourse have remained insensitive and virtually closed to the implications of segmentation inherent in the logic of modern unification. Gandhi—from the victimised part of the world—was perhaps the first to make an impassioned plea for taking note of the fact that the stupendous progress and prosperity of modern industrial civilisation in Europe was built on the ruin and plunder of other lands.[22]

To comprehend some of the annihilating implications of the cognitive closure entailed in the modern mode, consider the casual certainty of advanced formations that they understand the backward better than they could possibly understand themselves, since the backward mirrors the superseded childlike past of advanced formations. Hence the manifest irrelevance and worthlessness in modern cognition of self-understanding so far as it concerns archaic formations and thought. Whatever their past may have been, their future ought to be in the likeness of the present or at the very least like the more recent past of advanced formations.[23]

All this raises disturbing questions about the very basis of a civilisation which seeks validation and legitimacy in progress as the final quest for equality and unification. Could one regard the unequal segmentation of the world, bound to a common grid of production and validation, as mere transitional necessity? Is it possible to predicate, however loosely, the duration of this unhappy transitional phase? Or, is inequality inherent in the concept of 'division of labour'? Could it be, as Lohia feared, that the modern world is congealing into a caste-like global structure. If that is so, would modern civilisation survive the abolition of the division of labour? Would the prevalent techniques of modern production be viable in the absence of exchange and global division of labour? And what are its implications for notions of 'autonomy' and survival of distinctness as cultural–ethnic entities?

Autonomy in Modern Cognition

The sense of unique distance that marks out modern unification as the elaboration of the basis for a new human destiny merits careful thought. The grand certainty has been that modern unification would secure, beyond regression, conditions wherein Man free from all non-human constraints could work out the very ultimate in human possibility. Consider the implications of this vision of unflawed limitless freedom for autonomy and cultural distinctness.

True, modern unification is utterly unlike imperiums in the past. Its reach and effectiveness does not depend on direct political dominion. Colonial dominions all over the world have been dismantled in the past few decades. Yet, that has not impeded continual enhancement of the process of modern unification. Wallerstein, a firm votary of progress and a historian of exceptional empathy for the victims of progress, makes out the absence of a single centre of political power as the most hopeful and distinctive feature of modern universalism. The pivotal force which binds the world into a single unit, argues Wallerstein, is the global market. And this single global market comprises polities of diverse character, which are often engaged in fierce competition with each other.[24] Certain propositions implicit in such rendering of modern universalism merit elaborations.

Multiple centres of political power dwelling within an integral continuum of the global market are taken to represent a creative play of dialectical tension between what had hitherto been irreconcilable antinomies: the twin human impulses towards autonomy and universal human identity. The play of dialectical tension, often fierce and ugly, is seen as an unhappy transitional necessity until that ineffable final moment of repose in universal plenitude.[25]

To grasp in any meaningful sense the significance of autonomy in modern comprehension, the notion of autonomy has to be considered in terms of its cognitive placement in modern discourse. Individual and nation-states represent the legitimate twin loci of autonomy. They are recognised as appropriate instruments of historical reason. Through them, human expectations of justice may assert in the making of an ultimate universal space for all alike. Quite apart from the simple fact that individuals and nation-states do not represent anything like near uniform capacities and access to that ineluctable making of an ultimate universal space, this mode of comprehension does not allow for an abiding and legitimate mediation between the individual and universal. The modern faith is that once that universal space has become a reality, limitless possibilities unencumbered by petty parochial constraints would become available to all mankind. Hence the trenchant rejection of what are perceived as local or parochial (and therefore irrational) constraints, and the exclusive legitimacy of constraints (upon the individual) entailed in sustaining the universal.

Autonomy as a principle of self-governance is invariably represented in contrast to notions and situations of dependence. Self-governance has meaning only if its guiding principles are self-chosen. It is inseparable from its self-chosen guiding principles. Self-governance ceases to be itself the moment its guiding principles are disregarded. Autonomous assertion—in modern cognition as also in other cognitive modes—does not become valid simply because it is autonomously willed. Implicit in the very notion of guiding principles is a reference to something that lies clearly beyond the locus of autonomous assertion, be that an individual or a collective entity. Semantic bounds of self-governance or autonomy are inherently in relation to some notion of totality or ultimate purpose as definitive reference. Autonomy as an unconditional and absolutely self-contained quality is inconceivable. Autonomy can never be self-validating. As a self-validating principle, autonomy would cease to be itself (an assertion in freedom) and become a principle of supremacy: 'competing homogeneity'.[26]

The shrivelled space for autonomy in modern cognition and life has to be grasped in relation to the recognised modern principle of legitimate cohesions. For this principle predicates legitimate mediations between the individual and universal. Modern belief has been that progressive erosion of constraints, which had hitherto confined individual consciousness and loyalty within narrow limits, would enrich and enhance the substance and quality of space for autonomy. To invoke a parable from physics: just as the universal constraint of gravity makes possible rapid locomotion, progress as the only and universal constraint would extend the reach for autonomy to the infinite horizons of human imagination.[27]

Certain clarifications concerning the universal reach of gravity and history are of relevance in this context. Gravity is effective as a universal force by itself, and requires no mediation. To the absence of mediation is due perhaps its unvarying and universal quality. As matter, be it a living or non-living form, nothing could be said to represent an irreducible finality. Unlike gravity, universal history can only be thought of in terms of a primal constituent that belongs clearly to another order. Human logos, the first as also the final referent of history, represents an irreducible entity. It signifies a most unusual mediation, in that the human logos mediates what in the first place it has caused: at once the subject and the primal cause of history. The unavoidable necessity of mediation and the irreducible finality of the entity that mediates impart to the historical realm a character and possibility that could never be even distantly akin to the unvarying measurable universality of a natural force like gravity.

Questions and presuppositions concerning ultimate possibilities towards which modern discourse is oriented merit vigilant attention, not because they are always visible and to the fore in everyday living. It may indeed happen that they do not figure even indirectly in general formulations concerning everyday behaviour and practice. Presuppositions concerning what are perceived to be ultimate possibilities merit sustained attention of a meditative kind, because of their suffused inherence even when the stated calculus of the immediate and foreseeable seems to negate them. Their vitality endures over long durations, precisely because their presence is so invisibly suffused. They are of significance in that such presuppositions illuminate the orientation and texture of the cognitive terrain. In critical moments of decisive assertion they come sharply to the fore as lines of cognitive closure.

Class: Segment as the Potential Universal

Consider in this context certain implications embedded in the recognition of class as the primal category for legitimate cohesions. As a category that translates and embodies the compelling immediate historical functions for sustaining the grand mechanism of progress, class is seen as a formation in qualitative contrast to the essentially static primordial cohesions like family, kinship, clan, etc. In modern cognition class acquires the character of a faithful homologue of technology. And of the class segments spawned by the grand mechanism of progress, Marx noted, the industrial proleteriat by the very condition of its origin is by far the most swiftly expanding of all class formations.[28]

Proletarian class boundaries are seen to keep pace with the swift movement of industrial technology. Very like technology, the essential function of the proletariat is instinct with the power to shatter and transform the inert boundaries of primordial cohesions. Hence the historic resonance of Marx's invocation: the proletariat as the vital bearer of a universal human future in freedom.[29] True, in recent years that resonance and its promise have withered. Yet, that invocation remains significant and instructive. It clarifies a mode of comprehension common to the Marxist vision and the bourgeois world-view it sought to replace.

Proletariat is posited as a segment that has the potential of becoming the universal. Recognition of this potential is in terms of the inherently universal function of two entwined qualities: limitless extendability (the process of unification, the basis for universality) and virtual effacement of the past. As a formation more or less completely without a sense of its own past, the proletariat is seen to embody the robust certainty of emancipation for all humankind in a virgin future untainted by the awful burdens of a past. As a social formation constituted in the likeness of technology, to the proletariat is vouchsafed the power to secure complete and final release from parochial primordial constraints. Its historical power and moral grandeur flow from the certainty that in the proletariat human expectation for justice and the desire for ever more things were organically fused. Imperium of European nation-states, the prime bourgeois instrument for extending the reach of progress, could at its best be a contaminated half-way house: an 'unconscious tool of history'.

'Imperium of European nation-states' and 'proletariat as the vanguard'—invariably posited in a relationship of combat—represent in fact two distinct variants of the modern quest for universality. Differences between them are sharp, and of momentous consequence at several levels of detail. Yet, both arise from an identical cognitive terrain.[30] Both are premised on the certainty that limitless extendability would prise wide open the grand path to universality. Some of the definitive implications embedded in this belief could be indicated as follows:

1. Universality as inseparable from, and co-extensive with unification. Modern unification as essentially the process of extending the mechanism of progress in successive stages. Mechanism of progress represents a limitless possibility.
2. Progressive extension requires viable mediations. Worth and legitimacy of mediating instruments is to be ascertained in relation to their effectiveness in securing a universal future. Suffering and disruption of human lives, terrible and heartrending as it may be has to be accepted, provided it is no more than the unavoidable necessary price of progress.
3. Viable mediation requires rigorous consolidation of a referent and resource that would define and sustain the difficult process of transformation. Hence the grim imperative of what in the duration of transition could only be some variant of the 'centre–periphery' configuration.

The conception, 'proletariat as the vanguard' and its contemporary fate exemplify two apparently antithetical modern facts. As a formulation that seeks to encapsulate the neat logic of modern progress, its logical rigour is impeccable. Its firm theoretical basis is indirectly affirmed by the always uncertain theoretical placement of the bourgeois alternative: 'imperium of European nation-states'. The bourgeois alternative, despite its forbidding power for a very long time, was never sought to be legitimised as a class formation. Yet the stark fact: more than a century after Marx made known to the world his stirring vision, nowhere in the world is the proletariat anywhere near its assigned destiny of being the vanguard and maker of universal history. The Polish upsurge of the early eighties is perhaps the only instance of the proletariat becoming the voice of an entire society. And as the voice of society, its search has been for ways to affirm Polish identity. Not for a fleeting moment did this upsurge seek the role of a vanguard for the proletariat. The instructive fact is that the only time it was given to the proletariat to speak and be heard as the voice of an entire society, the proletariat was pitted against the entrenched might of the proletarian state.

How is one to read such a recurrent and abiding paradox: modern history negating the inherent logic of its framework of discourse and validation. Could it be that it illuminates that irreducible autonomous space given to even the most humble and helpless of our specie. A space so etched in the human condition that the most demonic tyranny is powerless to fully smother and tame its elusive resilience. Even as measurable space in the phenomenal world has been tamed and mastered almost to the last fraction, that elusive universal space unique to Man refuses to yield its wild quality. Reality, moulded in unquestioning fanatical allegiance to the blueprint of a particular vision of perfection, has unfailingly turned out to be very different from what was intended. That it should be so is a profound assurance of human freedom.

In the absence of the bourgeois vision of progress and the proletarian heresy ranged against it in fierce combat, modern reality perhaps could never have come to be what it is. But the enduring fact is that the actual reality as it has come to be is indubitably far removed from what either intended. Imperium of European nation-states has collapsed and is no longer regarded a viable instrument for extending the dynamic of progress. Dictatorship of the proletariat, which until recently could move millions to heroic struggle and sacrifice, is also no longer seriously believed to be the sure path towards the perfect realm of progress and universal plenty. Instead, a tacit consensus seems now to be more or less universal: the world market constitutes the universal binding force and principal instrument of what had begun as a quest for progress and universal plenty. And within the world market dwell 'sovereign nation-states' which mediate the universal.

Uncertain Cognitive Placement of the Nation-State

The nation-state, that most unyielding and resilient of modern facts, has come to be recognised as the legitimate mediation between the individual and universal. But its theoretical placement as a valid modern category remains ambiguous in an exceedingly interesting way.[31] Between 'class or class-like' formations, the primal principle of legitimate modern cohesions, and 'nation-state' stretches an impossible cognitive distance. The salience of nation-state as a modern fact has perhaps been definitive. Yet it has been impossible to posit a tangible link between 'nation-state' and what is believed to be the inherent logic of progress exemplified by 'class'. If 'class' could be said to embody the profound possibility of limitless extension inherent in technology and progress, 'nation' embodies the past and memory. 'Class' could be said to represent the form and ground of perpetual movement within which modern becoming unfolds; and 'nation', the unmoving anchor, the ground of repose. Class, like technology, negates distances. Nation, like memory, affirms certain distances as final.

The tension between the momentous vitality of nation as a modern fact and its uncertain theoretical placement illuminates the nature of actual space available for autonomy and cultural survival. True, in the absence of nation and nation-state as a salient modern fact, the world would have been far more sternly homogenous. Europe would have been, in a far more comprehensive sense than it is today, the true measure of human life and worth. But it would be a very serious mistake to read into the modern fact of nation and nation-state a principle of modern cohesion whose basic orientation is towards nurturance of autonomy and cultural distinctness.

Nation or nation-state does not represent what in a strict sense could be regarded as a principle of modern cohesion. It merely signifies the fact that a particular entity has generally come to be accepted as viable in the modern context. To complicate matters, viability cannot be postulated in terms of social facts that comprise a nation-state. Viability in this context can only be grasped in terms of the final outcome: ability of social facts to cohere into an effective instrument for sustaining, or at least coping with the world-wide requirements of progress. Nation-state represents the stern logic of modern survival: consolidation of a 'competing homogeneity'.[32]

Consolidation of nation-state as a competing homogeneity is a process substantially akin to and co-extensive with what could be characterised as the general, universal thrust of progress. This thrust derives its distinctive self-recognition and compelling power to reshape the world from its ever more rigorously enhanced ability to foreclose equations between Man and Nature in favour of modern technology. It is an all encompassing process of re-demarcation of definitive boundaries in space, and as cognitive categories.

Things as the Measure of Man

Foreclosure of possible equations between Man and Nature is pivoted to the first and foremost need of modern transformation: to extend and generalise certain unified grids of natural facts. These grids constitute the basic building blocks of a new natural space so restructured that its resources can be harnessed at an optimal level of efficiency. The notion of efficiency and its optimal level are determined by the scale and complexity of industrial technology. Just as division of labour and class formation signify social homologues of specialised technological functions, unified grids of natural facts signify the geographical–spatial homologue of division of labour.

Nature is reconstituted as a hierarchy of unified local segments bound to a single universal grid. Certain strands, that in Nature untouched by the modern dynamic subsist as elements in an intimate web, are prised apart and thereby sought to be released from the limits inherent in their natural placement. The essential guiding principle is of 'selection, cultivation and hierarchy'. True, this principle has been long familiar to Man. Its significance for human civilisation has perhaps been decisive since neolithic times. But prior to the modern breakthrough, this principle was never affirmed as a self-validating final referent. Its epistemic placement as also its actual salience in praxis was always modulated in relation to referents grounded in some cultural–religious vision. Modern discourse, in definitive contrast to perhaps all pre-modern sensibilities, elevates the principle of 'selection, cultivation and hierarchy' to a status akin to divine fate: a limitless finality, total and self-validating.[33]

Culture in modern discourse acquires value and significance in relation to its perceived implications for sustaining the self-consciously limitless process of reconstituting Nature. Hence the modern perception of culture as either a function or a manipulable fact[34] that has to be harnessed to the requirements of modern transformation. European culture as a reality rooted in a social substance that alone engendered dynamic self-movement has, however, come to acquire a very different cognitive placement. It represents much more than a mere contingent fact. European culture is seen to preserve and vivify all that is of value and worth in the past of all mankind. In the words of Gramsci, one of the more audacious heretics of the modern age, European culture is the only truly 'universal culture'. Other cultures are significant 'only in so far as they have become constitutive elements in European culture'.[35] Hence the instructive absence, so far as it concerns European culture, of a neat demarcation between 'tradition' and 'modernity'. And that remains true despite the fact that self-recognition as Modern Europe is inseparable from an anguished and deeply troubled quest to recover the ancient Graeco-Roman past of Europe as its classical referent.[36]

Perhaps the most perverse fact of our age of progress has been that communities and ways of life, towards which words like 'cultural survival' and 'ethnicity' direct our attention, have been reduced to linger on the margins of modern life and discourse. Words like 'cultural survival' and 'cultural plurality' signify a belated sense of remorse; an aftermath of the pitiless logic of modern transformation. Prior to the modern age, powerful kingdoms as also 'little communities' did indeed engage in brutal conquest and insensate slaughter for land, riches and slaves. For a 'little community' the prospect of capturing a few heads of cattle, slaves or brides could be reason enough to take up arms against a less powerful neighbour. Such conflicts were often the cause of cruel inflictions and terrible human suffering. But such conflicts never caused the wholesale extinction of communities and cultures. That is an achievement unique to our age of progress, so righteous in its belief that conquest of things was an unfailing assurance of universal freedom for Man.

Modern discourse, in its moments of fleeting serenity, has sought to invest these tragic vestiges of vanished rhythms of living, in the words of Levi-Strauss, with 'nobility' at the very time it was 'completing their destruction'. Unaware of having 'eliminated savage life', the modern sensibility now seeks to 'appease the nostalgic cannibalism of history with the shadows of those that history has already destroyed' in the ever more varied accumulations of its museums and libraries.[37] The utmost those vanquished by history may seek is to be remembered as well tended artefacts in museums and libraries.

The attenuated sense of certainty in recent years has engendered on the margins of modern discourse, serious concern for cultures vanquished by History. Categories like culture are affirmed as relevant and meaningful in the world today, in so far as they are co-extensive with an authentic humanist response. Implicit in such affirmations is the belief that what seems an unjust and cruel consequence of progress and modern technology represents, in fact, a perversion of the humanist vision. The assumption that all that exists on earth and beyond acquires meaning with the presence of Man remains basic to the modern faith. It abides in modern discourse as the starting point beyond proof and verifiability. For modern discourse, the humanist quest constitutes the ultimate referent and corrective for Man and life as it is, and as it ought to be.

Were the way out of the grave predicament of life and Man in our times so neat and facile, there would be no cause for serious concern and self-reflection. Were it so, notions like the 'human predicament' would merely signify mystical rhetoric devoid of tangible meaning. The task then, would simply be to measure and define more precisely the actual requirements of the humanist quest.

If one is to seek comprehension in any significant sense of the nature and implications of the modern predicament, the task is exceedingly difficult and inherently uncertain. Some of the most searing and intractable problems of our age are a consequence of the homocentric vision of progress. The need to consider 'cultural distinctiveness and diversity' as a problem in the modern context is a pointed confirmation of this fact. Surely tribal communities in India, as elsewhere, were never a problem for themselves or others prior to the colonial–modern onslaught. For thousands of years these simple folk managed to survive with a sense of profound worth and vitality on their own. The awful fact of the age of progress is that communities perceived as eternally stagnant on the brink of survival—the bottom-end of the evolutionary scale—have been smothered towards extinction. For the unfortunate victims of progress and History the unvarying choice has been either to linger as archaic dregs drained of memory and life, or to meekly submit to the steady erosion of their distinctness and identity as a step forward, towards integration at the lowest end of the skill and power spectrum of the modern production grid.

The homocentric vision of progress seeks to measure the significance of all that is or could be as moments in progression towards more developed and higher forms. Human specie is seen as the self-conscious and sovereign principle in the Man–Nature dialectic. His quest and possibilities are believed to be boundless and without limits. Power and mastery over nature is seen as an affirmation of Man's ability to measure a world destined to be recast in his image, and for his needs.

Forbidding gravity of the salient facts of our age of progress comes intensely to the fore in its stark paradoxes. Consider the tragic reversal in praxis of the modern vision: spurred by the vision of Man at last becoming the measure of things, the age of progress has created a world in which things have come to be the measure of Man. The comforting expectation of being able to replace the 'governance of Man' by the 'administration of things' has been actualised as a searing irony: a homocentric vision of the cosmos has come to place things at the very centre as the final arbiter of human worth.

The modern quest began with a firm and irrevocable demarcation between Man and Nature. Complete subjugation of Nature was to be the decisive step towards human freedom. Human freedom and equality are predicated on the hierarchic segmentation and subjugation of Nature. The belief is that, the hierarchic segmentation of Nature would secure complete mastery of Man over Nature, and thus make available an inexhaustible resource for a human life in plenitude, ever more varied and rich. Even as almost all of Nature has been segmented and remade into a unified hierarchy harnessed to human needs, modern civilisation is faced with the annihilating prospect of an exhausted and degraded resource base, incapable of sustaining life for very long on our planet. Future is the sovereign referent of modern civilisation. Yet, it is a civilisation that may so impoverish the wherewithal that makes human life possible and meaningful as to leave virtually nothing for the generations to come.

The original promise of the modern quest was to release human life from the demeaning realm of necessity and bare survival. Ceaseless struggle for bare survival in the past is seen as the degrading constraint on human creativity and freedom. Development of progressively specialised functions—as technology and as organisation—are perceived as an index of Man's march beyond the realm of necessity and bare survival. Ultimately, according to the modern belief, progress would create conditions for human life to unfold beyond the oppressive realm of bare survival. Hence the modern certainty that the fear of extinction that has never ceased to haunt Man could be exorcised once and for all.

Indeed the realm of necessity, so far as it concerns the advanced industrial world, has been abolished. But the concern for human survival and the fear of extinction has resurfaced in another, more extreme form: self-annihilation of the human specie. Nurtured on the promise of a world growing ever more plentiful, modern civilisation is perhaps the first in human history to develop a capacity for destruction that is far ahead of its admittedly impressive productive apparatus. Frontiers of its awesome technology are worked out in the demonic recesses of research and development in the science of war.

Perhaps the most tragic flaw in modern cognition is the systematic and self-conscious omission of death as a cognitive referent. Death, which has been the most profound preoccupation of spiritual–cultural reflection, has come to be regarded in modern cognition as the final dissolution into meaninglessness. This omission has grave implications. The obsessive and suicidal self-centredness of modern civilisation is due, in no small measure, to this systematic and arrogant unawareness of death.

The quest for freedom and equality loses its essential truth in a world oriented to a discourse that refuses to recognise distinctiveness and divergence as legitimate and meaningful. Perhaps the instinct to simultaneously distance and identify is too deep rooted in the human condition for Man to survive as a self-aware being, were the world to be reduced to an undifferentiated grey uniformity.

In modern discourse alikeness has come to signify equality. Differences and distances are seen to signify inequality, or stagnant isolation. Hence perhaps the modern disposition to accept uniformity and homogenisation, or at least that particular form of it which seems to promise maximal equality. Unification and uniformity are perceived as the twin vectors of equality and universal freedom.

Quite apart from the fact that radical attempts to organise living conditions that are substantially alike (and therefore equal) have failed the very notion of 'equality as alikeness' negates the possibility of meaningful cognitive space for cultural plurality. To this cognitive closure is perhaps due the near absence of serious notice in modern discourse of the unresolved tension between the conception of equality as alikeness and the quest for freedom.

The making of the modern world has unmistakably been towards something like a grey uniformity. Even where the modern mode of production has acquired merely a symbolic presence, modern categories dissolve the sense of legitimacy and hope of other modes of validation and existence. Meaningful existence of social formations and sensibilities that have somehow survived on the margins of the modern complex depends upon enlarging and consolidating spaces of sensitivity for very different modes of comprehension and validation.

Both physically and culturally what has survived the numbing modern onslaught are a few fragmented spaces. But India in this respect, as perhaps in several others, represents a situation of exceptional historical interest. Nearly 8 per cent of the total Indian population comprises 'scheduled tribes'.[38] Progress and power have always been less than sensitive and considerate to the plight of the weak and vanquished. Our pre-modern past also seethes with inflictions, grossly unjust and inhuman. But the sheer magnitude of the tribal presence in India indicates, both as fact and possibility, something qualitatively more than mere survival of archaic dregs drained of vitality. The simple statistical fact that one among every thirteen Indians is a tribal refers us to patterns of interaction between tribal social cohesions and the power of the world beyond that were qualitatively distanced from the inexorable 'historical process' which, in the brief span of a few centuries, utterly extinguished tribal cultures on the vast continents colonised by Europe.[39]

Responses to the contemporary tribal situation in India could be characterised in terms of two apparently polarised projects. Many of the more hard-headed modernisers among us harbour a terrible secret wish. Like Europe, they wish to consolidate a homogenous social order. The brutality such an outcome would inevitably entail is seen as the necessary price if we are ever to attain anything like parity with the West. There are others—no less destructive for all their well-intentioned concern for tribals—who would like, as it were, to reconstruct tribal entities as separate and neatly cauterised from the rest. Both these responses stem from a common cognitive terrain.

The foremost requirement, if tribal cohesions and sensibility are to survive as a meaningful presence, is to seek an authentic reaffirmation of modes of comprehension and validation that sustained tribal–non-tribal interaction in India for 3,000 years or more. It is imperative that we recognise the civilisational significance of our inheritance of 'interaction'. Interaction, unlike extinction, is inconceivable unless the interacting entities retain a sense of their distinct resilience. True, it was an interaction far from perfect and seriously flawed. What is more, that inheritance survives today as a shrivelled substance utterly unsure of the basis of its legitimacy in the modern world. But even so, the sheer magnitude of that survival embodies a profound promise.

Social magnitudes express a deeply suffused consensus as to what ought to be. Consensus, however suffused and deeply internalised, can perhaps never be a vital presence if it loses the sense of its own legitimacy. Such recognition could never be simply a question of reiteration and restoration. It entails both basic reappraisal of the nature of modern development and modern discourse as also reformulation of the idea of community as proximity wherein the village and region modulate diverse impulses and aspirations within a shared civilisational rhythm.

NOTES

1. Antecedents of the industrial revolution that began in the last quarter of the eighteenth century in England stretch far beyond the eighteenth century and the British Isles. Significance of this duration lies in the fabrication of instrumentalities that have since recast Nature with ever-increasing rigour to secure for Man the unchallenged mastery of all that exists or could exist.

   Antecedents, that suffused salience which renders fluid neat demarcations of historical space and duration, bring to the fore cohesive distinctness implicit in the nation-state as the working out of coherence in reference to a larger configuration.

   Concerning the relationship between the fact and idea of Europe-Christendom and the emergence of nation-states, see Norbert Elias, *Power and Civil Society: The Civilizing Process*, Vol. 2, Pantheon Books, 1982, pp. 91–228.

2. See Fernand Braudel, *The Mediterranean and the Mediterranean World in the Age of Philip II*, Vol. 1, Fontana, 1978, Part II-3: 'Is it Possible to Construct a Model of the Mediterranean Economy', pp. 418–61. Towards the end of the sixteenth century, the hub of this phenomenal outward thrust—the complex of techniques and economic arrangements—shifted to the Atlantic seaboard.

3. See Fernand Braudel, *Civilisation and Capitalism* Vol. 1: *The Structures of Everyday Life*, Collins, 1981, pp. 92ff. Braudel characterises the nomadic intrusion as essentially a 'marginal episode' of no enduring consequence.

   Lattimore outlines a very different quality of relationships between the shifting frontiers of nomadic regions and the sedentary world of settled cultivation. See Owen Lattimore, *Inner Asian Frontiers of China*, Beacon Press, 1962, In particular pp. 511–30.

4. Victory at Lepanto marks 'the end of the period of profound depression, the end of a genuine inferiority complex on the part of Christendom and a no less real Turkish supremacy. The Christian victory had halted progress towards a future which promised to be very bleak indeed.' Braudel, *Mediterranean*, Vol. 2, 1978, p. 1089.

   Consider in this context what Huizinga in his classic study calls the 'vehement pathos' and 'melancholy' that permeated the life and imagination of medieval Christendom. See J. Huizinga, *The Waning of the Middle Ages*, St. Martin's Press, 1984, in particular pp. 22–46.

5. For the Mediterranean as a dynamic frontier, see Braudel, *Mediterranean*, Vol. 1, pp. 168–230. For space as a hostile presence to be tamed and mastered, *ibid.*, pp. 355–93.

6. Claude Levi-Strauss, *The Savage Mind*, Weidenfeld and Nicolson, 1972, pp. 13–15.

7. See Charles Drekmeir, *Kingship and Community in Early India*, Stanford University Press, 1962, pp. 369ff.

8. 'Historical structure of being and becoming' refers primarily to the complex of beliefs which shape the sensibility of a civilisation. Between beliefs, as a statement of first principles, and sensibility, extends the mediating realm of 'working out' praxis. A particular historical sensibility is a specific appreciation–realisation of beliefs and actual historical configurations. Sensibility and material culture are intimately linked but not in the sense of cause and effect. Historical configuration could thus be characterised as 'grounded' or 'rooted' in a structure of beliefs rather than caused or created by them. For illuminating this crucial distinction I am grateful to Dr. R.K. Gupta.

9. Gandhi perceived in this a dangerously flawed quest of devising institutions that would make it unnecessary for Man to be good.

   From within the modern tradition, Gramsci in a searing critique of 'passive revolution' sought to restore human volition as a necessary and legitimate presence in historical praxis. But given his epistemological framework, the problem is merely postponed. Human volition is envisaged as a significant presence in historical praxis until the emergence of conditions in which humanity is destined to find its true significance: the classless society. See Antonio Gramsci, *Selections from the Prison Notebooks*, International Publishers, 1973, 'Problems of Marxism', pp. 381–416; 'Passive Revolution', pp. 106–14 and pp. 118–20.

10. See Mircea Eliade, *Cosmos and History: The Myth of the Eternal Return* (tr. W.R. Trask), Harcourt Brace & World, 1959, pp. 108ff, pp. 147ff.

11. To begin with, this humanist quest was directed, albeit in an oblique way, against theological fetters imposed by the Church and Christian dogma. It began as an attempt to recover the suppressed and nearly forgotten Graeco-Roman past. Francesco Petrarch (1304–75) pointedly chose to be honoured by the Roman Senate rather than Paris University dominated by theological scholasticism. Machiavelli invoked astrology against the doctrine of predestination to secure some play to human volition. Jules Michelet in his *History of France* (1855) gave to this sensibility and process a name that swiftly acquired universal currency: Renaissance or rebirth. Jacob Burckhardt's *The Civilisation of the Renaissance in Italy*, 2 vols., Harper, 1975, remains even after a lapse of a hundred years its classic conceptual referent.

Perhaps of foremost significance is the definitive shift in referents of worth and authenticity as much in relation to aesthetic appreciation as the constitution and form of everyday living.

'The heroes of the Italian Renaissance were no longer the great warriors in service of the Church and Emperor. Petrarch's life and works had made a heroic figure of the scholar and intellectual. Boccaccio's *Decameron* did much the same for the courageous innovative merchant trader. By the time the Renaissance drew to a close in the sixteenth century, Alberti had depicted the model family; Machiavelli had culled from examples both ancient and modern the superlative political ruler; Castiglione had eulogised the perfect courtier; and a new heroic individual had arisen to capture the Western imagination— the artist, celebrated in Varasi's *Lives of the Artists*, Cellini's Autobiography, and by the almost superhuman figures of Leonardo Da Vinci and Michelangelo.' Julia Conaway Bondanella and Mark Musa, eds., *The Italian Renaissance Reader*, A Meridian Book, 1987, p. xv. Also see Peter Burke, *The Italian Renaissance—Culture and Society in Italy*, Polity Press, 1991.

For clarifying subtle connections between astrology and legitimation of 'free will' in the works of Machiavelli, I am indebted to the unpublished study of Professor Anthony Parel of the University of Calgary, Canada.

12. Charles Darwin himself quite clearly refrained from taking the concluding step of fusing the idea of evolution and progress. He was severe in his rejection of Lamarck's idea of lineal biological progression. Darwin's definitive simile for evolution was of a mighty tree of many branches with its rising vertical trunk of evolution. But his theory of 'natural selection' distilled enticingly clear in that succinct rendering of Herbert Spencer, 'survival of the fittest'; as also his constant description of species as 'lower' and 'higher', 'lowly' and 'more advanced' lent itself well and easily to theories of social evolution. See Charles Darwin, *Origin of Species*, in particular the section, 'On the Degree to Which Organisation Tends to Advance', ch. 4, pp. 127ff.

Raymond Aron while castigating as 'false synthesis' the inherence in evolution of an 'internal thrust' towards 'hominization' concedes that it remains an 'understandable illusion'. His citation of Andre Laroi-Gourhan (1964) captures neatly its encompassing force.

Whatever explanations they may give for it, evolutionists are unanimous in believing that the stream which carries us along is indeed the stream of evolution. The lichen, the medusa, the oyster, or the giant tortoise are, like the gigantic dinosaur, nothing but eddies in the mainstream that flows towards us. If it is insisted that the creatures before us represent only one of the branches of evolution (the one which leads to intelligence, the others leading to other no less honourable forms of ultimate development), the evolution towards man still subsists, and the choice of illustrative linkages is legitimate. Whether, like Bergson or Tielhard, one sees in evolution the sign of an elan, the general quest for awareness culminating in Homo Sapiens, or (what amounts to the same thing on a material level) the play of a determinism culminating in living forms that are increasingly responsive to the motives for exploiting matter, the compartment of the mass from which man has sprung remains the same. Beneath the superstructure of explanations, the infrastructure of facts resolves itself into the same system.

Raymond Aron, *Progress and Disillusion*, Fredrick A. Praeger, 1968, pp. 209–10.

13. Karl Marx's observations concerning the analogous relationship between processes that have been at work in evolution and technology, albeit self-conscious and therefore clear and purposive in technology, articulate a salient strand in modern self-understanding:

Darwin has interested us in the history of Nature's Technology, i.e. in the formation of the organs of plants and animals, which organs serve as instruments of production for sustaining life. Does not the history of the productive organs of man, or organs that are the material basis of all social organisation, deserve equal attention?—human history differs from natural history in this, that we have made the former, but not the latter?

Karl Marx, *Capital—A Critique of Political Economy*, The Modern Library, p. 406.

14. Philosophically embarrassing though logically consistent consequence of thus defining value has been that Nature in itself can never signify value.

In recent years a deepening sense of discomfort with this sense of Nature has acquired sharp visibility on the margins of modern discourse in the ecology movement. But this critique is shackled by the fact, at least so far as the advanced industrial world is concerned, that the question is no longer of making the world in a particular way but of unmaking it in a substantial sense. One of its unintended consequences has been the attempt, likely to be more systematic in the future, of a global transfer of ecological and social costs of production in the form of 'dirty industries' to the less industrialised world.

15. Modern cognition seems quite unaware of the implications of the fact that the Italian Renaissance in the fourteenth century, seen to signify the first intimation of what eventually came to be the modern dynamic, occurred in the shadow of the Black Death and general economic decline in Europe. It began as a self-conscious attempt to recover the Pagan Graeco-Roman past from the amnesia systematically engendered by the Church and its doctrines for close to a millennium. Yet, in the context of Europe, 'modernity' and 'tradition' are never counterposed as antithetical categories. Extremely significant is the fact that scholarly consideration of this long interregnum of Europe withdrawing

into itself and seeking complete effacement of facts and memory of its pre-Christian past, focuses essentially on sociological–political explanations. Cognitive closures entailed by Christian theology in the discourse and self-understanding of Christendom-Europe are hardly ever seriously considered.

See, Agnes Heller, *Renaissance Man*, Routledge & Kegan Paul, 1960. Lamo Martines, *Power and Imagination: City-States in Renaissance Italy*, Vintage, 1980. E.F. Jacob, ed., *Italian Renaissance Studies*, Faber, 1960. For the Pagan perception of Christian doctrines and their epistemic-cultural implications, see Robert J. Wilken, *The Christians As the Romans Saw Them*, Yale University Press, 1984.

On the historical formation of Christendom, see the exceedingly learned and instructive study of Judith Herrin, *The Formation of Christendom*, Fontana, 1989.

16. Marx's characterisation of British rule in India as the 'unconscious tool of history' faithfully reflects the supreme value assigned in his conceptual schema to extending the reach of the industrial dynamic: the indispensable first step towards a truly universal human history in freedom. This belief remained unshaken despite Marx's acute awareness of the rapacity of colonial conquest and British rule. See Karl Marx, 'British Rule in India', *New York Daily Tribune*, 25 June 1853, and 'Future Results of British Rule in India', in K. Marx and F. Engels, *Selected Works*, Vol. 1, Progress Publishers, 1969, pp. 488–99. For a more stark, if crude, reiteration of the notion of the 'necessary price', see Friedrich Engels' pronouncements on Eastern Europe. Except the Poles and Magyars, the other 'races and peoples have the immediate destiny of going under in the world revolutionary storm.' Engels on the Austro-Hungarian Empire, cited in David McLellan, *Engels*, Fontana, 1977, p. 46.

17. Preoccupation with the magnitude of surplus and its appropriation has been of ambivalent consequence. It compels sustained attention to issues concerning deprivation and access to things. But its other consequence has been to further constrict and bind cognition of worth and value as entirely a function of things.

18. Cognitive closures demarcate the 'structure of attention' and 'hearing space'. The fact that the significance of the connection between ecological balance and survival of life on earth remained unrecognised until recently is instructive. It is not as if no one perceived such a connection, but even when someone of the stature of a Gandhi argued for its recognition, the argument was not seen to merit serious attention. See Gopinath Kaviraj's illuminating reflections on the Christian doctrine of creation *ex nihilo* and the absence in Europe, until almost the nineteenth century, of serious philosophical enquiry into origins of life and the cosmos, in Medard Boss, *A Psychiatrist Discovers India*, Rupa & Co., 1966, pp. 107ff.

19. Technology is posited as the prime mover that consolidates the distance between Man and Nature. For that distance is seen to constitute the firm basis of humanness. For instance, Marx was deeply touched by the 'kind of melancholy' heaped upon the victims of colonial conquest, but that could not obscure the fact that the reality marked out for destruction had brought about 'brutalising worship of Nature, exhibiting its degradation in the fact that man, the sovereign of nature, fell down on his knees in adoration of Hanuman, the monkey, and Sabbala, the cow', K. Marx and F. Engels, *On Colonisation*, Progress Publishers, 1978, p. 41.

20. Technology herein refers to what are posited in modern cognition as three analogous prime movers of all that exists or could be: Evolution (Nature's Technology), Technology (Evolution self-conscious and humanised), Social–Political Organisation (Technology Reified).

The idea of 'necessary price' commands legitimacy across ostensibly sharp ideological divides within modern discourse. Hence the incredibly swift acceptance of the 'price of transition to the Market' after seven decades of acceptance of the 'price of transition to socialism' in the erstwhile Soviet Union.

21. Ram Manohar Lohia in his remarkable essay, 'Economics After Marx' (1943), was perhaps the first to explicitly argue that modern capitalism and the Marxist vision are two variants within the same epistemic space predicated upon infinite plenitude of things as freedom. Lohia was also sensitive to the subtle mediation of cultural configuration (Europe) spawning the elements of modern technology and political economy. Hence his characterisation of Russia as a 'poor cousin' of Europe. Ram Manohar Lohia, *Marx, Gandhi and Socialism*, Navahind, 1963, pp. 1–90.

22. See M.K. Gandhi, 'Hind Swaraj', *Selected Works*, Vol. 4, pp. 83–208. For Gandhi, *Hind Swaraj* (1909) remained his definitive 'seed text'. A text of exceptional historical significance, it is a critique of the 'modern industrial civilisation' formulated in terms of categories that arise beyond the ambit of modern discourse. Hence the instinctive inattention and virtual denial of a 'hearing space' to it.

Ram Manohar Lohia, consciously in the tradition of Hind Swaraj, elaborated in the modern idiom a critique of development: the nexus of 'development' and 'continual retardation'. See 'Economics After Marx (1943)', in, Lohia, *Marx*, pp. 1–90.

But this issue—formulated as the problem of 'development of underdevelopment'—acquired compelling presence within modern discourse only with the critiques of Furtado, Seers and Andre Gunder Frank. For a succinct statement of the development of theory of underdevelopment see Harold Brookfield, *Interdependent Development*, Methuen, 1975, pp. 124–65. And Robert I. Rhodes, ed., *Imperialism and Underdevelopment—A Reader*, Monthly Review Press, 1970, Part I, Ch. 1, and Part 2, Ch. 2.

Wallerstein extends the formulation by postulating two level formations in the world political economy: global division of labour and cultural–ethnic entities within nation-states. But the conceptual implications of his critique are poised on the bend of a theoretical blind alley. From whence is to arise the sustaining force to reorder a world of equality and justice? See Immanuel Wallerstein, *The Capitalist World Economy: Essays*, Cambridge University Press, 1979; and *The Modern World System*, 2 vols., Academic Press, 1974.

23. For a sharp if somewhat crude nineteenth century projection of this faith consider Tylor's assertion in *Primitive Culture* that the 'trite comparison of savages to grown-up children is in the main sound', even though few 'educated Europeans' would recognise that 'they have once passed through a condition of mind from which races at a lower state of civilization never fully emerge'. And Comte's emphatic judgement that the comparison of the 'savage' with the 'child' is 'correct' and 'instructive'. Cited in Maurice Mandelbaum, *History, Man and Reason—A Study in Nineteenth Century Thought*, The Johns Hopkins University Press, 1971, p. 100.

Consider Darwin's first thoughts on seeing the Indians in Tierra del Fuego:

. . . how entire the difference between savage and civilised man is. It is greater than between a wild and domesticated animal, in as much as in man there is greater power of improvement' [December 18, 1832].
. . . a real barbarian—of man in his lowest and most savage state. One's mind hurries back over past centuries, and then asks, could our progenitors be such as these?

Charles Darwin's Beagle Diary (1832–36), *Metaphysics, Materialism and the Evolution of Mind—Early Writings of Charles Darwin*, The University of Chicago Press, 1980, pp. 170–71.

An instructive instance of the universal sweep of the faith in modern Europe as the ultimate destination for all Mankind is Ray Huang's lucid essay on the fate of History in China during the last 3,000 years. Huang's concluding note is of profound relief that at long last History in China is in full vigour and China is poised to completely be in the historical mainstream exemplified by Europe. Huang seeks to explore the grand question of the Modern historiography of China: why the 'industrial breakthrough' did not happen in the China of the eighth-ninth century. Implicit in that question is the absurd assumption that Modern Europe could have begun a thousand years earlier and in China. See Ray Huang, *China—A Macro History*, An East Gate Book, 1989.

24. See Immanuel Wallerstein, *The Modern World System I—Capitalist Agriculture and the Origins of the European World Economy in the Sixteenth Century*, Academic Press, 1974, in particular the chapter 'Theoretical Reprise', pp. 347–57.

25. Implicit in the modern faith in infinite plenitude as the basis of perfection in freedom is the paradox that making of a world of infinite plenitude has to be the outcome of incessant and bitter struggle. On this formative irony see Braudel, 'On Forms of War', in his *Mediterranean*, Vol. 2, pp. 836–91.

26. The distinction between autonomy as self-validating absolute imperative—be it in relation to a nation-state, community, ethnicity, class or any other form of cohesion—and, autonomy as an assertion in freedom is of crucial significance. For domination and coercion implicate the oppressor as much as the victim in unfreedom.

27. Autonomy in modern cognition is essentially in relation to the 'individual' as the irreducible constituent of the quest towards universality. Hence the absence of legitimate cognitive space for cultural or social distinctness, and the ineluctable sense of Universality and Equality as the making of all alike.

28. Despite the sense of intrinsic legitimacy associated with class in modern usage, class as a concept remains ambiguous. Marx himself spoke of class in several different senses. Peter Burke marks out two salient usages in Marx's writings: class defined in a 'broad' and a 'narrow' sense. Common interests and functions in the production process define class in the 'broad' sense. In the 'narrow' sense, consciousness of the unity of interests is posited as essential for designating human aggregates as class. Hence Marx's characterisation of French peasants (1850) as a mere aggregate akin to a 'sack of potatoes' devoid of the consciousness of unity of interests. See Peter Burke, *Sociology and History*, George Allen and Unwin, 1980, pp. 60–67.

Class in the 'broad' sense signifies the grid general to the Modern faith. Marx envisioned in the proletariat the perfect homologue of Technology:

> . . . in proportion as industry, commerce, navigation, railways extended, in same proportion the bourgeoisie developed . . . the rapid improvement of all instruments of production, by the immensely facilitated means of communication, draws all, even the most barbarian, nations into civilization . . . . It compels all nations, on pain of extinction, to adopt the bourgeois mode of production.'

And the self-generated negation—the perfect homologue of technology:

> Modern bourgeois society . . . is like the sorcerer, who is no longer able to control the power of the nether world which he has called up by his spells.
>
> But not only has the bourgeoisie forged the weapons that bring death to itself; it has also called into existence the men who are to wield those weapons—the modern working class . . . . The other classes decay and disappear in the face of Modern Industry: the proletariat is its special and essential product.

Karl Marx, 'The Communist Manifesto', in David McLellan, *Karl Marx: Selected Writings*, Oxford University Press, 1977, pp. 222–29.

29. In recent years as prospects of unity of the proletariat across nation-state frontiers have withered, radical hopes of revolutionary new beginnings have tended to pivot their faith upon a qualitatively different category of victims: victimised ethnic formations like Blacks, Tribals, unemployed, etc., or peripheral geo-political entities. For instance, Wallerstein in an attempt to clarify the theoretical locus of this hope within the structure of the Modern World System has argued that certain victimised formations identifiable in terms of ethnic-cultural formations within the advanced industrialised world and peripheral regions victimised by the global division of labour could be the basis of a universal new beginning. See Immanuel Wallerstein, *The Capitalist World Economy: Essays*, Cambridge University Press, 1979.

Marx's conception had at least the merit of logical rigour in that the proletariat was posited as the bearer of a new beginning by virtue of its location at the very core of the modern industrial system. Wallerstein's attempt, like other similar attempts, is poised on a theoretical blind alley. From whence is to arise the sustaining capacity to reorder the world?

30. Consider in this context Marx's appraisal of the significance of the world-wide hegemony of Europe:

> The bourgeoisie has subjected the country to the rule of the towns . . . and has thus rescued a considerable part of the population from the idiocy of rural life. Just as it has made the country dependent on the towns, so it has made barbarian and semi-barbarian countries dependent on the civilised ones, nations of peasants on nations of bourgeoisie, the East on the West. McLellan, *Karl Marx*, p. 225.

31. Attempts to define nation or nationality ineluctably end up in circular reiteration after the fashion 'it is that which is believed to be that'. Consider for instance Gellner's attempt:

. . . primarily a political principle, which holds that the political and national unit should be congruent . . . a 'sentiment' or a 'movement' in terms of that 'principle'.

National sentiment is the feeling of anger aroused by the violation of this principle, or the feeling of satisfaction aroused by its fulfilment.

. . . nationalism is a theory of political legitimacy, which requires that ethnic boundaries should not cut across political ones.

The modern form of the age old habit of making 'exceptions on one's behalf.

Perhaps George Santayana comes closest to lucid clarity:

Our nationality is like our relations to Women: too implicated in our moral nature to be changed honourably, and too accidental to be worth changing.

Ernest Gellner, *Nations and Nationalism*, Basil Blackwell, 1963, pp. 1–3. Another characteristic instance:

A national claim is called nationalist when an ethnic group, through those who speak in its name, aims at total independence, the right to constitute itself a sovereign state. *Progress and Disillusion*, Aron, p. 45.

Also see, Elie Kedourie, *Nationalism*, Hutchinson, 1985.

32. Its obsessive enveloping power is truly invoked in the metaphor of the 'Man without his shadow' in Chamirro's novel written during the Napoleonic period, Gellner, *Nations and Nationalism*, pp. 6–7. Yet Gellner concludes: 'The great, but valid, paradox is this: nations can be defined only in terms of the age of nationalism, rather than, as you might expect, the other way round.'

33. Hegel's affirmation that the nation-state signifies the ultimate destiny of a nation, though of little value in clarifying as to what constitutes a nation, is significant in that it demarcates the salient edge of the modern system. See G.W.F. Hegel, *Lectures on the Philosophy of World History*, Cambridge University Press, 1975, pp. 133ff.

34. Heidegger was perhaps the first in the modern west to reflect on the philosophical implications of the deep rupture and enclosement inherent in modern technology. Its essence is an 'enframing' that starts Man on a course wherein 'the real everywhere' becomes a 'standing reserve', and 'regulating and securing of the standing reserve' the basis of all knowing. And that 'destining' constitutes the extreme 'danger'. During recent years this rupture has come to be designated as problems of ecological disturbance and devastation. An irony of immense complexity is that Heidegger was a votary of the Nazi creed.

Martin Heidegger, 'The Question Concerning Technology', in David Farell Krell, ed., *Martin Heidegger—Basic Writing*, Routledge & Kegan Paul, 1978, pp. 305–10.

35. The instinctive faith in Europe as the final measure of human worth survived unscathed the grim experience of fascist terror and imprisonment, Gramsci, *Prison Notebooks*, p. 416, note 5.

36. The fact of utmost significance in this context is that no one would think of designating the Renaissance as a revivalist quest.

37. Claude Levi-Strauss, *Tristes Tropiques*, Penguin, 1984, p. 48. Of course anthropology is also informed by serious scholarly concern to discern in primitive cultures elements that could be of some use for modern life. Surely that offers little solace to those marked out for extinction.

38. *Census of India, Series-I, Paper 2 of 1984*, General Population of Scheduled Castes and Scheduled Tribes, Registrar General and Census Commissioner, India, 1984, p. 3; Statements 1 and 2.

39. Consider the poignant plea (1835) of a Chief of Chermis—a 'heathen' Finnish tribe in the till-then untamed expanse of Siberia—to the Church and the Czar: 'In the forest are white birch trees, tall pines and firs; there is little juniper. God suffers them all and bids not the juniper to be a pine tree. And so are we among ourselves, like the forest. Be ye the white birch, we will remain the juniper; we will not trouble you, we will pray for the Tsar, will pay the taxes and furnish recruits, but we will not change our holy things'. Alexander Herzen, *My Past and Thoughts*, Alfred A. Knopf, 1968, Vol. 1, p. 253.

2. SELF-PLACEMENT AND COLONIAL MEDIATION

In this place and on this day, a new epoch in the history of the world is beginning, and we shall be able to say that we have been present at its origin.

Johann Wolfgang von Goethe on
the French victory at Valmy
(20 September 1972)

A Chinese prose writer has observed that the unicorn, because of its anomaly, will pass unnoticed. Our eyes see what they are accustomed to seeing. Tacitus did not perceive the Crucifixion, although his book recorded it.

Jorge Louis Borges on
'The Modesty of History'
in *Other Inquisitions*,
New York, 1965, p. 167

At the gates of Lahore steeped in 'the magic of legend', Levi-Strauss sensed a profound loss. Keenly aware of the limits entailed in the moment of his seeing, he knows that limits have to do with what, given one's capacity, one may reach out to, as also what survives within reach. What survives is at best a fragmented and exceedingly uncertain intimation of what has vanished. 'Time the destroyer' always leaves behind a 'pile of rubble'.[1] Rubble transcribes, even as it signifies effacement. Therein transcription and effacement subsist in intimate distance. Reading something of the vanished in what survives is to seek to make absences perceptible.

One could represent the moment in which it was given to Levi-Strauss to see and perceive, as a moment like any other in its play of illumination and shadows. But Levi-Strauss is stirred by profound hope of another kind. So much of what he would want to see had ceased to exist. Others before him, like Bernier and Manucci, could and perhaps did see all or much of what had vanished. But so much of what they saw they failed to perceive.

Levi-Strauss concludes on a grave note his meditation on what is given to one to see and perceive. So much of what he would and could see, he would be unable to perceive. Hundred years later, someone in his footsteps on a similar quest may well rue his failing at having missed to record so much of what he would see. For, he had still to reach that 'stage of development' wherein reality, in the very act of flux and unfolding, could be fully comprehended.[2]

Levi-Strauss' illuminating reflections on the elusive distance between seeing and perceiving are marked by a sense of deep regret and uncertainty. Yet, they seem to conclude on a note of faith in the possibility of perfect comprehension of reality in the very moment, as it were, of its making. Implicit in this faith is the assumption that a definitive statement of first principles to which reality conforms is possible and the distance between what one sees and perceives could be steadily overcome. Hence the instructive contrast: acute uncertainty in relation to the past and the expectation of final clarity in relation to the future.

Memory and the Promise of Systematic Thought

Significance is inseparable from the selective nature of human observation and memory. Were human memory devoid of the capacity to discern and discriminate, systematic observation would be inconceivable. Selective attention is the basis of systematic thought. Selection denotes a certain definitive narrowing of attention. In the very act of noticing certain things, certain other things are overlooked.

In modern cognition, selective attention is seen as the primal impulse whose true possibility is to be grasped in systematic representation. Systematic thought is seen as the sure device for the gradual overcoming of limits. According to modern belief, the principle and process of selection would progressively encompass all that exists or could exist in its entirety. Selective attention thus acquires the quality of a movement in ascent, wherein limits engender their own progressive negation. To reinvoke gravity as a parable from physics: as gravity, that ultimate force and final limit which makes purposive movement possible even as it binds and keeps in place all matter, selective attention would eventually make possible all-encompassing comprehension even as it overlooks and narrows the focus of attention. Hence the expectation, in a future however distant, of a perfect mode of comprehension attuned to all relevant details of the cognitive universe in which significance in its entirety unfolds.

The sense of something lost in observation or historical remembrance is of profound significance, but perhaps in quite another sense. This sense of loss is exceptional in that there is no certain knowing of what has been lost. Clearly such a sense cannot be lineated on the threshold of facts, even though facts may suggest what they do not transcribe. It is an inchoate and exceedingly fragile intimation of the unsaid and unintended perceptible in what one sees and can reach out to. The illuminating sweep of geological metaphors so favoured by Levi-Strauss is itself seeded in a semantic reach of fluid boundaries. Metaphors, like life, signify the flow and latent power of what may abide unintended and unperceived. Often, even in negation of an extreme kind, something of the negated lingers. Memory translates reality in complex and subtle ways. Reality is etched in memory not simply as affirmation and identity but also as marks of distance.[3]

Facts do indeed modulate cognition and memory but perhaps never as an impermeable foreclosure. Facts are known not simply in terms of what they embody and intend to communicate. Distancing suggests the inherence in human cognition of a vital spark which facts can never fully predicate or control. The quality of restless play inseparable from this inherence cannot be grasped as a movement away to a known, even though dimly perceived ground of affirmation. Consider in this context, Brodsky's sense of profound incomprehension of the feeling which began to trouble him as a very young boy in Stalin's Russia. Facts and measures of judgement he had learnt and known told him beyond a shadow of doubt that Lenin represented the very best that a human being could aspire to be. Yet, a feeling of deepening dislike for Lenin began to haunt him. This feeling began as a dislike for the looks of Lenin. He had grown up seeing photographs of Lenin which presented him as the great exemplar: heroic, loving and selfless. In nothing that he had read and heard, or in the grand visuals of Lenin that he saw at home, in school and all over Leningrad, could he recognise any blemish. And for that very reason Brodsky felt impelled to distance himself from Lenin.[4]

Perceptibility of absence and the unintended is due, perhaps, to the peculiar ambivalence of distanciation and distance as fluid contact and latent intimation. The kind of possibility this quality suggests is not all-encompassing comprehension, but the impossibility in any final sense of all-encompassing comprehension as also complete forgetfulness. It negates both, unperceivable effacement and virgin beginnings.

Facts as the Arbiter of Value

Reading and comprehension—be it historical records or observation in fieldwork—is necessarily an act of self-placement. It is a choice of the ground of vantage and reprise. Self-placement defines the ground of repose that orients attention. But however unusual the lineaments of its self-chosen locus, self-placement is necessarily in relation to what subsists as clear and conscious remembrance, as also that which subsists barely perceptible and nearly forgotten. It is a relationship that subsumes affirmation and negation, remembrance and forgetfulness.

In India, the modern universal was mediated by colonial conquest. Colonial mediation set to work a process of forbidding sweep whereby the modern universal steadily came to be the final referent upon which all categories of description and judgement were sought to be predicated. It may often happen that the posited relationship to the 'modern universal' is flawed by severe contradictions. Such flaws when noticed are seen as evidence of contamination inherent in a stagnant social reality, powerless on its own of meaningful self-reflection. Invariably, the fact of such notice arouses bitter anxieties about the clinging viscosity of a deadening reality best remembered as dead. Such notice merely reaffirms the modern universal as the final referent of validation.

Self-placement could be considered in terms of two cardinal

orientations. One could begin by accepting the modern universal as the final arbiter of worth and significance. The task of self-placement would then be to clarify as precisely as possible the requirements for transforming the by itself inert social substance of the world beyond Europe. The final purpose and essential direction of such transformation would not admit of any serious differences. Of course, at the level of certain crucial details, differences could be very sharp and not always unimportant.

Eventual unification of all social facts is the basis of modern universality. In modern cognition the relationship between 'fact' and 'value'—'what is' and, 'what could and ought to be', 'fact' and 'possibility'—seethes with a perverse paradox. To clarify the nature and implications of this paradox, first consider the conception of universality and the placement of social facts in pre-modern cognition.

Pre-modern sensibility affirms universality as an eternal cosmic destiny. It accepts the boundless variability of natural and social facts. Variability in this mode of cognition signifies a quality very different from change and a conception of History as the limitless changeability of natural and social facts in continual progression. Social facts are seen as inherently imperfect and incomplete. Perfection is posited in undifferentiated origins. Hence the recognition of the need to nurture some legitimate space for efforts that seek to reach out beyond the bounds of realisable possibilities of social structures.[5]

Universality is conceived in an entirely different sense in modern cognition. It is affirmed as a historical process of unification of all social facts. Modern change seeks to actualise the universalist possibility that is believed to inhere in varying measure in a variety of social facts. Recognition of universalist elements in social facts is sought in terms of their actual and possible functions. Not all social facts, therefore, merit equal worth and legitimacy. Social facts acquire significance in the measure of their effectiveness as functions in the making of the modern universal. Facts in themselves—at least in theory—do not signify intrinsic value.[6] Strictly speaking, the notion of intrinsic worth is of relevance only in relation to value. No fact, however substantial and seemingly all-encompassing, merits recognition as signifying intrinsic worth.

Each social fact is seen to signify an identifiable range of functions. The objective worth of a particular function or a complex of functions—as also of the social facts in which those functions originate—is marked out in terms of its actual or possible capacity to facilitate or impede the progressive making and consolidation of the modern universal. Modern cognition does indeed concede that social facts as they exist, or have so far existed, are flawed and imperfect. Modern progress, as concept and reality, claims to furnish for the first time in human history the form and substance for limitless change towards perfection.

Consider the paradoxical salience implicit in this position:

Suppositions

1. Value denotes an absolute quality. Its truth abides at a clear remove from facts. Unlike facts, value signifies intrinsic worth and affirms the unconditional sovereignty of the future.
2. Value has meaning only if it can be actualised fully and completely as fact. Change denotes the steady erosion of distance between fact and value: what is and what ought to be. Progressive overcoming of distance between fact and value constitutes the very substance and process of historical change and progress.
3. Facts acquire value as functions in a process of negation-transformation. Negation-transformation of facts signifies the presence and unfolding of value in facts. Facts as functions acquire value in the measure of their effectiveness as homologues of technology. And like technology they are fated to be superseded by more advanced functions and formations. Hence the enormous variability in the magnitude and quality of the actual value that resides in different facts. Value of a fact ceases the moment a particular fact has exhausted its putative function in sustaining the modern universal. Sovereignty of the future and value as progressive negation of facts denotes the final purpose and definitive process entailed in historical change.

Implications

1. Positing value as the maker of facts has meant the consolidation of a stern and virtually unchanging hierarchy of facts. Facts at the apex of this hierarchy have come to denote the embodiment of value actualised in historical progression: the actual presence of absolute value as it really exists. Hence

the inversion: value as the maker of facts actualised as the absolute value of certain facts.

2. Social facts of the world beyond Europe, incapable on their own of self-movement, are seen to represent archaic forms devoid of historical substance. Affirmation of value therefore requires the more or less complete negation of such facts. Critical self-appraisal and self-recognition are thus inconceivable within the cognitive universe intrinsic to such facts. The utmost one could do is to ascertain and measure the relative receptivity of such facts to the dynamic of modern change.

3. Since no fact can legitimately claim intrinsic significance, the value of all that exists or could exist, be it language, memory, death, the earth or the cosmos itself, is made contingent upon historical progression of which the human logos is at once the cause and the instrument.

Refusal to accept facts as they are and have been defines the point of prime departure for the modern quest. Value in modern cognition signifies not just a statement of what ought to be, but as much, what could be. Could and ought are posited as congruent categories. Facts, like currencies in the world market, signify abstract value that is inherently unstable and subject to continual change. Hence the paradox: a quest that envisioned value as the maker of facts has come to accept facts as the arbiter of value, as also, actual as the possible.

Self-placement that proceeds from an affirmation of the modern universal as the final referent clarifies not so much the nature of pre-modern reality as it is and has been, but as to what ought to become of that reality in the future. Such self-placement is oriented to clarifying the requirements for transforming and reconstituting what is assumed to be an essentially inert substance in some variety of likeness to the dynamic substance of Europe. Such self-placement does not dissolve differences altogether. Differences concerning certain details could still be sharp and at times very bitter. Such differences concerning the tribal reality in India could be stated as follows:

1. Realisable pace and level of upward social-economic mobility of tribals. It is the cardinal consideration in debates concerning

programmes and policies of tribal development, education and political participation.

2. Tribal participation in the process of modern transformation. Perceptions on this question are often the cause of fierce disagreements. These could be about the nature of space available for tribal participation in the established framework of laws and political economy. More often, differences concern the perceived distance between what is allowed in law and denied in actual practice.

   Implicit in this question is an urgent moral concern. Inadequate flow of the benefits of progress is seen as the consequence of lack of human concern and respect for the potential capacity of the tribals. The argument is that, if the tribals were truly treated as equals and with sympathy, transformation would be more swift and less traumatic. Respect for tribals would also mean willingness to recognise those aspects of tribal culture and social ethos which could be of positive value in the process of transformation.

3. Implications of the traditional social ethos and the colonial inheritance. Perceptions on this issue differ essentially as to the extent to which this entrenched burden of inequality and exploitation impedes tribal progress. Invariably, colonial attitudes as distinct from modern concerns, and traditional caste sensibility are seen to mutually reinforce an ethos and structure of exclusion, dominance and exploitation.[7]

Self-placement that proceeds from acceptance of the 'modern universal' as the definitive referent is thus not quite free of uncertainties. It entails choices of a kind. But however sharp the differences, the basic orientation and final purpose of such self-placement is clear and fixed. The uncertainty is not with regard to what ought to be the state of things. Rather, it has to do with the precise details of how the state of things that ought to be, is to be actualised. So it is that even as the past keeps changing, the future remains certain and full of promise. Every detail of human life and consciousness is seen to be truly itself to the extent that it helps sustain the difficult process of transformation. Within this framework, the epistemic space for cultural autonomy and diversity remains precarious and sternly constricted.[8] Like life itself, the significance and truth of cultural facts and values are seen to be contingent upon their identifiable functions in the ineluctable sweep of modern transformation.

Concerning Rejection of the Modern Universal

The problem of self-placement is of a distinctly different order if one begins by rejecting the modern universal as the definitive referent. First, a clarification. Rejection of the 'modern universal' as the definitive referent does not mean that modern reality is to be negated in its entirety. It also does not mean that some kind of pre-modern restoration is possible or desirable.[9] Certain distinctly modern concerns, for instance, the level of surplus generation and the way in which it is appropriated and used, could continue to be significant and crucial. What then are to be the basis and criteria of judgement and choice? In other words, what is to be the ground of repose and frame of definitive reference for such self-placement?

To clarify the nature of the attempt, first an elaboration of what it definitely does not intend. The attempt is to clarify the possible ground of self-placement in relation to the tribal reality in India. 'Possible ground' is an issue and a problem precisely because this ground is to be grasped in terms that seek to exclude the 'modern universal' as the definitive referent. But this exclusion (of the modern universal) is not intended as the decisive grand discontinuity, so characteristic of the modern cognitive mode. Conception of change, as essentially an unfolding that begins with a grand discontinuity commands an irresistible attraction in the modern context. Whatever its implications as historical praxis, such a conception of change provides an epistemic referent of fierce clarity that visions of revolution and virgin beginning so devoutly cherish. Implicit in such a conception is the profound certainty that the meaning and reality of all that exists, or could exist, is pivoted on to an identifiable node of facts and beliefs.

Consider in this context two historic assertions, self-consciously formulated in polar opposition to each other. Our colonial rulers were convinced that to activate the dynamic of modern becoming in the tribal hinterland, the definitive first step had to be the creation and consolidation of the institution of private property.[10] From the other extremity of this cognitive horizon, the vision of proletarian revolution was premised on the certainty that the abolition of private property would clear the ground for a new and higher form of human living. The problem common to both formulations is to delineate precisely and correctly that pivotal node of facts and beliefs which binds and holds in place all that exists. And if the identification of, as it were, the pivot that binds things as they are in place be correct, its negation would secure the 'grand discontinuity' which would recreate and fill the primal ground for an altogether new kind of affirmation. In sharp contrast to the uncertain and inherently ambivalent emergence of something new in the past, this ground of affirmation would be consciously willed. Thus released from the awful burden of a flawed past, the very sense and quality of being and becoming would be forever transformed.

The phrase, 'the world turned upside down', or Marx's claim that he merely made Hegel 'stand on his head' denote much more than picturesque rhetoric.[11] They are an apposite metaphorical rendering of the salient feature of a cognitive mode. The image of geometrical inversion signifies, in its literal sense, an embedded deeper fact. In this image, the point of first beginning that orients cognition in this mode comes vividly to the fore: the belief that human life could be comprehended and governed as a vast and very complex mechanism of immensely varied parts. 'Overturning' and 'reversal' signify the unmaking of the world as it is, so as to clear the way for a consciously willed primordium of sheer positivity.

Categories like making and unmaking, order and chaos, form and formlessness as markers of that prime grid upon which life subsists in its complex flow, represents a sense of reality as old perhaps as Man on this planet. To this day, it is a sense alive and vivid in rituals and the everyday rhythms of tribal living in India. But that primal sense of a never to be concluded eternal play of chaos and order, form and formlessness, is sought to be transmuted, in the image of geometrical inversion, into a concluding final act. The modern quest is to prepare the ground for the final decisive battle against uncertainty and chaos: the triumph of order over chaos, possibility over fact.[12] Thereafter, all that is or could be (fact and possibility), would be amenable to form and order. True, the staggering profusion of parts that comprise the vast mechanism of human living and the forbidding complexity of their relationship make the task of comprehending its regulating principles exceedingly risky. But the belief is that there exists that pivotal node wherein all the varied and prolix parts intersect. If that could be correctly identified and appropriate levers devised to reach and regulate that node, human civilisation could be recast truly as the unflawed realm of freedom and creativity. Hence the recurrence of that awful arrogance implicit in the faith that it is given to some individual or group to use past failures to perfect ways to wage and win the concluding awesome final battle for a future in perfection.

Self-placement that seeks to be beyond the definitive reach of the modern universal has therefore to be grasped in terms other than those of 'reversal' and 'grand discontinuity'. Rejection of 'reversal' and 'grand discontinuity' does not deny the fact and legitimacy of change. But it does negate the notion of virgin beginnings and the possibility of unflawed value as the maker of facts. Value does not signify pure possibility, detached and sanitised from the contaminating realm of imperfect facts. How then is one to read the word, value? What kind of a mediation does it signify between what is, and what ought to be?

Value as a recognition and indication of categorical preference lineates the distance and tension between 'what is', and 'what ought to be'. As a referent of what could and ought to be, value does suggest possibilities, near and distant, for facts to become very different from what they happen to be. But value is not merely a cognitive instrument for historical change and progression. Perhaps it signifies, a presence exceedingly more subtle and intricate. Value, even as it invokes that realm which has never been but could perhaps in some measure be, affirms the truth of a profound self-sense that subsists away and beyond historical progression. It is an affirmation of life as it is and as it ought to be not simply as a metaphor of change, but also as a metaphor of the eternal return: order and chaos, form and formlessness, life and its negation, birth and death. Change and progression are subsumed in the metaphor of eternal return. Historical progression seeks to exclude repetition and the cycle of eternal return from the universe of significance. At best 'eternal return' is seen to merit significance as routinised function: the as yet unmastered segment of Nature and Biology.[13]

The attempt in the present study is to seek the 'possible ground' for self-placement indicated by the texture of interaction between tribals and the world beyond, worked out in the midst of a historical terrain untouched by the modern universal. Fragments of this texture are taken note of in modern discourse. It could often be that some of these fragments are cherished as artefacts of unusual aesthetic value, or useful skills.[14] But the significant fact is that whatever the nature of notice (favourable or dismissive) recognition and assessment is always in relation to fragments. Certain parts—not necessarily unchanging and stagnant—which arise and unfold as elements in a certain texture of coherence and possibility and noticed as interesting are designated as 'tradition'. Tradition in this context signifies no more than a collection of fragments. Hence the near absence of recognition in modern discourse of the essential texture within which what survive as fragments subsisted as elements in a complex of reference and meaning.

The word tradition, in the context of the world beyond Europe, involves a crucial but little noticed definitional sleight. Tradition is posited as manifestly incapable of self-movement and self-appraisal in counterposition to modernity. What is more, modern discourse assumes as axiomatic its authority to measure and judge the worth of tradition entirely in terms of its own categories. Yet, the very suggestion of assessing tradition and modernity in terms of categories that arise from a cognitive realm untouched by modernity, would invariably be seen as vacuous sentiment. But that is precisely what self-placement beyond the definitive reach of the modern universal seeks. The attempt is to shift the locus of cognition and judgement.[15]

Such a shift of cognitive locus requires a careful look at the historical texture of transmission of tribal remembrance. What is the historical context in which 'self-placement' becomes an issue and a serious problem? And what are the constraints and considerations which impinge upon our understanding of tribal remembrance?

Colonial Mediation and Perception of Tribal Reality

Perception of tribal reality prior to the colonial impingement is oriented to two distanced resources: archival–historical records and folk-memory. Archival–historical resource commands clear preference in modern discourse as the more accurate representation of things as they were. Folk memory is recognised as valid remembrance only in so far as it amplifies and confirms what is explicitly stated or at least discernible as implicit in historical records.

Almost the entire body of extant historical material refers to a tradition of historiography instinct with a concern to discern and measure the potential for transformation that may be present in the virtually immobile realm beyond Europe. Often the person who transcribed in meticulous detail a particular situation or event may feel resigned to the irretrievably dim prospects of transformation for that situation or community. But transformation as the desirable possibility remains the supreme measure and point of vantage. Colonial governance of a barely known and unfamiliar land had to begin as a concerted effort to render it in some measure known and familiar. Hence the enormous volume of diverse information and comment that began to be assembled during the last quarter of the eighteenth century.[16] Prior to that the desire to know and control was defined within a severely restricted threshold of political possibilities.

Records assembled during the early phase of colonial governance were concerned primarily with areas of settled cultivation along the main river lines. Their foremost concern was to map local social–political arrangements and ascertain their implications for acceptable levels of revenue demand. Revenue yields were a decisive consideration. The minimal expectation was that the area over which colonial control was extended should at least yield revenue sufficient to meet the costs of local administration.

As effective colonial control extended deeper into the hinterland (early nineteenth century), areas of 'intermittent' and 'shifting cultivation' (primarily tribal areas) began to be noticed in somewhat greater detail. The passion to know and control in this context was modulated to:

1. The imperative need to consolidate the nuclei of settled cultivation to facilitate regular flow of revenue; sufficient at least to defray the cost of local administration.
2. Securing tacit acceptance and loyalty of influential segments of the tribal–peasant communities.
3. Securing continuous supply of timber, other forest produce and, later during the nineteenth century, minerals (notably coal and iron) at minimal cost.[17]

As the sense of an enduring imperial destiny for the 'British dominion' in India deepened, detailed ethnographic data of no direct consequence to the needs of revenue administration began to be collected.[18] The Court of Directors of the East India Company, in a despatch dated 7 January 1807, instructed the Bengal Government to 'undertake a statistical survey' of the area under their 'immediate authority', as it was certain to be 'attended with much utility'. The intent was to map out certain crucial details: 'condition of local inhabitants, prevalence and prevention of disease, social organisation, religious customs, and precise details concerning emoluments and power of local priests and chiefs'. The foremost concern was to ascertain: 'what circumstances exist or may probably arise that might attach them to government, or render them disaffected'.[19]

The sheer magnitude and what appeared to those intrepid imperial administrators from the British Isles to be the near chaotic diversity of belief and social configurations was not something that could in a few years be bound into manageable classification. After seven years of incessant effort, the first Surveyor, Dr. Francis Buchanan, could barely manage to report on nine districts of the Bengal Presidency.[20] The structure of attention of colonial rulers was intimately shaped by the perceived fate and aspirations of British rule. The census of 1881 signifies the first comprehensive classificatory rendering of India in modern categories. Towards the end of the nineteenth century, the colossal enterprise of measurement and classification initiated in 1807 was consolidated to the point of a substantive statement: District Manuals and Gazetteers, Settlement Reports, Census Records, Tribes and Castes Handbooks, Linguistic Surveys, Archaeological Surveys, travelogues, monographs and articles.[21]

These records signify an elaborate and truly stupendous exercise of placement within neat and relatively inflexible boundaries. As perhaps in all situations of encounter with the strange and unknown, observation was oriented to known, familiar categories and patterns of interaction. Distance and discontinuity between the known and unfamiliar was sought to be located in terms of elements that negated, or indicated in some instances, similarity with a known remote past.

Colonial Rule as the Instrument of Unification and Progress

Colonial sensibility was very earnest in its faith in the inherently liberating power of Man's continually enhanced ability to reshape material reality. The belief was that to British rule is given the historic mission to firmly posit Man as the active, supreme and self-conscious principle in the Man–Nature dialectic. Progressive elimination of distances—geographical and social—was grasped as the prising of possibilities to render fully known what had hitherto been barely perceived. Colonial rule was seen as the only viable instrument for binding into a workable historical substance what on its own would remain forever inert and atomised: an unavoidable necessity in historical progression towards 'Man as the measure of things'. Unification was genuinely believed to be the precondition for universality. That inevitably nurtured a sense of awesome responsibility: extending the dynamic of modern civilisation into a realm stubbornly unreceptive to the profound promise of universal progress.[22]

Colonial conquest as a conscious instrument in the service of the modern universal was unlike any other that had preceded it. It was the outcome of a distinctly modern impulse to measure and tame the world around. Colonial self-perception was emphatic in demarcating its manifest superiority to all pre-modern conquests. Whereas the principal object of pre-modern conquest was to secure control over less powerful human groups, colonial conquest as a modern enterprise sought mastery primarily over things. The implicit colinearity of subjugation and universal progress, so strident and salient in colonial self-perception, requires careful thought. It flows out of what could be characterised as the formative paradox of the modern quest: progress and universal human freedom are predicated on the progressive and complete subjugation of Nature.

Consider some of the implications of this paradox that are of direct relevance to the remembrance of the pre-modern tribal reality.

Homocentric values have come to be so intimate a part of contemporary sensibility and discourse that their absolute pre-eminence is simply accepted as axiomatic. The posited equation between subjugation of Nature and universal human freedom seems unexceptionable. Without seeming at all illogical, one could speak of subversion of Nature as natural. It is a position which bristles with serious philosophical embarrassments. To clarify the problem of self-placement in relation to remembrance of the pre-modern tribal situation, it would suffice to focus on certain implications of the posited binary equation between human freedom and subjugation of Nature.

First and foremost, subjugation of Nature requires that the

distance between Man and Nature be unyielding and impenetrable. Demarcation of this distance requires that Nature as an integral complex be systematically dismantled, and the existential space be rationally split into a manageable hierarchy of useful segments. In modern cognition these requirements represent an absolute norm. They are accepted as cardinal indicators of meaningful historical movement towards an ultimate threshold for all mankind. Its universalist promise is believed to inhere in what is perceived as the actual presence of absolute value in measurable facts. The belief is that the release of these facts from the constraints of their inherited placement within narrow specifities of cultural texture and parochial allegiance, would set in motion the dynamic play of absolute value. The re-making of the existential space—boundaries of private property and state control, as also cognitive demarcations for legitimate cohesions—is thus affirmed as the limitless sweep of a universal epistemic space: the tangible working out of the sovereignty of human reason and systematic thought.

From this cognitive vantage, colonial administrators as the actual and living 'measure of things' confronted the tribal native: so little removed from Nature that the things he could call his own seemed unworthy of being measured. Other natives, subsisting primarily on settled agriculture, also seemed nowhere near being the 'measure of things'. But clearly the existential situation of the 'tribal native' seemed frozen at a threshold far lower than that of the 'Hindu' or the 'Muslim' native.

The tribal hinterland signified a social space least touched by purposive human activity. It was perceived as a romantic virgin field, somewhat akin to the state of Man and things in Europe of thousands of years ago.[23] It demarcated the lineage, albeit frozen, of a universal human trajectory. And this frozen lineage manifestly incapable of self-movement towards something higher and better, could only be pushed towards purposive movement by the coercive power of colonial rule.

The compelling and immediate reason for altering, however slightly, the sensibility and social reality of the tribal native stemmed from the need to secure acceptance of colonial rule. This compulsion engendered an ironical twist. Legitimacy of colonial rule was dependent on the clear demonstration of a near impossible distance between the 'Native' and 'Man as the measure of things'. Colonial discourse and colonial governance could never quite master these conflicting impulses. Colonial ethnography of the tribal native tended to subtly transpose these conflicting impulses into an affirmation of the legitimacy of colonial mediation.

In Ethnology Levi-Strauss perceives the remorse of the West.[24] Ethnology does not negate progress. But the affirmation is in the tradition of critiques of progress. Its vital impulses flow out of both secular social concerns regarding exploitation and oppression, and the older Christian invocation of concern for the other and critique of power. Ethnology in this sense, at least so far as it concerns tribals in India, had a remarkably weak presence.

Colonial perception of the tribal in India, quite unlike the European perception of the American Indian or the Australian aborigines, was mediated by a third presence: variously characterised as Hindu, Mughal or Maratha. Remorse was directed, as it were, outwards. Concern for the other, in this context, meant restraining this 'third presence'. Hence the emphatic and in certain situations genuine self-perception of colonial rule as the 'protector and saviour' of powerless marginal communities like tribals.[25]

In colonial discourse the 'third presence' came to acquire a peculiar, convoluted significance at two related levels. First and foremost, it seemed to confirm the colonial belief that the word 'India' essentially represented a geographical space. Contacts and linkages between diverse castes and communities living in India were seen to be no more than the compulsions etched by geology. Hence the impassioned colonial refrain: India prior to British rule was no more than a geographical expression. Whatever attenuated historical substance the word India may seem to signify, was the outcome of railways, telegraph, English language and colonial courts established by British rule.[26]

The most unsettling complication for British rule was that India, unlike Greenland or the vast continents of America colonised by Europe, was a land with a vast and dense human presence. Greenland or America could be dealt with as virtually empty of human presence. True, these vast spaces were not entirely empty of human presence. But the scale and capacity of this presence to harness the wherewithal to resist and impede the march of progress was not of much consequence. These vast spaces could be effectively appropriated and humanised to the last detail as a New Europe.[27] There were no insuperable impediments to constrict and contaminate the vigorous play of the modern Man–Nature dialectic. The quality of the human presence in India was not seen as radically different from that in the vast spaces remade as New Europes. Clearly the human presence in India, frozen at a bare remove from Nature, was powerless on its own to harness the energy and direction for meaningful self-movement. But India, so far as colonial rulers were concerned, represented a geographical space complicated by a human presence on a vast scale. To extend the range of reference, human life in China was also seen to subsist on a rudimentary threshold of Man–Nature interaction. Like India, the human presence was dense, and on a vast scale. But very unlike India, China was seen to be linked into a unity not just by geological contiguity, but in a real and substantial political-historical sense.[28]

India, in colonial perception, represented a most unusual situation. The Man–Nature dialectic all across the vast stretches of the subcontinent remained for the most part frozen at a rudimentary threshold. Within this threshold, two clearly separable and distinct levels could be demarcated. Both levels co-existed with little change in a state of immemorial suspension. Settled agriculture denoted the relatively advanced and therefore dominant level in the Man–Nature equation. Shifting cultivation, the predominant mode of livelihood in tribal areas, denoted Man–Nature interaction frozen at a level where human claims on Nature could have no legal legitimacy.[29] At both levels human life was constrained to be perpetually repetitive and stagnant. But communities which subsisted on an essentially static economy of settled agriculture could muster far superior coercive power. These communities, each a world unto itself and engaged in bitter incessant conflict with each other, comprised the 'third presence': a juxtaposition of dispersed conflicting entities.

In terms of colonial cognition, India represented a perfect instance, to transpose a category favoured by Geertz, of social and cultural 'involution' on a stupendous scale.[30] Man–Nature equations remained virtually frozen. Life within these equations conformed to an unchanging pattern of immemorial repetition. The worth and legitimacy of each moment and action was sought in the degree of perceived resemblance with an exemplary past. That past represented the ultimate and eternal referent for validation and judgement. Similar, or even exactly identical, Man–Nature configurations sustained a confounding variety of diverse social–cultural textures. Even worse, nothing in the beliefs, values, or the existential interaction of these dispersed disparate entities held promise of a possible ground for enduring unity. Hence the recurrent assertion in colonial discourse that colonial mediation represented fortuitous convergence of the imperatives of progress and human justice.

Colonial placement of the tribal reality in India brings to the fore an issue that touches in a fundamental sense the problem of self-placement: meticulous transmutation of a complex civilisational texture of intensely varied cultural–social facts into a turbulent dispersion of unrelated and unrelatable facts. Self-placement that seeks release in some significant sense from the definitive bind of the modern universal, has to begin as an attempt to clarify the nature of this civilisational texture. The sheer magnitude and resilience of tribal distinctness in close proximity to what colonial demarcation designated as the 'non-tribal' would be inconceivable in the absence of a texture of interaction which allowed configurations rich in cultural diversity to co-exist in close proximity for several millennia.

Victims as Participants in Colonial Discourse

To comprehend the self-perception of colonial rule simply as a form of moral convenience and self-indulgence on a grand scale would be a serious error. Even the most despicable human phenomenon can never completely suppress some semblance of moral awareness. Notions of self-justification and sense of shame are for that reason never without some significance. The most persistent if not always discernible aspect of the colonial mediation is its mode of discourse and comprehension, which still serves as our definitional resource for legal substance, human worth and valid cognition.

The true measure of the potency of colonial rule inheres, not in the political structures so self-consciously dismantled by the nationalist upsurge, but in the subliminal reach of colonial discourse that has come to be so intimate a part of us. Words like colonial discourse and colonial sensibility have been used in the preceding section to refer to the discourse and mental disposition of our colonial rulers. But there is another dimension to it, or should one say, another recreation of it lived by the colonial subjects. Colonial discourse in this sense is as much a creation of natives as it is of the colonial rulers.[31] Of course, the dissimilarity in the terms of participation is of crucial significance. Natives participated as victims. Being victims in this sense means something deeper and far more annihilating than crude physical subjugation.

Victims, as participants in colonial discourse, can and indeed do acquire rare and complex skills. But the cardinal referents which orient recognition of discrete information and skills in an existential situation to the rhythm of a self-validating knowledge complex are located beyond the universe of colonial discourse. Life and movement in this universe of discourse is akin to the play of shadows. Even as the mighty presence that casts shadows seems to recede into the far distance, shadows loom and lengthen, enclosing all in their insubstantiality.

Any attempt to step away from the play of shadows is constrained to be on an uncertain, fragile threshold. Colonial discourse is so intimately with us that its categories and modes of comprehension cling to what may appear as its most categorical negation. Perhaps precisely for that reason Gandhi's critique of colonial rule began as a search and affirmation of intellectual and historical spaces least touched by the colonial impingement. Both as historical fact and possibility tribal social cohesion and sensibility in India signify such a space in Gandhi's vision.[32]

Limits and the Curse of Mediacy

Understanding social–historical facts is also inherently a suggestion of possibilities. 'Hermeneutics' and the recently felt need for vigilant attention to 'apperception' has resulted, in the rendering of Clifford Geertz, in a 'scattering of frameworks'. One likes to believe that this drift is towards a 'realm of creative uncertainty'.[33] It is oriented to two distinct philosophical impulses in modern discourse.

For Habermas, the specific conditions under which understanding unfolds are a constraint, an unavoidable (given the structure of historical being) disturbance that contaminates understanding. Such 'disturbance' and the consequent contamination, though not easily exorcised, has to be steadily controlled and gradually reduced.[34]

Understanding as a problem of Hermeneutics, according to Geertz, suggests social science homologues to the philosophical premonition of Wittgenstein: the 'highway' visible and transparent but 'permanently closed'; and human cognition forever an exploration of alleys and byways meandering sometimes close to the 'highway'. Ambivalence and disturbance signify in this vision the ineradicable condition of human cognition, as also its creative possibilities.[35]

Recognition of the presence of 'disturbance' in the process of comprehension as the first step towards its eventual eradication constitutes the definitive thrust in modern discourse. In certain specific contexts neat notions of accurate representation and categorical certainty have been discarded. Yet, in the apposite rendering of Ernst Cassirer, 'this standpoint represents a typical attitude which is ever recurrent' in 'theory of art as well as in theory of knowledge'.[36] Persistent recurrence of 'disturbance' and the intrusion of 'limits' is regarded in 'scientific intellectual investigation' as akin to myth; not a particular kind of power of formulation, but a 'mental defect'. The quest continues to be to some day and somehow rescue the power of systematic formulation from the 'curse of mediacy'. In other words, the systematic reconstruction of a mental universe wherein 'true forms of objects' would stand forth accurate and unshakably firm in language uncontaminated by 'forms of thought'.[37]

The modern search for an unflawed mode of comprehension is intended to be the basis for structuring its perfect existential homologue. Distance between the world as it is and as it ought to be has perhaps always caused grave anxieties. Uniqueness of the modern sensibility inheres not in the perception of that distance, or the way it is defined, but in the belief that for the first time it is given to the human logos to so recast the existential situation of Man as to vanquish for all time the distance between 'what is' and 'what ought to be'.[38] Affirmation of the possibility of unflawed comprehension is a declaration that the final and irreversible triumph of order and form is a realisable project. The seductive power of this arrogant belief could perhaps be most truly represented as an inverted form of magical bewitchment. The magician knows that the powers of magic can never be more than a fleeting conquest; something grasped unbeknown from the vastness of chaos. Magicians know that their most amazing conquests are but a fragile and fortuitous occurrence: form forever on the brink of formlessness. In modern knowledge this relationship is inverted into a linear movement of progressive consolidation: chaos and formlessness steadily edged closer to form and order.

Cognitive Shifts and Hearing Spaces

Recognition of social facts takes place in relation to some structure of historical reference. This structure is constituted by categories in terms of which facts are sought and investigated. Categories and perceptions are bound by a relationship of intimate distance. It is not a relationship of mirror-like reflection. Each category lineates amidst the paronymia of references the nature of attention. It marks out the flow of access to a certain range of significance. Access, inevitably, conditions and forecloses what lies within reach, as also that which is reached and recognised. Like space, categories are bounded by perspective.

Each word and concept refers to other words and concepts. And this reference is infinite. Signification and meaning unfold in a particular structure of reference. Reference is never linear. It tends always to return to that which in the first instance impels reference beyond itself. Semantic value can only be comprehended as a space of inherently uncertain and fluid boundaries lineated in a particular reference structure. Boundary itself cannot be discerned simply as a firm inflexible line that divides and separates. It can only be comprehended as a texture and space that converges into two, or more, recognisably distinct semantic values. Boundaries divide but perhaps always as fluid extensions. In such a structure of reference a final terminal reference is inconceivable. Hence the potential which inheres in the language and comprehension capacity of each human collective to assimilate and express an infinite range of new meanings: rendering the unknown comprehensible and meaningful. And that is a process mediated by the dialectic of reference to what, prior to the encounter with the unknown, was known and somewhat familiar. An ineradicable tension therefore seems to inhere in the distance that never completely dissolves between comprehension and that which is comprehended.

Cognitive shifts signify much more than a meticulous elaboration of hitherto unnoticed facts. They denote shifts in the mode of placement and signification. Cognitive shifts happen precisely because cognitive boundaries, etched as they have to be in the paronymia of reference, are prone to inherent disturbances. Cognitive boundaries are never entirely stable or foreclosed, and, cognitive shifts do happen.

The impulse towards a shift stems from the very cognitive ground which in some cardinal sense that impulse seeks to negate. In that sense, the most trenchant negation is an act of modulation. New beginning in the distinctly modern sense of 'grand discontinuity' brought forth by human volition, somewhat like the act of creation ex nihilo, has so far simply never happened. Cognitive boundaries do shift and long entrenched cognitive limits may indeed rupture in most unexpected ways, but never perhaps in the sense of a grand leap on to a threshold created, as it were, ex nihilo.[39] Such shifts may linger unnoticed for long periods on the margins of a particular discourse. They acquire a presence in relation to intricate strands of receptivity, or what could be termed as the available 'hearing space' in a discourse. Not everything that is said is heard or remembered. And even when something or someone is heard, it is perhaps rarely in the sense in which it has been voiced.

Hearing space in its basic sense denotes the range and complexity of cognition in a particular civilisational–cultural texture. In that sense, the fact that something said seems to linger barely noticed on the margins of a discourse, remains exceedingly significant. In civilisations and traditions that seek to engage and measure complex and conflicting strands of memory, a kind of primal hearing space is available to sharply opposed varieties of thought and ways of thinking. Not to forget completely is a function of deep complexities without which no civilisation can perhaps last for long.[40]

Hearing space in the sense of assertive historical presence denotes a different kind of mediation. It has to do with the structure of immediate attention. The relationship between the immediate structure of attention and the enduring primal spaces which orient cognition can at best be indicated. Consider in this context the plight of some of the largely forsaken voices in India soon after the end of colonial rule.

To those of us who were in school during the fifties and the early sixties, the Nehru era seemed vibrant with promise of better times to come. Bhakra Nangal as the 'temple of modern India' was a metaphor that stirred our fondest hope that in time the modern realm of prosperity and power, hitherto the exclusive domain of Europe and America, shall surely also be vouchsafed to us.

The few lonely voices, like Ram Manohar Lohia speaking of the oustees of Rihand Dam (1960) as the 'victims of development', were swept aside virtually unheard.[41] Such voices seemed unfortunate and irritating obstructions on the grand highway of development. Among some they harkened dark fears of an unconscious 'anti-national conspiracy' to keep India backward: something like a death wish.

Another instructive instance in this context is the recent recognition of the problem of 'bonded labour'. This social fact came into pointed national focus only after Indira Gandhi chose to include it in her 'twenty point programme'. The manner of its inclusion is a telling comment on the self-confidence and sensitivity of even the most radical and vigilant segments of our intelligentsia. According to Indira Gandhi, she came to know of the existence of 'bonded labour' when someone told her of its prevalence at Bhubaneshwar airport just before she boarded a flight for Delhi. And she instantly recognised that 'abolition of bonded labour' would glow bright and radical in her twenty point banner to legitimise the Emergency.[42] Whatever the intent, the fact that bonded labour became an issue of serious national debate only after its inclusion in the 'twenty point programme' remains significant. The fact of bonded labour had long been known to many people. Details concerning its incidence and extent had been meticulously recorded year after year in the reports of the Commissioner for Scheduled Castes and Tribes.[43] And yet, prior to its inclusion in the twenty point programme, bonded labour never became an issue of serious concern and debate for our social science or politics.

Consider another telling instance. India has its modest share of Fukuoka devotees.[44] But they are unable to grasp the simple and very large fact that Fukuoka's 'natural farming' is a close kin of the 'penda' and 'jhum' in our tribal hinterland. To see the close identity between them requires no great skill. What is more, it is a question that could be considered in precise technical details.

In the first decade of this century, Gandhi in *Hind Swaraj* invoked the everyday rhythms of folk-tribal living as the truly resilient realm of Indian civilisation, least touched by colonial mediation. Implicit in this invocation is a recognition of tribal reality as a vital strand in the texture of Indian civilisation. Through the long years of struggle against colonial rule Gandhi never ceased to speak of 'Tribals, Harijans and Women' as the cardinal categories of suffering and injustice. But even that voice, incomparable in its effectiveness when it came to waging battle against colonial rule, seemed distant and unreal; indeed, so far as our dominant modern colonial elite was concerned, an unfortunate burden of archaic sentimentality.[45]

Most details outlined in the sections that follow concerning the pre-modern tribal situation figure in some form in recorded colonial remembrance. Certainly, recorded colonial remembrance does not negate them. The need is to work out the placement of this remembrance in terms of an orientation that seeks affirmation from another cognitive realm.

Notes

1. Claude Levi-Strauss, *Tristes Tropiques*, Penguin, 1984, pp. 49, 51.
2. '. . . I may be insensitive to reality as it is taking shape at this very moment, since I have not reached the stage of development at which I would be capable of perceiving it.' *Ibid.*, p. 51.
3. Levi-Strauss speaks of music in post-Renaissance Europe as akin to myth in its intellectual as well as emotive function. Like myth, the meaning of music can only be comprehended if in each 'variation you keep in mind the theme you listened to before' and remain 'conscious of the totality of music'. Claude Levi-Strauss, *Myth and Meaning*, Routledge & Kegan Paul, 1980, pp. 46–49.

   A theme illumined as mediations in the minutest of everyday utterance and living of the infinite and eternal in Claude Levi-Strauss, *The Raw and the Cooked*, Basil Blackwell, 1970.

   Octavio Paz speaks of poetry as akin to myth and music in its 'indissoluble unity' for the 'tiniest change alters the whole composition'. As in myth and music, each listener is a silent participant. Poem is 'frozen speech'. Beyond it nothing but 'noise or silence, a senselessness' beyond words. So it is that a poem says something which it alone 'can say, without ever saying it entirely'. Octavio Paz, *Claude Levi-Strauss—An Introduction*, Dell Publishing Co., 1974, pp. 57–60.

   Foucault has argued that the quest since the sixteenth century has been to make language speak precisely 'that which is' and to rigorously restrain it from saying 'anything more than what is said'. Pure meaning. As it were, the spelling out of human intent so entirely clear and conscious as to be immune from representations other than the one intended. A possibility never really available because:

   > Language stands half way between the visible forms of nature and the secret conveniences of esoteric discourse. It is a fragmented nature, divided against itself and deprived of its original transparency by admixture; it is a secret that carries within itself, though near the surface, the decipherable signs of what it is trying to say. It is at the same time a buried revelation and a revelation that is gradually being restored to ever greater clarity.

   Michel Foucault, *The Order of Things—An Archaeology of the Human Sciences*, Tavistock Publications, 1982, pp. 43, 35–36.

   Foucault's seminal intervention arises precisely from a cognitive terrain of elusive unintended persistence. The form and prime impulse of history, he knows, are not to be grasped as complicated details to be resolved in their appropriate duration as moves towards 'growing perfection'. Rather it is to be grasped as 'conditions of possibility'.

4. J. Brodsky, *Less Than One*, Ferror Strauss Giroux, 1986.

5. For instance, the ascetic and the magician confront and seek to grapple with a reality beyond the ken of social structures and everyday experience. That reality is seen to impinge upon and determine the fate of established structures and everyday experience. In that may also be perceived the inherence of power to impart to everyday living and experience dazzling possibilities, in themselves unflawed and perfect, but actualised in fleeting cosmic fragments.

In being in touch with that numinous reality Man senses his 'profound nothingness'. Yet, in the minutest of earthly living, Man seeks 'cosmic valence'. His habitation, so very essential and universal to human living, is not perceived as an 'object', or as Le Corbusier would induce us to believe, 'a machine to live in', but the very 'universe that man constructs for himself by imitating the paradigmatic creation of the gods, cosmogony.'

Mircea Eliade, *The Sacred and the Profane—The Nature of Religion*, Harcourt, Brace and World, 1959, pp. 11ff, 50–57, and 63ff.

On the concept of city and its numinous referent, see Ananda K. Coomaraswamy, *What is Civilisation? And Other Essays*, Oxford University Press, 1989, pp. 1–12.

6. Of course, in modern practice certain facts are treasured literally in freeze. The unique value placed upon first editions, anniversaries, manuscripts, originals as opposed to copies even if they conform to perfection with the original, brings to the fore the sense of deep unease at the heart of the modern faith. Witness the recent hysteria and quick retraction by a Japanese millionaire of his last wish to have his collection of paintings by European masters cremated with him. Most instructive perhaps is the preservation of the bodies of the great warriors of a faith that seeks complete mastery over all facts as manipulable functions: Lenin, Stalin, Mao and Ho Chi Minh.

Belief in the eventual human ability to control and mould all facts has been the basis of modern optimism and energy. Its philosophic basis, however, remains, exceedingly fragile. See Ernest Cassirer's succinct and illuminating note on 'The Problem of Optimism', in his *Rousseau, Kant and Goethe*, Harper & Row, 1963, pp. 35–43.

7. Revealing and instructive in this context is the debate in the 1930s and 1940s between nationalists and the colonial administrators with pronounced anthropological concerns. Though marked by bitter differences, the root predicate from which consideration of the tribal situation proceeded in both cases was that it represents the 'lowest substratum' in the hierarchy of social facts. Both acknowledged the imperative of transforming, as quickly as possible, this substatrum into something closer to a modern fact. Differences concerned the pace of transformation and details of political–administrative arrangements.

Nationalists were fearful that the policy of demarcating predominantly tribal areas as 'excluded' from the operation of general laws and political process would isolate tribals into museum survivals to edify the curiosity of anthropologists and strengthen the stranglehold of colonial rule. Colonial administrators were as certain that uncontrolled operation of general laws and political process would mean ruin and destruction of tribals at the hands of greedy

Hindu money-lenders and a peasantry hungry for land. For the national position see, A.V. Thakkar, *The Problem of Aborigines of India*, Gokhale Institute of Politics and Economics, Poona, 1947. A.M. Somasundaram, 'Segregation or Assimilation?', *Man in India*, Vol. 27, No. 0, 1947, pp. 66–73.

For the colonial administrative point of view see, W.V. Grigson, 'The Aboriginal in the Future India', *Man in India*, Vol. 26, No. 2, 1946, pp. 81–100. J.H. Hutton, 'Problems of Reconstruction in the Assam Hills', ibid., pp. 101–17.

For a self-consciously anthropological intervention deeply sympathetic to Indian nationalism, see Verrier Elwin, *The Aboriginals*, Oxford University Press, 1943; and Sarat Chandra Roy, 'The Aborigines of Chota Nagpur—Their Proper Status in the Reformed Constitution', *Man in India*, Vol. 26, No. 2, 1946, pp. 131–51.

The Constituent Assembly debates reflect without exception the definitive power of the 'root predicate'. The most frequent invocation is the 'desire for advancement' and 'bringing the backward tribal communities on par' with relatively more advanced formations. Issues discussed are: special measures of legal–administrative protection and welfare, realistic and rational demarcation of a schedule of tribes and partially excluded areas. As for the direction of this advance, it is simply assumed as given and axiomatic. See H.S. Saksena, *Safeguards for Scheduled Castes and Tribes—An Exploration of the Constituent Assembly Debates*, Uppal Publishing House, 1981, pp. 41–42, 83–100, 475–539.

A.V. Thakkar, as Chairman of the Sub-Committee on Excluded and Partially Excluded Areas, reiterated that benefits of exclusion were not 'particularly noticeable'. But the recommendations of the Committee firmly endorsed the imperative of demarcating excluded areas. See *Constituent Assembly of India*, Government of India Press, 1949, Vol. 7, pp. 143–205.

This mode of consideration continues more or less unchanged. See for instance, *Approach to Tribal Development in the Sixth Plan*, Ministry of Home Affairs, Occasional Paper no. 17; *Proceedings of Conference of Tribal Commissioners* (14–15 July 1977), Ministry of Home Affairs, Occasional Paper no. 18; and B.D. Sharma, *Planning for Industrial Development of the Tribal Areas*, Ministry of Home Affairs, Occasional Paper, no. 7.

8. Museum encapsulates as metaphor and as physical locus the legitimate epistemic space in modern cognition for archaic survivals. Museumified care and preservation seeks to recover from fragments of dead facts whatever could be of use and value in the modern quest.

The utmost that Alfred Kroeber, an anthropologist of rare empathy, could seek when face to face with the 'last speakers' of 'virgin languages' polished in oral transmission to 'idiosyncratic perfection' was to rush with 'notebook and pencil', and in recording 'rescue from historylessness' all languages and cultures 'still living'. Theodore Kroeber, *Alfred Kroeber—A Personal Configuration*, University of California Press, 1970, p. 51.

Kroeber knew that this kind of rescue and preservation infuses in what is rescued functions and significance that have nothing to do with the living texture of which it was once a part. He likened the accession entry given to each 'specimen' in the museum to the 'birth certificate' of a person, and the 'accessions catalogue' to the 'museum's Bible'. *Ibid.*, p. 70.

A very different kind of quest is exemplified by the magnificent *Rupankar* experiment of Swaminathan at Bharat Bhavan, Bhopal. For Swaminathan, tribal art is not a surviving fragment of an 'archipelago' to be laid bare in the manner of an archaeological excavation. It exists 'amongst us and alongside us' and therefore could still be one of the 'contemporary expressions' of our time. See J. Swaminathan, *The Perceiving Fingers*, Bharat Bhavan, Bhopal, 1987, pp. 7–13.

9. The intent is to clarify a certain mode of consideration. For instance, to contrast the enduring quality of public works represented by a spectrum of Mughal buildings from the Red Fort to obscure *kos minars* along the Old Grand Trunk road with the mean and shoddy public structures built during the last forty-five years, is not to argue either for the restoration of the Mughal empire or even the abolition of modern schools of architecture and planning.

10. The 'Permanent Settlement' (1793), perhaps the most audacious attempt by colonial rule to transform the hitherto 'stagnant' countryside by fixing revenue demand in perpetuity, was conceived as a measure to regulate accumulation of surplus in the hands of a 'dynamic' class of landowners. For a meticulous exploration of the 'intellectual ancestry' of this idea, see Ranjit Guha, *A Rule of Property for Bengal*, Orient Longmans, 1982.

11. The title of Hill's study of radical groups (Diggers, Ranters, Levellers and others) and the 'social and emotional impulses' from which they arose is an apposite valorisation of the decisive in modern expectation. Christopher Hill, *The World Turned Upside Down*, Penguin, 1976.

12. This very modern expectation is akin to sorcery (as distinct from magic) as a 'form of controlled and conscious power' devoid of any 'built-in device' against abuse. Mary Douglas, *Purity and Danger*, Pelican Books, 1970, p. 119. Also see, for an insightful discussion on the play between form as power, and the play between form and formlessness, pp. 72–89, and pp. 114–36.

13. This belief is rooted in the humanistic certainty that Man is and ought to be the 'master of all creation'. In isolating 'man from the rest of creation', the human species is cast 'defenseless' and exposed to an existential situation that it can never fully encompass. Claude Levi-Strauss, *The View From Afar*, Basil Blackwell, 1985, pp. 22ff.

14. Skill, in contradistinction to knowledge, signifies a discrete fragment available for appropriation into a larger framework of reference and meaning.

15. Gandhi's *Hind Swaraj* (1909) represents precisely such an attempt in the modern context. For Gandhi, *Hind Swaraj* remained his definitive 'seed text'. It is a critique of the 'modern industrial civilisation' formulated in terms of categories that arise beyond the ambit of modern discourse.

    See M.K. Gandhi, 'Hind Swaraj', in Raghavan Iyer, *The Moral and Political Writings of Mahatma Gandhi*, Clarendon Press, 1987, Vol. 1, pp. 200–70. For instance, Gandhi posited 'vivisection' as the principal moral failing of modern civilisation in that it valorised human life as an absolute value. See Gandhi's remarks on science and civilisation, *ibid.*, pp. 310–15.

16. Establishment of revenue administration—settlement reports—was the first indispensable step towards providing a firm basis for imparting an imperial destiny to British rule. Moreover, colonial conquest was carried out as a self-financed enterprise. Hence the revenue conscious character of official observations. This attitude in itself marked something of a qualitative ascent from

crass personal profiteering which characterised 'information gathering' expeditions (Motte's Journey to Sambhalpur, Orissa, at the behest of Lord Clive, 1766) during the early years of British rule. But human cognition, however rigorously bent to specific purposes, has an ineradicable element of playfulness. Hence the transcription of details—to this could be added differences regarding best possible ways of realising the imperial mission—of human significance but quite beyond concerns of revenue.

17. Notion of land as private property was at best exceedingly fragile, even in the valleys of dense rice cultivation. Migration was a common fact of life. Colonial revenue settlements elevated revenue collectors to the new status of landowners. They were to be nurtured as a 'rural aristocracy' with 'a strong stake in the stability of the British rule'. See C.B. Lucie-Smith, *Report on the Land Revenue Settlement of Chanda District*, 1870, note 54, 'Note by Commissioner C. Bernard', paragraph 32. Concerning migratory habits and the prevalent notions of property in land, see J.W. Chisholm, *Report on the Land Revenue Settlement of Bilaspore District*, 1868, note 41, paragraphs 240, 343–45.

18. Ethnographic information of no direct consequence to revenue administration remained incredibly fragmentary until the mid-nineteenth century. As examples of the confined perception of colonial rulers, consider: Walter Hamilton in the second edition of the *East India Gazetteer* (1828) could only name two tribes in the Chota Nagpore region.

   Ethnography composed in London makes even more dismal reading. R.G. Latham, Vice-President of the Ethnographical Society of London, in 'Ethnology in India' (1859), after emphatic assurances that the 'Nilgherry Hills' were the 'best investigated' part of British India, could only manage the following entry on the Todas: 'The Todas—Infanticide polyandrists, who are few in numbers, and less Hindu than their neighbours.'

   Justice Campbell of Calcutta could not go beyond vague generalities even with regard to the Bhadraloka Baidya caste in Bengal, in 'Ethnology in India' (1866): '. . . peculiar to Bengal, the Baidyas or Physicians. They are not very numerous, are, I believe, often learned and respectable, and rank high among the Hindus, but in truth I do not know very much about them. It would be interesting to know more.'

19. Cited in Sarat Chandra Roy, 'Anthropological Research in India', *Man in India*, 1921, Vol. 1, No. 1, pp. 20–21.

20. *Ibid*, p. 22.

21. This massive enterprise remained almost entirely a government and British affair. Monographs and articles constitute but a small part of the immense volume of official data. Indians participated, as in all other departments of colonial administration, in the capacity of loyal assistants and translators. Contributions of ethnographic interest by Indians during the nineteenth century were few. According to Sarat Chandra Roy's computation of the articles on ethnography published in the influential journals of the nineteenth century: (*a*) *Journal and Proceedings of the Bengal Asiatic Society* (1784–1884); of the 100 papers only 3 by Indians. (*b*) *Calcutta Review* (1843–1883); of the 53 articles published, 10 were by Indians. (*c*) Dr. Burgess' *Indian Antiquary* (1872–1883); of the 260 articles published, 12 were by Indians.

Contributions by Indians increased during the next forty years: (*a*) *Proceedings and Journal of the Bengal Asiatic Society* (1884–1920); of the 215 articles, 65 were by Indians. (*b*) *Calcutta Review* (1884–1920); of the 76 articles, 30 were by Indians. (*c*) *Indian Antiquary* (1884–1920); of the 477 articles, 132 were by Indians.

It is noteworthy in this context that even non-official institutions like the Bengal Asiatic Society initiated sustained effort to solicit and publish articles of ethnographic interest at the behest of the government and with the help of government subsidies.

22. For an unusual and stark affirmation of this belief—unification as the first essential step toward universality—consider Surendranath Bannerjee's invocation of British rule as a 'civilising mission' in the tradition of Roman Legions. It is significant that this invocation was genuinely meant to rouse Indians to their common destiny as a Nation. Surendranath Bannerjee, 'Address on Indian Unity' (Calcutta Students Association, 16 March 1879) in K.P. Karunakaran, ed., *Modern Indian Political Tradition*, Allied Publishers, 1962, pp. 31–45.

23. The 'comparative method', as it was termed in the nineteenth century, insisted that one could learn of Europe's distant past from Asia's present. 'The great difference between the East and West is that the Past of the West lives in the Present of the East. What we call barbarism is the infant state of our civilisation.' Sir Henry Summer Maine, *Early Law and Custom*, John Murray, 1890, p. 131.

    Maine's argument is instructive. Hindu legal usage in the nineteenth century Punjab exhibits 'close resemblances to the most Ancient Roman Law'. *Ibid.*, p. 8. That resemblance demarcates the survival of a primal stratum relatively untouched by the deadening influence of Brahmanic thought. But it could not develop into something higher and more refined because it was enclosed within the Brahmanic Hindu Universe. See *ibid.*, pp. 8ff and 26–51. Primitive customs and usages perform functions useful to Man, but they remain frozen since primitive sensibility is unaware of their actual rational core. See *ibid.*, pp. 24ff.

    Sir Alfred Lyall, a firm believer in the 'comparative method', perceived the continual fragmentation of identities—caste and sects—as evidence of unawareness of the functional implications of beliefs and rituals. The chief failing of Brahminism, he argued, was that it never attempted to 'centralise and organise' religious beliefs, and hence the 'disorderly supernaturalism of pre-Christian ages'. See Sir Alfred C. Lyall, 'The Religious Situation in India', *Asiatic Studies*, Vol. 1, Cosmo Publications, pp. 286ff.

    The inevitable consequence of this failure to organise and control: '. . . luxuriant growth of religious fancies and usages; of superstitions and philosophies, belonging to very different phases of society and mental culture,' *ibid.*, Vol. 2, pp. 291ff.

    For the use of 'comparative method' during the nineteenth century see, E.E. Evans Pritchard, *Essays in Social Anthropology*, Faber and Faber, 1962, Ch. 1.

24. Levi-Strauss, *Tristes Tropiques*, pp. 48ff.

25. Consider the implications of the political fact that British rule in the moment of its greatest peril (1942) found support from incredibly diverse and opposed segments in India: Hindu Mahasabha, RSS, Muslim League, CPI, M.N. Roy,

Ramaswamy Periyar and B.R. Ambedkar, and of course the Indian princes. This strange and complex mix of votaries of radical social restructuring and assertions rooted in what are seen as primordial memories and arrangements raises basic questions concerning the structure of cognition and legitimacy in colonial India.

26. This belief represents a uniform consensus from Curzon to Nehru, Savarkar and M.N. Roy. Gandhi was perhaps alone in his categoric rejection of the belief that Indian identity was the unintended outcome of 'railways, English language and the British legal system'. See *Hind Swaraj*.

27. See, for instance, Andrew Hill Clark, *The Invasion of New Zealand By People, Plants and Animals*, Rutgers University Studies in Geography, Greenwood Press, 1970.

28. See Edwin Reischauer and John K. Fairbank, *East Asia the Great Tradition*, George Allen and Unwin, 1948.

29. Colonial officials, anxious to harness the large reserves of timber for the modern world, noted the universal hankering in tribal areas for the 'freedom of the forest'. To slash and burn patches of forest. A freedom they were determined to curb and eradicate. See Baden Powell's remarks in *Report of the Proceedings of the Forest Conference Year 1873–74*, pp. 3–7. Also Horsley, 'The Khandesh Satpura Forests and Their Bheel Inhabitants', in D. Brandis and A. Smythies, eds., *Proceedings of Forest Conference, Simla, October 1875*, Calcutta, 1876, pp. 23–27. Papers on Forest Policy conferences.

Instructive in this context is that 'slash and burn' cultivation was seen as a form of Man–Nature interaction that did not merit legal recognition of human claims on Nature for sustenance and survival. Hence the unqualified claims of the state:

> . . . the ruling of the Government stands that *Jhum* land, which the owners have bought or inherited as immovable property which can be validly held by an individual or a clan, is all unclassed State forest at the absolute disposal of Government, on which there is no liability to pay compensation in the event of its being taken over.

J.P. Mills, *Census of India, 1931*, Vol. 1, Part III B, pp. 147ff.

30. Geertz defines 'involution' (first proposed by Goldenweiser, 1936, as 'variety' and 'complexity' within a 'uniform' frame for Moari art) as a cultural pattern which, 'having reached what would be a definitive form, nonetheless fails to stabilize or transform themselves into a new pattern but rather continue to develop by being internally more complicated.' Clifford Geertz, *Agricultural Involution—The Process of Agricultural Change in Indonesia*, University of California Press, 1969, pp. 80ff.

31. In speaking of 'colonial discourse' as a creation as much of the colonial victims as of the colonial masters the intent is to affirm:

1. Even in the most degraded situation of ferocious repression, human victims can never be so completely reduced as to be entirely manipulable.
2. The reality of a certain distance, ineliminable and impossible to predicate, between human intent and its realisation. Hence the inherence of negation

in the most awesome and seemingly effective forms of control and repression.

See the meticulously documented study of submission and subtle resistance in Nazi concentration camps, Barrington Moore, *Injustice: Social Bases of Obedience and Revolt*, Macmillan, 1978.

32. See Gandhi on History as interpretation, and the realm least touched by it as the source of renewal in *Hind Swaraj*, Iyer, *op. cit.*, pp. 244ff.

33. Clifford Geertz, *Local Knowledge—Further Essays in Interpretive Anthropology*, Basic Books, 1983, pp. 4ff.

34. See Jürgen Habermas, *Legitimation Crisis*, Beacon Press, 1975. Also his, *The Philosophical Discourse of Modernity*, Polity Press, 1987, pp. 294–326.

35. See Geertz, *Local Knowledge*, pp. 6ff.

36. Ernst Cassirer, *Language and Myth*, Dover Publications Inc., 1953, p. 5.

37. *Ibid.*, pp. 4ff.

38. Douglas, *Purity*, pp. 73–89.

39. The intent is not merely to indicate that grand discontinuities, however immense their sweep, have been incomplete. Residues of varying resilience and magnitude always somehow escape untouched. But that such survivals indicate a structure of validation, perhaps inherently beyond the ambit of self-conscious cognition. Consider for instance Foucault's mode of considering the 'suddenness and thoroughness of the epistemic shift in sixteenth century Europe', and his question

. . . whether the subjects responsible for the scientific discourse are not determined in their situation . . . by conditions that dominate and overwhelm them.

Foucault, *The Order of Things*, pp. XII–XIV.

40. Primal space signifies not merely the lingering reality of notions and modes of judgement–appraisal of a constricted salience within a civilisational texture, but also the inherence within them of deep and inseparable links to what is perceived as the truth and authentic quest of that civilisation.

41. Conversations with Shri Shyam Kartik of Waidhan (MP), active in the cause of those displaced by the Rihand dam since the first satyagraha in 1959. Lohia visited the area (1959) and in his speeches frequently characterised the displaced as: '*Vikas ke sharanarthi*' (refugees of development) and '*Vikas ke sataye huai*' (victims of development). Also see interview with Shyam Kartik in *Vikas ki Keemat* (in Hindi), SETU, Ahmedabad, 1985, pp. 139–40. For a brief reiteration of this position, see, *Mankind*, Vol.3, October 1961, pp. 71–79.

Lohia was also perhaps the first political leader after Gandhi to link the questions of ecological pollution, livelihood and cultural self-esteem. See, 'Rivers of India' (24 February 1958, Benaras speech) in Ram Manohar Lohia, *Interval During Politics*, Navhind Prakashan, 1965, pp. 88–90.

42. It brings sharply to the fore the question as to what constitutes the basis in any discourse for recognition of something as a serious problem.

43. See section entitled 'Bonded and Forced Labour', in *Report of the Commissioner of Scheduled Castes and Scheduled Tribes* (1971–1972 and 1972–73), New Delhi, 1974, pp. 216–20. Also 'Forced Labour' in the *Report* (1966–67), New Delhi, 1967, p. 24. And the *Report* (1965–66), New Delhi, 1966, pp. 59–60.

44. See M. Fukuoka, *One Straw Revolution—An Introduction to Natural Farming*, Friends Rural Centre Rasulia, Hoshangabad, 1985.
45. The fact that radical modern critiques perceived in it a cunning stratagem to fudge the correct categories of exploitation is of secondary importance. The significant fact is that these categories have subsequently been incorporated in political practice simply as skill and technique for enhanced political mobilisation.

3. PROXIMITY AND APPROXIMATION

To clarify the meaning and significance of 'proximity and approximation', first, a brief reiteration concerning the cognitive locus of the 'centre–periphery' configuration. Transformation, the cardinal referent in modern change, to be meaningful has to meet two conditions: definitive demarcation of that which is to be transformed, and a centre and a resource which would carry through the process of transformation. At least in theory, such a process may be informed by genuine sympathy for that which is to be transformed. However intense and genuine the feelings for that which is to be transformed, transformation implies that at some point distinctness would cease to be substantial and definitive. Views may differ very sharply as to the duration and precise details of the process of transformation. Even so, the utmost that may be allowed to an entity which proves unreceptive and unwilling to be transformed is to linger as an archaic survival, interesting and harmless. Such an entity can claim no legitimacy in its own terms. Hence the imperative of the centre–periphery configuration in modern cognition and political economy.

Modern transformation seeks to secure the eventual elimination of all distances (in space, cognition and between facts) through a process that begins by positing clear distances and neat demarcations. However its point of grand departure from all that had preceded it is believed to be not in having created distances and demarcations but in activating an irreversible process which would eventually dissolve distances and differences. The assumption is that in the pre-modern context, distances and differences have been unyielding and incessantly elaborated. But this incessant elaboration and the consequent variety of forms is seen as akin to a play of shadows, for they denote directionless involution of an inert and virtually frozen social substance.

Consider in this context the scholarly search for a neat theoretical demarcation for the term tribal. The difficult complication is that the term tribal, in the context of India, cannot be defined as a racial or ethnic category.[1] The prevalent and accepted definition of a tribal is essentially legal–juridical. Certain groups and communities are listed in the government schedule—periodically revised, the last revision in 1976—as tribes. Hence the prevalent usage: 'scheduled tribes'.[2]

Criteria used for classifying a particular group as a tribe comprise an uncertain mix of race, ethnicity, socio-economic and educational backwardness. Groups that are classified as 'tribes' in one province may not be listed in the schedule of tribes for the adjoining province.[3] Troubled by this flagrant lack of precision social scientists have sought to define tribes in India in more precise and neatly scientific terms.

The instructive fact is that this scholarly effort has yielded very little beyond elaborate reiterations of and references to theoretical debates in Europe concerning the precise content and significance of 'pre-capitalist' societies'.[4] It makes no attempt to examine the relevance in relation to India of the basic assumption that, if only precise identification of the level of Man–Nature equations reflected in production techniques could be worked out, a scientific scheme to provide for the correct placement of all pre-capitalist formations could be formulated. For instance, how does one assign 'levels' to Man–Nature equations of two proximate communities in constant interaction: one community subsisting on terraced agriculture and the other on shifting cultivation. As to a more precise and scientific definition of a tribe in India, it offers next to nothing that could add or alter the current usage: scheduled tribe.[5]

This scholarly failing has little to do with the acquisition of a clever felicity in using all that the craft of social science has to offer. It is instructive as an instance of the kind of misattention to which our contemporary discourse is often prone. A social configuration that is stubbornly chaotic and still fluid on the ground is sought to be represented in terms of neat demarcations firmly identified. Boundaries that demarcate a 'tribal' from a 'non-tribal' continue to be uncertain and fluid. This fluidity tends to deepen and become more intense in social textures that have survived as most distanced from the modern world. Another fact of some consequence is the sheer impossibility of locating a particular period or happening as the climactic point, from which one could measure the beginning of the 'tribal–non-tribal' interaction in India.[6]

Fragmented Tribal Presence and Tribal Contiguity

Tribal presence in contemporary India, as also in the past, can be located at two distinct but intrinsically related levels:

1. Fragmented and fragmentary 'tribal' presence in the very midst of 'non-tribal' life; and
2. Tribal presence in 'tribal contiguities' comprising regions that continue to be, or were until recently, predominantly tribal.

The historian Kosambi, in the early fifties, had merely to step outside his house in Poona towards 'a little valley bounded by the land of the Law College (which teaches post-British law in English), the Bhandarkar Oriental Research Institute (whose collection of Sanskrit manuscripts and edition of the *Mahabharata* are known all over the world), the Fergusson College, several country houses of Bombay millionaires, and a sheep breeding farm run on scientific lines', to encounter the still unfolding 'historical processes' of 'interaction of obsolete with modern forms'.[7] As a characteristic illustration of the fragmented and fragmentary 'tribal' survivals in the midst of a 'non-tribal' milieu, consider the following observations made by Kosambi:

Nearest to me in location are a tent dwelling nomadic group of *Ras Phase Pardhis* whose basic costume (for the man) is a simple loin cloth, who never take a bath, but who retain the natural cleanliness, mobility, superior senses of wild animals. They have six exogamous clans or septs whose names have become surnames of feudal Maratha families: Bhonsale, Powar,

Cavahan, Jadhav, Sinde, Kale. The last is actually a Citpavan brahman surname; the penultimate once denoted 'son of a slave girl' (without acknowledged father) till it was ennobled by the rising to the kingdom of Gwalior. . . . Besides begging and petty stealing, these Pardhis are expert bird snarers. . . . There never was any question of racial purity, for strangers used to be adopted into a clan on payment of a fee. The real basic reason for their new willingness to abandon tribal life is its impossibility: game has almost vanished, while none of them can afford a hunting license.[8]

Within the 'tribal contiguity' (predominantly tribal region), tribal presence signifies a different historic quality of tribal–non-tribal interaction. Choices available to tribal communities in working out their own equations between Man and Nature have not been entirely foreclosed in favour of a more advanced mode of livelihood. Powerful rulers from the world of settled cultivation did seek to control the tribal contiguity. But pre-modern conquest could never exact more than a nominal annual tribute. The divide between resistance and restraint, submission and defiance was always somewhat fluid. Nature, little touched by Man, remained a secure refuge beyond the reach of invading armies. The texture of interaction this presence signifies could be rendered as a complex of impingements and relationships between several distinct social cohesions and modes of livelihood subsisting in close proximity.

Kheti and Penda as Proximate Modes of Living
Kheti (settled cultivation) and Penda (shifting cultivation)[9] represent two sharply distinct modes of livelihood. They signify very different kinds of statements concerning the human presence and Nature. Technological and social mediations within these modes are ordered very differently. In a rough and ready sense, the world of kheti is linked to non-tribal ways of life. And the world of penda is linked to tribal ways of life. But it is extremely important to remember that any kind of demarcation between tribal and non-tribal is subject to substantial exceptions of an intricate kind.[10] Between these two modes, kheti represents what in modern cognition would be designated as the manifestly more evolved and higher level of Man–Nature equations. Quite in accord with modern

expectation, the region of *kheti* even in the pre-modern context tended to expand and enclose new areas. But in the long process of extending and reaching out, *kheti* in the pre-modern context did not completely displace *penda*. In fact, the very process of reaching out came to be mediated by varied modes of livelihood which partook of the world of both *kheti* and *penda*. Hence the use of the term, 'mode of livelihood', in preference to 'mode of production', which encodes the notion of total reordering of the space that happens to be within the reach of its technological grid.

The salient features and forms of relationship between the world of *penda* and *kheti* encapsulated in Chart 1 express the unfoldment of a process stretching over 3,000 years or more. The texture of tribal–non-tribal interaction is outlined primarily in reference to the Gangetic Doab, the prime region of *kheti* and the Vindhyan highlands, the prime region of *penda*.

Gangetic Doab, the prime region of *kheti*, comprises a vast stretch of more or less level plains. Along its northern periphery rise the snow-covered Himalayan ranges from which flow the perennial Ganga and Yamuna, as also several other rivers, which give to these plains their distinctive description (Doab, or the land between two rivers). Towards the south extend the Vindhyan highlands.

Kheti marks out a permanent human presence riveted to a particular piece of land. The same plot of land is cultivated year after year, from one generation to the next. From that plot of land Nature is sought to be more or less completely banished. Survival of any stretch of land as *kheti* is inconceivable in the absence of constant human intervention. It requires constant care: ploughing, manuring, watering, weeding, etc. In the event of withdrawal or failure of human care, Nature does return to the lands of *kheti* but almost always in a shrivelled and degraded form. Viability of human intervention in sustaining *kheti* depends on the ability to harness animal power (mostly bullocks in the Gangetic plains) for ploughing and transport. The spatial boundaries worked out in *kheti* tend towards more or less straight-lined geometric patterns.

Village sites, like the fields of *kheti*, are also fixed and permanent. *Kacha* rutted tracks which could support wheeled carts for most of the year connect fixed sites of work and living (*kheti* fields, villages and towns) over great distances. Movement in the world of *kheti* is bound to fixed and permanent sites of work and habitation. They

CHART 1
Definitive Features of the Existential Space Prior to the Reordering Initiated by Colonial Rule

Space as Encapsulated Historical Sequence (Diachronic)	Space as Nexus of Relationships (Synchronic)
Gangetic Doab—prime region of settled cultivation (kheti)	Intensive cultivation. Irrigated crops (wheat, rice, etc.). Extensive use of animal power (mainly bullocks) for ploughing and transport. Permanent village sites linked by rutted kacha tracks. Wheeled transport.
	Dense demography. Large urban concentrations. Considerable surplus and trade. Periodic famines and epidemics.
	Regular revenue for the rulers. Hence large armies and imperial aspirations.
	Centres of crafts and skills, pilgrimage and knowledge, along riverlines as also high up on the hills and mountains.
Vindhyan hills—prime region of shifting cultivation (penda, podu, jhum, etc.)	Extensive dispersed cultivation. Crops cultivated (kosra, kodon, media. etc.) Not dependent on irrigation. Absence of the use of animal power. Unrestricted access to produce of Nature. Shifting village sites linked by narrow footpaths. Absence of wheeled transport.
	Sparsely populated. Absence of demographic concentrations. Insignificant surplus and trade. Absence of famines and epidemics.
	Nominal tribute for the Chief. Absence of standing army. Lack of clear demarcation between political authority and the social realm. Centres of pilgrimage, learning and skills in the fluid mediating zone between areas of shifting and settled cultivation.

* Flat stretches between hill ranges—enclaves of limited settled cultivation (*kheti*)	Crops cultivated of both the irrigated and the non-irrigated variety. Limited use of animal power. Unrestricted access to Nature. Fixed village sites. In some cases, rutted *kacha* tracks linked villages to the fields of settled cultivation. Infrequent and limited use of wheeled transport.	Thinly populated. Bigger villages but no large urban concentrations. Small surplus, limited trade through periodic and shifting *hats*. Absence of famines and epidemics. Tribute in place of revenue. Absence of standing army. Petty kingdoms or chiefships. Fluid demarcations between political authority and the social realm. Centres of pilgrimage, learning and craft skills.
** Dispersed flat stretches—areas of intermittent cultivation Unbounded, undemarcated spaces—regions of hunting, foodgathering and cattle grazing.	Approximates to settled cultivation in technique (ploughing, weeding etc.) and to shifting cultivation in its migrant character. Untended nature little touched by Man.	Emergence of fluid mediations: in technique, crafts, rituals, worship, beliefs and language, between entities linked to a vertical cultural-technological spectrum.

Note:
* Valleys and long flat stretches along riverlines in the region of shifting cultivation.
** Isolated flatlands and flat hill tops in the region of shifting cultivation.

denote the space from whence movement of Man and things proceeds and terminates. This engenders a profound ambivalence of momentous consequence: the inseparableness of the apparently contrary qualities of permanence-cessation of movement, and the enhanced capacity to move Man and things over long distances.[11]

Kheti secures enhanced and steady yields of crops useful to Man by banishing Nature completely from a certain stretch of land. Over that stretch Man's mastery is complete and unrivalled. Nothing that Man does not like or find useful can survive and grow within that stretch. The considerable surplus this activity generates makes possible trade and exchange of goods and services, emergence of large urban centres, as also varied range of skills, crafts and cultural links across immense distances. Along with all that, it also makes possible the consolidation of mechanisms of coercion and domination: steadily enhanced revenue demands, standing armies and imperial ambitions. In years of scanty rainfall or severe epidemics, the land of rich harvests is ravaged by hunger and death.

The Vindhyan highlands, a prime region of shifting cultivation, comprise a combination of densely forested hill slopes and valleys. Numerous little streams and three large rivers (Son, Narbada and Mahanadi) water its slopes and valleys. But unlike the Gangetic plains, riverlines in the Vindhyan region do not exert the kind of formative influence so characteristic of the plains of settled cultivation.[12]

Penda, in sharp contrast to *kheti*, marks out but a fleeting human presence in the midst of untamed Nature. Every year a fresh hill slope is cleared for *penda* cultivation. In the *penda* clearing, Nature in all its wild resilience and variety retains its sway, albeit a little subdued. Crops sown on a *penda* slope require virtually no human care. Viability of shifting cultivation has nothing to do with the use of animal power.[13] After the crops have been harvested, *penda* slopes merge back into Nature. The spatial boundaries worked out in *penda* tend to be somewhat like the diffused uncertain lines found in Nature.

Living sites, like the *penda* slopes, keep shifting.[14] Narrow little foot tracks which connect villages and *penda* slopes are just wide enough to allow movement of man or animal in single file. At no time of the year can they support wheeled transport of even the most rudimentary kind. The absence of permanently fixed sites of work and habitation engender a distinctly slower but unbounded pace of human movement.

Penda secures an ample supply of crops useful to man. Its yields in comparison to a *kheti* field are much smaller.[15] By allowing Nature to linger on *penda* slopes, this mode ensures that harvests never fail completely. Famines simply never happen.[16] True, a *penda* clearing denotes human intrusion of a fairly decisive kind. But this intrusion does not seek to completely banish and master Nature. Plants of no use to Man are allowed to grow along with crops sown afresh each year. The surplus generated is meagre and can at best support extremely restricted exchange and trade through shifting *hats*.[17] But the very little surplus available and the absence of permanence–fixity characteristic of the shifting cultivation mode of livelihood also forecloses the possibility of creating mechanisms of coercion and oppression. Chiefs in the world of shifting cultivation have to rule without the help of an army or a regular supply of revenue.

Until barely a hundred years ago the vast highland expanse of shifting cultivation was characterised by dispersed enclaves of settled rice cultivation (*kheti*) in the valleys and highland plateaus, and shifting cultivation (*penda, podu, bewara, jhum, dahiya*, etc.) on hill slopes. Immense unclaimed and undemarcated spaces mediated between the level fields of *kheti* and the slopes of *penda*. Nature almost untouched by Man reigned supreme.[18] In this fluid mediating region, hunters from the world of shifting cultivation and cattle grazers, artisans from the world of settled cultivation worked out varied equations and intricate adjustments between diverse modes of livelihood, sensibilities and social cohesions. What came to be designated as 'intermittent cultivation' in colonial revenue records—close to *kheti* in technique and to *penda* in its migrant character—represents a characteristic instance of the fluidity of this process which allowed for the working out of diverse and varied adjustments. *Kheti* and *penda* as pre-modern proximities signify the co-persistence of distinct modes of livelihood at several complex levels of intimacy and distance.[19]

Mediations in Tribal Sensibility

The word proximity is intended to indicate the fact and substance of interaction in the pre-modern context. Proximity as mediation, unlike modern mediations, does not seek to embody the logic and substance of some remote presence. Proximate entities may be grounded in diverse modes of livelihood. But each proximity possesses a life and viability of its own.

Tribal sensibility has been accustomed to seeking comprehension of the alien and unknown in reference to relative proximities. Vital impulses of this reference complex flow from the nature of placement assigned to a particular mediation in tribal sensibility.

To clarify the nature of the distinctive substance of proximity, first a statement concerning the placement assigned in tribal sensibility to modern mediations:

1. Mediations are perceived as extensions of a powerful presence, remote yet irresistible.
2. Mediations, even when they seem to help, are felt as abstractions; difficult to define, and unrelated to the actual mediating social formations.
3. Response to such mediations is conditioned by an acute sense of the near total connectedness of all modern activity.[20]

Implications

1. Modern mediations are thus perceived, both in existential and logical sense, as organic and integral to the forces that necessitate mediation. Consider for instance the seemingly unreasoning remark of a tribal that electricity in their homes while making things within the house nice and bright, would also reveal to outsiders what hitherto had been only for the eyes of those within the house. Implicit in this remark is the inherent and ineliminable connectedness of modern mediations. Thus the question is not simply of the condition of dependence entailed in the use of unmastered skills, but the acute sense that what sustains such skills would always be well beyond reach and comprehension.[21] Hence the sense of the enduring outsideness and unyielding alienness of modern mediations in tribal sensibility.
2. Modern mediations are seen as alien and inherently beyond assimilation. The impossibility of construing references in terms of a specific social–cultural locus imparts to modern mediations, however innocuous or demonstrably good, a demonic character. In tribal perception they acquire limitless

powers seething with hidden dangerous possibilities. This sense imparts to them an utterly unpredictable and arbitrary character. Hence the response, almost instinctive, of distrust and fearful withdrawal from things alien and unknown.

3. Stated intents and objectives of mediations remain suspect. Individual equations nurtured on implicit trust are powerless to efface, except in a severely restricted sense, this pervasive suspicion. Clearly, the question is not of individual distances and distrust. At issue is the cognitive distance and the inherent incomprehensibility of all that emanates from the modern complex.

'Pre-modern proximities' as mediations were recognisably different and distanced from the forces and entities they mediated. They were not seen to be radiating centres of transformation. Proximity as mediation signified a process towards mutual approximation.[22] Despite the diminishing resilience of this existential and reference complex, communities still oriented to pre-colonial textures sustain to this day sensibilities and life-rhythms that make them simultaneously very like and yet distinct from the tribal. That is perhaps what makes it possible to encounter a Brahmin living among tribals, yet meticulous in keeping his sacred thread; but his gestures, facial expressions and body postures unmistakably tribal.

Bronze has absolutely no function or place among the techniques and tools of production used by the Abujhamad tribals of Bastar. Yet, the Garhwa tribals over the centuries have perfected skills and techniques to cast lumps of bronze into exquisite artefacts. The inspiration that nurtures the Garhwa's creative craft can only be comprehended in reference to tribal sensibility.

For centuries Agaria tribals have practiced their exceptional skills of smelting and forging iron. But in building their houses they do not use one bit of iron. Hence perhaps the sense, in the pre-colonial tribal context, of the alien as relatively distanced proximity.

Distinctness, Limits and Approximation

Approximation, in contradistinction to transformation, is inconceivable in the absence of distinct proximities. The inherent constitutive structure—in cognition and as cohesions—of each fact and possibility entails its own distinct mode of being and becoming (*swabhava, swadharma*). Distinctness in relationships of approximation is not something in the sense of being frozen and utterly untouched by the other. Proximate entities do not remain exactly as they were in the process of approximation. Certain elements in each proximity are elaborated and redefined in ways that would be inconceivable in the absence of the other as an intimate presence. But such reformulations derive sustenance from spaces within the constitutive structures of the very cohesion or entity which they seek in some measure to change. They signify an actualisation of certain inherent possibilities. And that may entail negation of even large facts, perceived as integral constituents in the life and history of a particular cohesion.

Pre-colonial proximity allowed for legitimate spaces for redefinition and restructuring of concepts, techniques, rituals and worship. Co-persistence became viable in a framework of validation that recognised the existence of distinct entities as legitimate in their own right. Boundaries—in space, and as social category—remained fluid. Hence the simultaneous existence of divergent modes of livelihood, as also of different rituals of worship practised by different communities for the same deity, and in the same temple.[23]

Distinctness as distance, within this texture, cannot be meaningfully grasped as a measure of the relative capacity of a particular cohesion to control and appropriate the available surplus. Hence perhaps the fact, at best exceptional in modern contexts, that distinctness as distance and distanciation was not perceived as threatening. True, in certain contexts, distinctness signified hierarchical segmentation. For example, the chief, the *gaita* or *gunia*, were accorded a clearly elevated placement. Certain functions, regarded as vital to the sanity and survival of the prevalent social order, were their exclusive prerogative. This quality of distance as elevated placement essentially refers, not to privileged access to surplus, but to a prime ritual space.[24]

To clarify the basic difficulty—in terms of modern cognition—implicit in this fact, consider it as a paradox. The prime terrain—control over surplus—of which symbols and rituals associated with the exercise of power are supposed to be essentially an expression, is virtually non-existent. Yet the fierce persistence of elaborate rituals and symbols that elevate the exercise of power as a function of an exalted ritual space.

Recognition of legitimate limits is seen in tribal sensibility as the pre-condition for order and human sanity. Limits and legitimacy are defined in terms of cosmic placement. Knowing one's true placement defines legitimacy and affirms order. Effectiveness does not in itself constitute validation. Authority—as knowledge, and as power—is legitimate only in so far as it confirms and conforms to the true order of placement of men and things.

This formulation would only seem to confirm the modern comprehension of tribal sensibility as irrevocably bound within unvariable, self-prescribed limits. But an extremely significant, if somewhat ambivalent, consequence of defining legitimacy and order as authentic cosmic placement also inheres in this mode of comprehension. Since all legitimate existence is subject to limits defined by correct placement, logically, nothing can be absolutely opposed or absolutely superior.

NOTES

1. The word *adivasi* is of recent modern origin. The word *jati* denotes genus or kind.
2. The word 'schedule' is defined in the Constitution:

   Schedule means a schedule of this Constitution.
   And,

   Scheduled tribes means such tribes or tribal communities as are deemed under article 342 to be Scheduled Tribes for the purpose of this Constitution.

   H.S. Saksena, *Safeguards for Scheduled Castes and Tribes—An Exploration of the Constituent Assembly Debates*, Uppal Publishing House, 1981, p. 524.
3. For example, in Uttar Pradesh Agaria, Kol, Baiga, and Gond are enumerated as 'castes', whereas in neighbouring Madhya Pradesh they are all enumerated as 'tribes'. See Census 1981, note 13; Series I India, part II–B (iii), Primary Census Abstract Scheduled Tribes, pp. lvii–lviii, and lxxi.
4. For a statement of this kind of theoretical concern see, Joel S. Kahn and Joseph R. Llobera, eds., *The Anthropology of Pre-Colonial Societies*, Macmillan, 1981, pp. 57–108.
5. See Jaganath Pathy, *Tribal Peasantry—Dynamics of Development*, Inter-India Publications, 1984, pp. 1–43.

6. This absence is indicative of not just details lost in the long duration of tribal–non-tribal interaction, but also of the inherently dispersed and fluid quality of this interaction.

7. D.D. Kosambi, *An Introduction to the Study of Indian History*, Popular Book Depot, 1956, p. 25.

8. *Ibid.*, pp. 26–27.

9. The term *penda* is used for cultivation practices designated in English as shifting cultivation. The term *jhum* is used over a far more extensive area. I use the term *penda* because (*a*) my direct familiarity with shifting cultivation is based on the field experience in Abujhamad, Bastar; and (*b*) *penda* as still practised in Abujhamad perhaps best represents a living mode of livelihood least touched by the world of *kheti*.

10. Such exceptions concern not just the inherent fluidity of boundaries between tribal and non-tribal, but also the incidence of groups seen as non-tribals taking up shifting cultivation. See the chapter entitled 'The World of Shifting Cultivation'.

11. This refers to a paradox of far deeper cultural consequence than Zeno's second paradox of motion: more rapid the pace of locomotion, greater the fixity and closure of the boundaries of nodal points of locomotion.

12. Flowing water is indeed considered clean and preferred to water from a well or a pond. But rivers do not touch the aesthetic imagination of the world of shifting cultivation. Their shrines and spontaneous gestures of sanctity are associated with hills and the narrow passes between hills and forests.

13. The absence of animal power on a slope of shifting cultivation is complete. Not only is animal power not used in ploughing, sowing, harvesting or casting, but not even for manure.

14. In Abujhamad Bastar, the living sites began to acquire permanence during the 1920s and 1930s.

15. *Penda* yields are small only in terms of optimal yields. But if one were to compare yields on *penda* slopes and *kheti* fields in adjoining areas, the former would be comparable and at times more plentiful. See Sardindu Bose, *Carrying Capacity of Land Under Shifting Cultivation*, Asiatic Society, 1967.

16. The immunity against famines is inherent in the kind of Man–Nature equation implicit in *penda*. See the chapter entitled 'The World of Shifting Cultivation'.

17. The surplus essentially comprised that which could be garnered from natural forests rather than the produce of *penda* slopes. As for their desire for things from the world beyond their hills, it was confined to salt and colourful trinkets till well into the twentieth century in Bastar.

18. Even in the relatively densely settled valleys and plains of Chhattisgarh, *kheti* fields converged on to forests or just unclaimed open spaces. Such proximity has been intense and dramatic in areas like Bastar. As recently as 1983–84, the forest around the thousand years old ruins of Barsur (near Jagdalpur) was just a few hours' walk. Nature virtually untouched by Man in close proximity with enclaves recast by human activity could endure because *kheti* within the 'tribal contiguity' did not embody the logic of limitless extension.

19. Lucie-Smith estimated that the state had effectively appropriated around 50 per cent of the hitherto 'common resource' from forests and wastes. C.B. Lucie-Smith, *Report on the Land Revenue Settlement Chanda District*, 1870, note 54, paragraph 303.

Settlement operations systematically refrained from taking legal cognisance of the rights of those engaged in 'scattered' or 'intermittent cultivation', subsequently designated as the *varg char* or *shaskiya zameen*. Problem of *varg char* or *shaskiya zameen* has its origin in the revenue settlements effected by colonial rule, see Lucie-Smith, *Report*, paras 315 and 320; and J.W. Chisholm, *Report on the Land Revenue Settlement of Bilaspore District*, 1868, note 41, para 166.

As forests came to be rigorously enclosed by the state, these mediating forms were the first to dissolve and make a fragile transition to *kheti* in its most unproductive form. For instance, in the Singrauli region (1985-86) one could see slopes which were obviously cultivated as forest clearings a few generations ago being ploughed by emaciated bullocks.

Other crucial mediations in this relationship of intimate distance: cattle herders, potters and Agaria iron smelters.

20. Perception of total connectedness is both in terms of the 'legal framework' and the way skills and knowledge are constituted. In Chhattisgarh I was struck by the filth around the water handpumps in tribal villages, otherwise clean and well tended. In a long conversation the *sarpanch* of Patiyapali village (Bilaspur district) explained: 'water pumps are owned by the *sarkar*. If it needs mending, villagers are afraid to touch it. They may damage it. Water pumps have to be drilled. Drills are made in large factories. We cannot have a factory in every village. So how do we keep it clean and functional.'

21. In the metaphorical rendering of the Gunia of Patiyapali: 'Like the bird struck by the arrow of an invisible hunter we try to imagine the form and power of whence the arrow come.'

22. For directing attention to the possibilities of 'approximation' as a concept of change and historical interaction, I am indebted to some of the audacious and seminal essays of Lohia, 'Ram and Krishna and Shiva', *Interval During Politics*, Navhind Prakashan, 1965, pp. 29–49; see also Ram Manohar Lohia, 'Approximation of Mankind', *Wheel of History*, Navhind Prakashan, 1963, pp. 48–55.

23. Man, in this vision, was not seen as the sovereign referent of value and judgement. Nature was not regarded as a hostile presence to be reduced and mastered. All that was given to all forms of life (human and non-human) was to know and be in their legitimate place and function.

This allowed for diversity and autonomy. But the searing paradoxes that it engendered also merit close attention. Even as life moved in close proximity to Nature, it often came to be lived so close to the gutter as to be indistinguishable from it. And a social order of cosmic harmony nurtured on non-attachment to property came to prize the most demeaning forms of caste exclusion and property. For drawing pointed attention to the reversal in practice of the ideal of non-attachment. See Ram Manohar Lohia, *The Caste System*, Navhind Prakashan, 1964, pp. 49–73.

24. This is not to suggest that authority so situated was never used unfairly. But this fact does indicate that critique of power in such contexts can only be meaningful at a clear remove from forms of property relations and appropriation of surplus.

PART II

PRE-MODERN PROXIMITY AND TRIBAL SOCIAL COHESIONS

4. PRE-MODERN TRIBAL CONTIGUITY

Plains and Hills: Iron and the Making
of Historical Space

For more than 3,000 years after the disappearance of the Indus Valley civilisation, the Ganga riverline has been the artery of communication, pilgrimage and settled cultivation. Gangetic *doab*, as the pivotal space for the unfolding of this civilisation was defined, noted the historian Kosambi, by the new civilisational imperative of securing ample access to iron ore.[1] As the use of the heavy iron ploughshare spread, vast stretches of virgin forests were tamed for settled cultivation (*kheti*).

The centre of civilisation and political power in ancient India tended to shift steadily eastwards. Mohanjodaro or the Indus Valley Valley civilisation, the earliest known urban civilisation (3000 BC to 1500 BC), flourished in the north-west (present-day province of Sindh in Pakistan) of the subcontinent.[2] From what we know, its end was sudden. Great deal of uncertainty persists regarding the cause of its sudden end. Recent excavations suggest that perhaps the end was not so sudden and complete. Substantial continuity persists in what was earlier represented to be a completely new beginning: the pastoral Vedic civilisation.[3]

A perplexing fact concerning the Indus civilisation is the near absence of any memory about it. Early in this century, chance discovery of terracotta seals—an unintended consequence of the modern enterprise to overcome distance—dug up along with bricks from ancient mounds that were being worked to provide cheap ballast for the railway line, led to the discovery of the stupendous ruins of Mohanjodaro.[4] Mohanjodaro's existence came as a complete surprise to scholarship and folk memory alike. Consider yet other and no less interesting perplexities that touch upon forgetfulness and continuities. To this day peasants in villages around Mohanjodaro yoke their bullocks to carts crafted in the very likeness of terracotta clay carts housed in the Mohanjodaro museum.[5] It is unlikely that the peasants who use these bullock carts and the craftsmen who make them would have ever visited the museum. This memory signifies the silent survival of a skill utterly unaware of its origins. Bronze figurines cast by the Garhwa tribals in distant Bastar continue to depict the hairstyle so characteristic of terracotta female figurines crafted 4,000 years ago in the Indus Valley. To cite another perplexing fact from the dim premodern realm of 'no-change', Mohanjodaro was a large city. Nearly 40,000 people are believed to have lived in its neatly laid out structures of well-fired solid bricks and lime. Yet, it was a city devoid of the expansive vigour that iron is believed to vouchsafe to Man in the incessant struggle to tame Nature. Structures which are believed to have housed ordinary workers were infinitely better than houses of working people in cities of the subcontinent ever since.[6]

For nearly a thousand years, after the sudden disappearance of the Indus Valley civilisation, large urban settlements were unknown. They began to emerge once again around the sixth century BC in the eastern Gangetic plains. In an audacious sweep, Kosambi pivots this continual shift towards the east—of surplus, trade and political power—to the need for securing a sufficient supply of iron ore. His foremost concern is to mark out the relationship of iron to the movement of Man and things, their scale and structure of organisation; concerns defined by the acute sense that Man embodies the profound possibility towards which evolution in Nature over countless millennia has tended. And Nature, as it were, transcends itself in Man. Iron, that grand vitaliser of Man and things in those far off times as also in the modern age, is seen to represent the primal force for movement and change: the point of recurring return in historical explanation. Kosambi argues that unlike the relatively thinner vegetation in the Indus Valley, the dense forest vegetation in the Gangetic *doab* could not have been cleared for settled cultivation (*kheti*) without extensive use of the heavy iron plough. In a telling and characteristic use of contemporary evidence, Kosambi demonstrates the striking identity between ploughshares still used by peasants in the Gangetic plains and the one carved in stone 2,000 years ago.[7]

The long millennium-and-a-half that separate the Indus Valley from the rise of Magadha as the pre-eminent power in the plains of north India, was a period of steady expansion of the area under *kheti*. Iron in the Gangetic plains meant the spread of fixed sites of habitation and work, separated by immense distances but in constant communication with each other. The steady and ample harvests from the fields of *kheti* sustained regular exchange and trade over long distances. For the rulers this meant enhanced revenue and power. Villages in the remotest hinterland were connected by rutted *kacha* tracks for bullock carts. Steady surplus appropriated through tax and trade from a settled peasantry facilitated specialisation, varied crafts and skills, as also large armies and imperial aspirations. But in years of drought, crops withered. The land of ample harvests was ravaged by hunger and famine. Ample harvests, while facilitating large and dense clusters of human habitation also created conditions for the breeding of pathogenic germs, which in periodic bursts of epidemic frenzy decimated large segments of the populace.[8]

The Gangetic plains in the north—the prime region of *kheti*—are separated from the Deccan plateau in the south by the sprawling Vindhyan highlands. A feature of some consequence for routes of trade, cultural influences and political hegemony is the considerably heavier rainfall in the eastern ranges of the Vindhyas. Forests in eastern Madhya Pradesh and central Orissa have therefore been far more dense and inaccessible than in the western districts along the Satpura hills.

Conquest, trade and pilgrimage between the northern plains and the Deccan plateau followed routes almost parallel—northeast to south-west—to the rivers Son and Narbada. Trade and armies on the march tended to cling to the western passes across the Vindhyas. Unlike the eastern hill ranges of dense forests, the western Vindhyas have been more intensely exposed to influences from Rajasthan, Gujarat and Maharashtra. Eastern Vindhyas have also felt and known the impact of the region of *kheti* for more than a millennia. But in the denseness of the eastern hills those influences tended to more sharply dissolve and approximate to other rhythms of life and livelihood. From the eastern seaboard in Orissa, Man and things could and did reach out far into the deep hinterland as remote as Bastar. Like Son and Narbada in the north and west, the Mahanadi riverline marked the route into the dense vastness of the eastern Vindhyas. But the forbidding terrain of its hills and forests compelled movement of Man and things to conform to a rhythm strikingly different.[9]

Vindhyan Highlands

The Vindhyan region, the prime region of shifting cultivation (*penda*) could be differentiated as three tracts of highlands alternating with two of plains country. The Malwa plateau in the north-west at an elevation of 1,500 to 2,000 ft., comprising the districts of Damoh and Sagar, is situated on a sheer rise north of the river Narbada. It slopes towards the north, and its rivers flow into the Yamuna and the Ganga. Forest cover on this side of the Vindhyas has always been sparse and stunted. Narbada Valley, which adjoins this plateau, comprises a long and narrow stretch—about 200 miles long and on an average 20 miles wide—of fertile land scoured by rapid monsoon streams which flow down from the Satpura hills. It has been for a long time a substantial enclave of intense settled cultivation in the midst of hill slopes of dispersed shifting cultivation (*penda*). Another tract extends across about 100 miles from Amarkantak to Saletkeri hills in Balaghat district. Its spurs run westwards for nearly 400 miles. Its narrow valleys are rich in fertile deposits of soil drained year after year. Satpuras form the great watershed for the plains lying to its north and south. Most of the important rivers of this region—Narbada, Tapti, Wainganga and Wardha—rise in these hills.[10]

Along the southern and eastern face of the Satpura ranges stretch the plains of Nagpur, Chhattisgarh and Sambhalpur. These abundant stretches of plains country are intersected by two ranges of hills. The western part of the Nagpur plains, watered by the Wainganga and Wardha, has for a long time been a rich cotton-growing area.[11] Its eastern half, with its heavier rainfall and numerous irrigation tanks, has been a large enclave of rice fields of *kheti.* Towards the east lie the extensive plains of Chhattisgarh, comprising mainly the districts of Raipur and Bilaspur. Mahanadi, the other great river of the Vindhyan region, flows east through the southern part of the Chhattisgarh plains. East of the Chhattisgarh plains lies the middle basin of the Mahanadi, comprising Sambhalpur district and the chiefships of Sonpur, Patna and Kalahandi. South of these level plains extends the vast expanse of hills and valleys comprising the chiefships of Chanda, Bastar and Kanker.[12]

The Vindhyan geography is akin to concentric weaves of plains and hills, little valleys and steep hill slopes. This weave persists all across and on a varied scale. Etched on a scale clearly modest in comparison to the lofty sweep of the Himalayan ranges, it represents a space remarkably different from the even regularity of the Gangetic plains. The relentless reach of the modern dynamic has tended to soften and dissolve this difference. Something of the immemorial quality of Man–Nature rhythms that prevailed in this region is conveyed in what was sketched in the early years of this century as a matter-of-fact description of the landscape:

> . . . recurring contrast of woodland and tillage and the alteration of hills and valleys, wood and rivers. In the Narbada Valley during the pleasant winter months the eye may range over miles of green corn land, broken by low black boundary ridges of twisting footpaths. The horizon is bounded on either side by hill ranges which seem to rise abruptly from the plains; but on coming nearer to them, the heavy green of their slopes is found to be divided from the softer hues of the young wheat by broad belts of gravelly soil, carpeted with short sward and dotted with noble trees, recalling the appearance of an English park . . . the high and abrupt hills—clothed from summit to base with forest, and seamed by the deep course of the streams, up which the roads twist and turn . . . little valleys cultivated like gardens . . . .[13]

And the more deeply lush and densely wooded eastern ranges after the rains in September:

> . . . from some such point as the hill overlooking the Mahanadi at Sambalpur, can be seen miles of continuous fields heavy with

irrigated rice . . ., while in the background wooded hills covered
with darker coloured foliage fringe the horizon . . ..[14]

Geological formations, like the incredibly diverse and distinct
communities of this region, are characterised by an unceasing play
of distancing and convergence. Son and Narbada, two important
rivers of this region, originate within a mile of each other at
Amarkantak and flow in opposite directions. Son flows north-east
into the Ganga, Narbada flows west into the Arabian sea. Mahanadi
emerging a little lower south-east carves its own course to the Bay
of Bengal. Further south originate the principal feeders of Godavari
in the southern peninsula. Recurring play of movement, towards
and away, is as true of the very large as of little formations. In the
meticulously vivid rendering of Forsyth:

> The drainage of the great Mahadeo block. Two streams rise
> near its southern face, the Denwa and the Sonbhadra. Both
> flow nearly south, away from the Narbada, for a short way,
> when the former turns to the east, and the latter to the west.
> Presently however, they find two vast cracks in the range, and
> turn sharp to the north, passing through them to the northern
> face, where they unite and fall into the Narbada after all.[15]

Valleys, as aptly noted by Forsyth, a district officer of the early
adventurous phase of colonial rule, 'everywhere penetrate the hills.'
And the 'rich cultivation of the flat land' is everywhere bounded
by 'unclaimed waste and rugged forest cover steeps'. Hills above
2,000 ft. have a 'tendency to spread out in the form of plateaux'.
Some of them comprise the 'top of only one hill and a small area'.
Others run along the 'summits' of several hills which support like
'buttresses' large level 'undulating plains'. A few 'solitary flat
topped hills' shoot up 'still higher' to nearly 3,500 ft., coalescing at
times into a 'plateau at about the same elevation'. But summits
that rise to 'nearly 5,000 feet above the sea' never assume 'the
character of a plateau'.[16]

Prior to the penetration of the railways[17] in the second half of the
nineteenth century, and of metalled roads in the twentieth, the
eastern Vindhyan hill region (spilling into the present-day states of
Uttar Pradesh and Bihar in the north, Bengal and Orissa in the
east, and Andhra Pradesh in the South) constituted an almost

unbroken tribal contiguity. Its northern extremity almost touched the Ganga riverline in the present-day district of Mirzapur. Yet, within a few days' walk from the formidable fortress of Chunar, the tribal kingdom of Singrauli survived in this area until 1947. Towards the west, the tribal contiguity extended, albeit dispersed and somewhat broken, into Maharashtra, Gujarat and Rajasthan.

Until barely a hundred years ago this vast tribal contiguity was characterised by dispersed enclaves of settled rice cultivation in the valleys and plateaus, and shifting cultivation (*penda, podu, jhum, bewara, dahiya,* etc.) on the hill slopes. Immense unclaimed and undemarcated spaces mediated between the level fields of *kheti* and the wooded slopes of *penda*. Nature, barely touched by Man, reigned supreme. In this mediating region of fluid boundaries hunters from the world of shifting cultivation and cattle grazers, artisans, mendicants, itinerant traders and others of varied description from the world of settled cultivation worked out varied equations and adjustments between diverse sensibilities and cohesions.

The pre-modern texture of tribal–non-tribal relationships, as also the relationship between tribal social cohesions and political authority is outlined primarily in reference to Bastar and the regions proximate to Bastar.

1. The Bastar region, comprising the former princely states of Bastar and Kanker raj in Madhya Pradesh, constitutes for this outline the hub of the tribal contiguity.

2. Proximate regions, akin to Bastar in their ethnic–social composition as also in the dense wooded remoteness of their hills, comprise the former principalities of Kharonde, Jeypore, Kalahandi, Board and Goomsur in Orissa, and Chanda in the present-day Chandrapur district in Maharashtra.

3. Chhattisgarh region comprises present-day districts of Durg, Raipur and Bilaspur, and the hills of Mandla and Balaghat. From within this region arose powerful kingdoms—Haihayas, the Rajput rulers of Ratanpur, and the Gond rulers of Garh Mandla—which sought to extend their paramount sway over the entire region.

4. Northern extremity of the tribal contiguity: the Singrauli region in Madhya Pradesh and Uttar Pradesh comprising the former principality of Singrauli and parts of the present-day district of Mirzapur.

Bastar, until barely thirty years ago, remained an area utmost distanced from the modern world. With an area of 15,091 sq. miles, Bastar district is larger than the state of Kerala.[18] The present-day district is made up of the former Bastar principality (13,061 sq. miles) and the territory of the Kanker raj.[19] In recent years there has been a large influx of immigrants from Chhattisgarh and other adjacent areas in the wake of large-scale iron ore mining in south Bastar, timber extraction, public works and various other government schemes. Under the Dandakaranya project thousands of refugee families from Bangladesh have been settled in the district. But, despite all that, Bastar remains predominantly tribal. Of its 1,842,854 inhabitants enumerated in the 1981 census, two-thirds (1,249,197) are tribals. Tribals in Bastar have been—to extend and transpose Srinivas' concept—the 'dominant caste'.[20]

Distance as the Measure of Space and History

Distance, according to Braudel, was the 'principal enemy' of the modern world struggling to emerge in Europe.[21] Conquest of distance has been seen as the making of the grand highway for the steady march of progress and freedom. In the absence of railways and roads—two principal elements in the modern communication grid—distance acquires a different quality and resilience, it defines the limits within which unfamiliar ideas and influences may assert. Distance, as an attribute of untouched Nature, is also an unfailing refuge against the tyranny of rulers. It imposes a severe limit upon the oppressive reach of even the most formidable political authority.

As recently as 1958 Bastar was listed by the Dhebar committee as the district most backward in modern communications.[22] Nearly fifty years before that, Lt. Col. E. Clementi Smith, in command of a detachment of 225 rifles and in desperate hurry to reach Jugdalpur in time to put down a tribal rebellion (February 1910), records in telling detail the beginnings of the slow conquest of distance in Bastar.

Time and speed were critical for the success of Smith's mission. Railway staff and the district authorities had done their very best to expedite things. Yet to cover the forty miles between Raipur and Dhamtari on the narrow gauge railway line took five hours. The rail line terminated at Dhamtari. Bullock carts, mobilised in Dhamtari for the 140-mile journey ahead to Jugdalpur, were harnessed to water buffaloes of 'the wildest description'. As often with animals and humans in a situation of sudden encounter with the utterly unfamiliar, 'unnerved' by the 'smell of the Punjabi Sepoy' most of the buffaloes 'bolted' into the wilderness.[23] Provisions for the entire duration of the expedition, along with bullock carts to carry them, had to be mobilised from Raipur. The road to Jugdalpur, which follows the ancient *banjara* trade route,[24] bristled with sharp bends and steep slopes of the as yet untamed forests and hills. Around 1886-87 the road had been surfaced under British supervision. A telegraph line along the road ensured instant transmission of news between Raipur and Jugdalpur. But road construction had also caused considerable resentment. To escape *begar* (forced labour) on road construction, villages close to the road were deserted.[25] Even twenty years later some of its effects were still visible. Col. Smith was struck by the 'very few villages near the road'. Water along the road was 'scarce'. As the imperial detachment crossed unhindered the '9 hairpin turns' to the bottom of Keskal Ghati enclosed 'between high hills covered with thick jungle which comes right down to the road', the Colonel felt understandably relieved to leave behind what, in the event of any kind of resistance, would certainly have been a 'death trap'.

The return journey along the jungle tracks entailed even greater effort and hardship. 'Getting the transport carts' over the numerous 'deep nullahs' along the way 'necessitated a great deal of digging of ramps and laying a temporary road of boughs and grass over the sandy bottoms'. At numerous places where the approach was very abrupt and steep, about '8 to 10 men per cart were required to act as brakes' during descents over the rocky inclines of 'nullahs'. Apart from marching, the only military task the expedition performed was burning two Madia villages near Chote Dongar. After thirty-two days and 400 miles, the imperial expeditionary force with 'clothes, or what remained of them' in 'rags', boots 'worn out and equipment torn'[26] marched out of Bastar. And this was true of a campaign undertaken during the best part of the dry cold weather.

For Glasfurd in 1862,[27] distance in the hills and wilds of Bastar signified something intrinsically more unacceptable than mere exhaustion after a difficult journey. It blurred what was believed to be the basic divide between Man and Nature. Distance in this case signified Nature constricting Man within limits so closed as to make the human presence no more than a mild variation of rhythms of recurrence and repetition intrinsic to Nature. It marked out the impossible constrast between the little communities of these wild hills and Man as he could and ought to be. Sixty-seven years earlier, Blunt (1795),[28] on a long journey of exploration from Chunar to Ellore experienced a similar emotion but felt powerless to change the state of things.

Motte on his way to Sambhalpur in the mid-eighteenth century[29] also noticed the striking absence of a clear separation between Man and Nature. But he was keenly aware of the fragility of the colonial presence. For that reason, perhaps, Motte's rendering of details, which remained unchanged into the time of Glasfurd a hundred years later, conveys a very different sense. He knew that so far as this wilderness was concerned his presence was condemned to be as fleeting and fragile as the human presence generally in these remote parts. As the hills rose and the Balasore plains receded beyond sight, tracks which could support the most rudimentary type of wheeled transport disappeared. Supplies had to be carried on the back of pack animals. Motte's soldiers, like the tribals of these hills, had to walk in single file. Like a comforting instinct, Madia tribals to this day nurse this habit as they walk single file on the wide metalled roads recently built in Bastar. Movement, be it of humans or animals, had to adjust within limits defined by surroundings little touched by human activity. Soldiers and armies could do little to alter these limits.

In Glasfurd's time, even as the rhythm of Man and things continued as of old in and around the hills of Bastar, much had decisively changed in the world that was relentlessly closing in upon these hills. That vast region of *kheti* and steady surplus, the Gangetic plains of the north, had been firmly harnessed to sustain and enhance the reach of British colonial control. The colonial empire had come to be a settled fact. The march of progress was no longer constrained by the absence of a firm and dynamic centre of authority. Glasfurd knew that his mission and report would give form and force to the colonial enterprise of 'opening up' Bastar to the world.

Obstacles to the march of progress seemed formidable in the extreme. Glasfurd sharply noted that the 'Dependency' of Bastar was without a 'single road' which could support wheeled transport. The entire country was one long expanse of 'interminable forest'. Regular cultivation was confined to a 'small tract around Jugdalpur'. Even across this little cultivated tract ran steep 'mountain ranges which present serious obstacles to traffic'.³⁰ As for the human presence:

> The inhabitants are composed of rude, uncivilised tribes of Gonds; in some parts almost savages, who shun contact with strangers, and have but few wants which they cannot supply themselves, honest and interesting to the Ethnologist perhaps, but a race who prefer the solitude of forests to the bustle of towns, and the freedom of the savage to all the allurements and comforts of civilisation.³¹

In Glasfurd's perception Man and Nature were unacceptably close. Human proximity to Nature was in inverse proportion to the unyielding quality of distance in the wild hills of Bastar. Its inhabitants, rather than truly engage in the grand struggle to make Nature yield in full measure the very forms civilised living required, seemed content to subsist on whatever Nature on its own may choose to yield. Hence the warning:

> . . . with such a country and such inhabitants, rapid progress and improvement cannot be looked for; and any effort to open out the Dependency, with the hope of immediately stimulating trade, or rather creating it where it never existed, would end in disappointment.³²

To remove the 'bars to civilisation', the first essential step had to be the conquest of distance. Progress and civilisation were inconceivable in the absence of roads that could support movement on wheels. Glasfurd outlined the critical steps: the immediate task should be to 'open up a few important lines on which traffic already exists'. He knew that for its inhabitants there was simply nothing in the wide world beyond these wild hills for which they had any use. But that could hardly be a reason for leaving the 'Dependency' to stagnate within its immemorial cycle of repetition and immobility. So much of what was locked up in its inaccessible remoteness was of great value and use to the world beyond these wild hills. A regular flow of rich timber from the southern part of the 'Dependency', could be quickly secured by opening up traffic on 'a navigable Godavary'.³³

Glasfurd knew that building roads, and more so keeping them in a state of good service entailed much more than the simple application of technical skills. At the bare minimum, it required some softening of the sense that the human possibility had to be confined within more or less inflexible limits defined by Nature. Hence his insistence that a 'better system of criminal and judicial procedure' than the one 'in force in Jugdalpore' be extended to Bastar. The need was to awaken and create demands which would 'send traders into parts they never ventured before, and the inhabitants would receive cloth, salt, tobacco and other articles in exchange for their rice, lac, wax, etc. in the interior'. But all this could easily regress and be lost to the wilderness. Scattered ruins of powerful intrusions from the world beyond these wild hills were a grim reminder of the fate which could well overtake the colonial enterprise. If changes and improvements were to be 'material and lasting' it was imperative that the 'facilities of communication' be effective enough to forever shatter the remoteness of this hinterland.[34]

To sustain this long and difficult enterprise required an enhanced and assured flow of revenue. The prevalent revenue assessment, in Glasfurd's estimate, was 'light', averaging from 'half a rupee to a rupee and quarter' per plough; and 'four annas to a rupee' per axe.[35] Besides, the shifting nature of village settlements dispersed in wild hills and dense forests made it a 'difficult matter indeed to collect the land revenue with regularity'. But regular roads and a little irrigation would in a 'short time treble the revenue of the country'.[36] Glasfurd felt confident that all this could be accomplished without much use of direct force:

> The police now distributed over the Dependency will also be of great use in gradually accustoming the people to us, and the location of a news-writer at Jugdalpur would be attended with equally good results.[37]

Nearly three-quarters of a century later, when most of Glasfurd's recommendations for 'civilising the Dependency' had been more or less fully executed, Grigson, another distinguished officer of the Empire in Bastar and, unlike Glasfurd, exceptionally sensitive to the tribal condition, perceived in Glasfurd's comments and sweeping plans only the most recent instance of conceit and grand self-delusion to which builders of empires succumbed even in Bastar.

To Grigson British presence seemed but another occurrence in an invariable pattern:

> As the Maratha Amil sixty seven years before, so now the Victorian Englishman, develop trade, and civilisation would follow. The isolation of centuries was to end, Bastar to be opened to the world and its savages to exchange their freedom for the 'allurements and comforts of civilisation', trade and traders, clothes, tobacco, a better system of criminal and judicial procedure, vaccination and copper coin. Did, and do, the ghosts of old builders of the ruins of Barsur, Bhairamgarh and Kuruspal smile to hear a newer race decree that 'Bastar must be civilised!'[38]

Grigson's allusion to the by then forgotten builders of the splendid temples and tanks of Barsur of 800 years ago is profoundly suggestive; but perhaps not in the apparently intended sense of a warning. The invocation of these surviving fragments from another past is meaningful at another level. It is a referent of the difference and distance in the meaning of change before and after the modern intrusion in Bastar.

To the imperial officers despatched in the mid-nineteenth century to pioneer the opening-up and eventual integration of this remote 'dependency', Bastar appeared a land governed by changeless primeval forces stubbornly indifferent to the world outside. It was their mission to soften and erode this indifference. They sought an enduring presence for the colonial mediation not through a simple enforcement of superior armed might. They believed that in transforming the landscape and Nature itself, the sense of oneself and the world would irrevocably change even among the rude inhabitants of this hinterland. Glasfurd as well as Elliot before him, knew, and in impressive detail, the non-tribal origins of the Bastar ruling family. The fact that political conquest had been so manifestly powerless to tame the primeval forces—their resilience and power so little affected after nearly 500 years of conquest—was a grim reminder of the danger to British rule of also regressing into the familiar stagnant mould. Prior to the colonial conquest the primaeval forces in Bastar had found it possible to tame and limit the reach of conquests, and to orient to its own vital impulses what to begin with was an alien presence.

Bastar: Mediations as Proximities

The rulers of Bastar were a cadet branch of the Kakatıya dynasty which ruled Warangal (1150 to 1425). The Kakatiyas of Warangal (in present-day Andhra Pradesh) established their rule as feudatories of the Chalukyas. Prataprudra Dev, the last Kakatiya to rule in Warangal, was defeated and killed by Ahmed Shah Bahmani early in the fifteenth century. His brother, Anam Dev, retreated into the safety of Bastar forests across the Godavari river.

Long before Anam Dev's conquest of Bastar, the Kakatiyas exercised a loose control over certain territories in Bastar. Grigson mentions the survival of a tradition among the Koyas of southern Bastar of 'visiting King Prataprudra's court at Warangal'.[39] Bastar's amorphous links across the Godavari persisted well into the eighteenth century. 'Bastar retained several zamindaris south of the Godavary . . . before Anam Deo's arrival there was a nominal suzerainty of Warangal over most of Bastar, and real authority resting with local chiefs or in the hands of old tribal organizations that was so marked a feature of medieval kingdoms.'[40]

Traces of a much earlier external presence survive in a Barsur inscription which records that the Nagavansis (of Telegu origin) ruled in Bastar (near Dantewada) and Kuruspal (near Chitrakoot falls) during the eleventh century. Other inscriptions record raids into Bastar between AD 844 and 1150 by Chalukya, Chola and Hoyasala princes.[41]

Extensive ruins of temples and irrigation tanks in Barsur and Bhairamgarh testify to a long and substantial external presence in Bastar. As surviving fragments of another past, the splendid 800 year-old temples and tanks in Barsur are profoundly suggestive. They signify an elemental force and quality far removed from the possibility of 'regression' which Glasfurd and Elliot feared, and which Grigson accepted with calm detachment.

Distance in this context signifies not merely the unalterable limits which constrain the reach and effectiveness of an outside presence, but also something intrinsically vital. It signifies the emergence and resilience of a distinct cultural–cognitive space. The true significance of the surviving archaeological fragments is to be sought in the cognitive terrain which made possible the creative elaboration of skills and crafts which to begin with were perhaps unfamiliar and unknown in the tribal contiguity. One could argue that the severely restricted appropriation of surplus and the undiminished vigour of tribal cohesions could be explained as the ineradicable attribute of a backward technology of conquest and colonisation. But the still alive tradition of bronze casting and the now almost extinct craft of iron smelting furnish quite another kind of referent in this context.

Barsur, the site of the twelfth century ruins of the Nagavansi rulers of Bastar, is even now on the edge of the forest; just a day's walk from the still little touched hills of Abujhamad. Yet, the grandeur and aesthetic vigour of these monuments remain incomparable to anything built since in Bastar. Glasfurd counted 100 brick-lined irrigation tanks around Barsur. After 'five hundred years' the bricks were amazing for their solidity and finish, and looked as if 'just taken out of a brick kiln'.[42] Unlike the debased and wretched nth rate imitations with which Bastar has been so profusely and shamelessly littered in the last forty years, the buildings of Barsur are not pale imitations of something else. They are their own measure. Perhaps the only thing that can be said in favour of the shoddy structures of the last forty-five years in Bastar and other regions on the periphery is that they are certain not to last for long. The quality of modern construction visibly withers as one moves away from the road. The farther away from the road, the worse the building. In instructive contrast the quality of houses built according to traditional skills and techniques of the region tends to improve as one moves away from the road.[43]

The ancient buildings of Barsur represent an immense effort which must have taken many years to complete. It is not as if the tradition of crafts and aesthetics which made these buildings possible originated in Bastar. In that sense there is hardly anything, at least in India, that has not touched or been touched by something other than itself. But the framework, which made this kind of interaction possible and defined its terms, was oriented to a different order of things. The tradition of craft and aesthetics associated with the ruins in Barsur, in moving into Bastar was not moving away from some centre to an obscure periphery. The movement into Bastar in this instance signifies an organic shift of a complex from one centre to another, of a very different texture.[44]

What is true of the tradition of building skills under royal patronage in Barsur is perhaps even more true of skills and crafts that continue to be practiced to this day in the distant villages of Bastar. Bronze has absolutely no function or place in the techniques and tools of production used by the Madia and Muria tribals of Bastar. Yet the local Garhwa craftsmen have perfected skills and techniques to cast lumps of bronze into exquisite artefacts.

The Garhwa's craft was perfected in the mediating cluster of villages on the fringes of settled and shifting cultivation. Bronze metallurgy was unknown in this region. The metal came from outside. But apart from the metal, all other materials and tools used in bronze casting were and continue to be locally obtained and fabricated.

Garhwas are a recent offshoot of the Ghasia caste. Most of them can trace a Madia ancestor within two or three generations. The inspiration that nurtures their creative craft can only be located in reference to the Madia tribal sensibility. Encounter with things utterly unknown and beyond the range of all previous experience has been, in a more self-assured past, an elevating and creative experience. The story of the origin of the Garhwa craft, related by one of its greatest living practitioners, Jayadev Baghel of Konda-gaon,[45] evokes the sense of profound and subtle play between Man and Nature stirring human imagination to the creative act.

The first hesitant impulse to touch and hold a glimmering lump of metal is remembered to have been kindled in the midst of an utterly unlooked for and dimly comprehended happening. Some nameless ancestor, wandering through forests and hills in search of game and food, came upon bright lumps on the edge of large stone crevices. It was the peak of summer. As in the burning heat of summer now, so in that distant past, forests suddenly set themselves ablaze. As the shimmering lump beckoned him to the first fumbling touch of metal, he felt overwhelmed. Very gently he carried the solid bright lumps home. A few days later, upset by its dulled glimmer he swept its surface; the more he swept and handled it the brighter it glimmered. Full of joy and very excited he swept and tidied up a little corner in the house for this wondrous thing. In awe and reverence he would touch, and fumble. Soon in this wondrous play of touching and fumbling he began to recognise the skills of the Garhwa's craft. Neighbours began to notice that the Garhwa's house was now so bright and beautiful. And so it came about that the Garhwa began to cast figures of bronze, and every-one worshipped them.

For the Garhwa craftsmen this story is much more than just a colourful tale. Each movement in the elaborate act which transforms lumps of metal into artefacts is alive to the memory of that distant ancestor and all those who in following his example have kept the craft alive. The first self-distancing from Nature happens in moments of awe and reverence. Self-awareness of distancing unfolds as skills. And those skills, even as they shape new and dazzling forms, are nurtured with a sense of deep humility. Before skills emerge as recognisable elements in the creative play, the irresistible aesthetic emotion stirred by the glimmering lump of metal is expressed as an activity to clear and create spaces that would never have been, were it not for the creative impulse inherent in Man.[46]

Iron as a Tribal Mediation

Iron, that irresistible mover of things and Man long before the age of steam, has been known and used by tribals in this region since antiquity. For centuries Agaria tribals have practiced their ancient skills of smelting iron from ore, and forging it into implements. Unlike the craft of the Garhwa, the Agaria craft tradition and skills are consciously directed towards the practical and functional requirements of everyday life.[47] Their craft, like the metal they smelt and forge, is bare and matter-of-fact. But Agaria smelters know something of the sheer sweep and potency of the metal they shape. 'If you think Iron is nothing', reminds one of their proverbs, 'look out of the house and see it wandering all over the three worlds'.[48] Iron is sanctified in the Agaria origin myth as the substance which rivets and keeps the earth itself in its place. It is remembered not only as the mighty mover and vitaliser, but as the very thing without which life on earth could never have endured:

In the first moments of cosmic uncertainty, when the earth, like a thin pancake, buffeted in all directions on the primaeval expanse of water; the nails with which Nanga Baiga secured the world in place were made by Agar Sai—the First Agaria![49]

Agarias, known by various names in different places, belong to the great Gond family of tribals in central India. In 1940 Verrier Elwin found them to be 'most numerous' and far away from the 'roads and railways, in the Maikal hills and in the lovely zamindaries of Bilaspur'.[50] Bilaspur and Mandla, almost the mid-point in the Vindhyan tribal contiguity, form the 'real home of the Agaria'.[51] Like the Agaria myth of creation and the origin of their craft, Agaria smelting techniques belong to a distinct and independent tribal tradition of metallurgy. In the last hundred years or so, the *lohar* (blacksmith) of the plains has rarely been known to have engaged in the smelting of iron. Agarias engage in both smelting and forging iron. Certain Agaria families in Mirzapur specialised exclusively in smelting iron from ore. Iron is extracted from ore in 'small clay furnaces' fired by burning charcoal.[52] Bellows are of a 'particular kettledrum pattern' and worked by Agarias 'with their feet'. Bellows of the 'lohar' are always 'worked by hand'.[53] Available evidence suggests that iron smelting and forging has been a skill that was known and practised by tribals in this region from ancient times. During his extensive and systematic exploration of central India in search of deposits of iron ore during the 1880s, P.N. Bose of the Geological Survey was struck by the fact that the only metal for which there is a word in Gondi is iron.[54]

Experts of the Geological Survey of India noticed the exceptional resourcefulness of smelting techniques, and the extensive prevalence of the industry of iron smelting deep in the remote hills far removed from the plains of settled cultivation:

> Iron smelting was at one time a widespread industry in India and there is hardly a district away from the great alluvial tracts of the Indus, Ganges and Brahmputra, in which slag heaps are not found. For the primitive iron smelter finds no difficulty in obtaining sufficient supplies of ore from deposits that no European iron-master would regard as worth his serious consideration.[55]

Iron smelting activity could be fairly intense in certain village clusters favoured by easy access to iron ore and firewood from the forest. Prior to the enactment of the stern colonial forest laws, perhaps the largest cluster of Agaria clay furnaces was around Amarpani–Tendukhera in the Narsinghpur district. According to the estimate of Sir L.L. Fermer of the Geological Survey, 'about 70 to 80 furnaces' were being worked in this area in the years 1855–57 to produce about '140 tons of iron annually'.[56]

As the effective reach of forest and land revenue laws extended deeper into the hinterland in the last quarter of the nineteenth century, the Agaria craft of iron smelting began to register a steady decline. A notice concerning the state of iron smelting in the Balaghat District Gazetteer is instructive of the tragic fate that was beginning to overtake this ancient craft all over central India by the first decade of this century:

> Iron smelting was widely practised all over Dhansua and Bhanpur forests, till the practice was prohibited in those belonging to Government. There are now only one or two furnaces working in Bhanpur.[57]

Before the onslaught of the modern forest laws, Raipur district supported one of the largest concentrations of Agaria smelters. In 1887, when the Agaria craft was already on the decline, P.N. Bose had seen numerous clay furnaces still being worked in this area by a 'class of Gonds who style themselves Agarias or Pardhans'.[58] By the 1930s, the name Agaria was 'scarcely heard' in Raipur district.[59] The following extract from Elwin's *The Agaria* encapsulates the salient details concerning the situation and forces which smothered this ancient craft:

> In 1891 no fewer than 1,850 persons returned themselves as Agaria, but this number dropped in twenty years to 273. The number of furnaces also dropped from 28 in 1898—a total which was maintained until 1913 or later—to only 1 in 1925; and the industry has probably expired before the competition of market iron which is particularly strong in a district with such good communications. When Grigson was Deputy Commissioner of Jubbelpore in 1937, he saw several abandoned furnaces along the border of Jubbulpore and Sihora Tehsils; and he noted that the blacksmiths attributed the abandonment of iron smelting to the forest rates, the raising of which they said had made it cheaper to buy the raw material from the bazaar.[60]

Clearly, what is of exceptional significance is not the continual decline to extinction of the Agaria craft, but the fact that for close to sixty-seventy years these tribal smelters persisted with working their clay furnaces in the fierce shadow of modern industrial technology and colonial forest laws. What does this survival signify? Two considerations merit a close look:

1. Could it be that the quantum of iron produced was always small and never of much consequence. The fact of decline, then, is of relevance only in so far as it concerns the restricted and inflexible reach of a primitive technology.
2. Survival of Agaria smelting could have been due to the rather slowly enhanced capacity of industrial technology to reach out into the hinterland. Instances of survival in situations well exposed to industrial technology merely indicate either the compulsion to accept an inferior technology because it is cheaper, or simply the persistence of blind habit.

Firm estimates for iron extracted by indigenous techniques before the decline set in are extremely problematic. To illustrate the difficulty, consider a few details of an estimate cited as apparently reliable. According to this estimate, during the period 1909 to 1913—years when the Agaria craft was already in sharp decline—the average annual production was estimated at 557 tons from 428 clay furnaces. Assuming this estimate to be the optimal base line, Elwin concluded that at the end of the 1930s production was 'probably less than [a] third of this'.[61] Elwin, it may be noted, was exceptionally vigilant in not accepting government estimates and reports uncritically. But in this instance, the illusion of fact which the printed word comes to acquire despite one's basic inclinations—particularly when it concerns figures of dispersed aggregates difficult to verify—seems to have flawed Elwin's judgement. Certain other figures cited by Elwin himself clearly suggest that this figure grossly understates the actual quantum of iron smelted.

In 1938, according to Elwin, 486 clay furnaces were being worked to produce 839 tons of iron in the principality of Jashpur. In the adjacent and much smaller principality of Udaipur—formerly part of Sarguja—according to information Elwin characterised as 'admirably documented', 109 furnaces and 134 forges were being worked by 'iron workers of all types'.[62] And this was true of a time when the Agaria craft is believed to have become almost extinct.

Precise estimates of iron yields prior to the competition from iron smelted in modern furnaces in England would perhaps always be difficult. The crucial fact is that before the modern colonial onslaught began, iron tools and implements used by peasants in the plains of settled cultivation were forged from iron smelted in primitive clay furnaces in the tribal hinterland. Therefore, whatever may have been the precise quantity of iron smelted, the fact of decline and eventual extinction remains of immense significance.

The Agaria craft survived the longest and best in areas which were far removed from the reach of modern law and communications. For instance, the principalities of Udaipur and Jashpur, where as late as 1940 Elwin confirmed the survival of a considerable cluster of Agaria clay furnaces, were areas which had only distantly felt the modern impact. Hence the relative freedom from the constraints of the colonial political economy. But that certainly does not constitute evidence of an inherently closed and therefore exhausted possibility.

Encounter with the unfamiliar and manifestly more powerful modern metallurgy, far from being an invigorating experience, gradually foreclosed the sustenance and viability of Agaria craft. It would be a mistake to see in the slow destruction of this ancient craft the end, even though tragic, of a tradition that had already exhausted all its intrinsic possibilities. It need not have been so. That other creative possibilities could have emerged in a different framework of political economy and cognition is affirmed by what Elwin characterised as the 'heroic resistance' of Agaria craft for close to a century in the shadow of fierce modern competition and laws systematically unhelpful.

To comprehend the significance of the survival of the Agaria craft tradition for so long after its demise had been ordained by the new colonial order of things, certain crucial details concerning their craft merit attention. Iron smelted in Agaria clay furnaces was invariably from ores with a low iron content. No 'European iron-master', in the considered judgement of the Geological Survey, would have considered these ores worth working.[63] It was not as if the Agaria iron-masters were indifferent to considerations of quality. But the considerations were of a different order. Agarias of Mandla graded the local ore into six categories.[64] The best quality ore according to Agaria classification, on the basis of chemical analysis in the modern laboratory of Tata Iron Works (1930s), was rated as 'low grade ore' with a low iron content.[65] It was the sort of ore for which the modern economy of scale simply had no use. For the

Agaria, 'economy of scale' was of no consequence. Agarias graded ores in terms of the softness of the iron they would yield, and from which implements of high tensile quality could be forged.

The survival of Agaria iron smelting was linked to the stubborn preference among the peasants of the plains of intense settled cultivation and the shifting cultivators of the Vindhyan highlands for iron smelted in their clay furnaces. Iron was as much of an essential requirement, and perhaps more so, in the areas of shifting cultivation as it was in the plains of settled agriculture. Settled agriculture, and on a substantial scale, is known to have flourished in India and elsewhere long before the discovery of iron.[66] But cutting and clearing a fresh patch of forest every year for shifting cultivation seems inconceivable without the use of an iron axe. Consider the extraordinary implicaton of this fact for the pre-modern texture of tribal–non-tribal interaction. Agaria craft as the largest, if not the only, provider of the vital ingredient so indispensable to the 'settled cultivation mode of livelihood' in the plains and valleys; and the 'shifting cultivation mode of livelihood' in the hills constituted an unusual instance of an exclusively tribal mediation.

The demand for implements forged out of iron smelted in 'primitive clay furnaces' persisted well into the twentieth century. At the Ahraura *hat* in Mirzapur (close to the Gangetic plains), on an average 1,400 axes forged from iron smelted in Agaria clay furnaces were sold every year in the first decade of this century.[67] This persistence, ostensibly in the face of better technological choices, may well seem an instance of blind habit or superstitious preference. Hence the need to invoke expert testimony concerning the quality of iron smelted from low grade ore by the tribal iron-masters of Central India.

Elwin is emphatic that the peasants' preference for the 'soft and malleable' ores was due to the simple fact that they could be shaped into tools and implements which were better to work with and easier to maintain.

One reason for this heroic persistence is the peasant's preference for tools made from the soft and malleable ores used by village smelters. For example, in the iron head of the small axe, the hole which takes the wooden handle is made by hammering it out with a large nail while the iron is hot—which would be impossible with English iron. Again, the 'karrahi', a sort of

large plate with handles, made in Jubbelpore, is made by continuous hammering of the cold iron—a process which gives the
metal a fine polish, but could not be applied to more brittle
iron. The peasants also believe that tools made with the village
iron are easier to mend when broken.[68]

In the considered judgement of Wallace, published in the *Journal
of Iron and Steel*, 'Charcoal iron' could survive long years of
exposure without gathering rust:

I have seen native-made iron, forged on a stone anvil, and have
observed that it does not rust like English iron when exposed to
the weather. The ironwork of the car on which the Gods of the
Kulu valley take the air has a fine brown patina and no rust
flakes. It is all charcoal iron.

Sir L.L. Fermer of the Geological Survey of India thought iron
smelted at Tendukhera (Narsinghpur district) was of exceptional
quality.

This metal was of unusually good quality, and a portion of it was
converted into steel by reheating, hammering, rolling in burnt
cow dung, and plunging into water.[69]

The intrinsic resilience of the sensibility—in the sense of grasping
unfamiliar new possibilities—that nurtured the Agaria craft tradition comes alive in another detail of its early encounter with the
modern world. Iron for the suspension bridge built over the Beas
river in Sagar (1830) was smelted in the clay furnaces of Tendukhera.[70] Until the end of the nineteenth century, smelting on a
considerable scale—140 tons in 70 to 80 furnaces, i.e., an average
of 2 tons per furnace in a year—continued in the environs of
Tendukhera. According to the detailed assessment (late 1880s) of
Bose of the Geological Survey, and the Agricultural Ledger of the
Central Provinces Government (late 1880s), despite the annihilating colonial onslaught, iron smelting continued to be fairly profitable.[71] Clearly these skills, at least among some of the iron masters,
were susceptible to interesting and creative possibilities.

Unlike most other tribals, the Agaria community is singularly
matter-of-fact. Yet, years later when the Agaria craft was on the

verge of extinction, railways—that wondrous combination of 'iron and fire' in a 'gigantic moving furnace'—could entice an Agaria in the 'wilds of the Motinale forest' to compose a Karma song:

> At every station the engine takes coal and water
> In front run the wires to give the news.
> Behind we sit clutching our tickets in our hands
> In front goes the motor,
> Behind goes the cycle
> Leaving their food, the children run to see.[72]

Perhaps, in a different framework of validation and political economy, these tribal iron-masters would have assimilated the age of 'iron and steam' as a revitalising element within the tradition of their craft. Had that been so, the advent of the railways to India, rather than levelling out its crafts and tradition, could have in a significant measure helped to redefine at another level and in different terms the situation in which Indian civilisation encountered the West and its 'modern dynamic'. The construction of railways in no small measure contributed to directing nationalist attention towards the colonial character of British rule.[73] But the nationalist critique, penetrating and far more perceptive than the contemporary understanding in other parts of the colonised world, seems to have been utterly blind to the implications of the destruction of the ancient craft of iron smelting. Even Gandhi, so profoundly sensitive to creative possibilities in the everyday life rhythm of Indian civilisation, witnessed without a word the withering into oblivion of this stupendous craft tradition.

So large a phenomenon of persistent unseeing reflects perhaps the constraints to which perception even in its most emancipated moments is bound. Individual perceptions may perceive and affirm far beyond the bounds implicit in a particular framework of discourse and validation. But the 'hearing space' available to such affirmations within that discourse is far more severely foreclosed. The fate of much of what Gandhi perceived and affirmed in our colonial discourse is a tragic illustration of how unyielding these constraints can be.[74]

The nature and salience of some of these constraints surface rather strikingly in the inverse relationship between information concerning the quality and viability of indigenous iron smelting, and the stubborn incapacity to recognise its significance. Iron smelting was mentioned in numerous settlement reports and district gazetteers. In 1868, the Bhandara District Exhibition gave an award to a specimen exhibit of locally smelted iron.[75] Experts of the Geological Survey were emphatic in their very favourable estimates of the quality of indigenously smelted iron. The Agriculture Department of the Central Provinces recorded in considerable detail the economics of 'native iron smelting'. Yet the Braboune Committee (1931), while listing the 'village industries' worth rescuing, does not so much as mention iron smelting or the name Agaria.[76] By this time, a fairly well informed and vigilant nationalist press was well established. But no one thought it worthwhile to at least register a protest. A few years later, S.C. Roy, the leading figure of early Indian anthropology,[77] and Verrier Elwin published meticulously researched studies on the craft of iron smelting. Again, 'The Aboriginal Problem in the C.P. and Berar' (1944) by Grigson, the most comprehensive statement on the condition of tribals in central India, does not mention the Agaria craft. And Grigson was extremely knowledgeable about tribal affairs, and exceptionally sensitive to the tribal condition.[78]

Significance in Modern Cognition and Limits in Tribal Perception

Gandhi could never forget that human beings, even when engaged in the service of an evil system like colonialism can and indeed do good. That signifies an irreducible autonomous space, inherent and ineradicable in human existence. Without it, human perception and memory would lose much of their resonance and meaning. But between perception and its recognition as a legitimate presence in human life mediate notions of significance and valid comprehension. Acts and statements that appear absurd or perverse often dramatise the limits of cognition implicit in the accepted notions of significance and valid comprehension.

Certain observations of Col. Ward, Settlement Officer of Mandla district (1869),[79] on the Agaria are instructive in this context. Ward characterised Agarias as 'inefficient' and 'lazy'. His reason for this characterisation: Agarias invariably locate their clay furnaces close to the sources of ore. The sheer absurdity of this remark is incredibly heightened if one remembers that as a representative of the leading industrial power, he could not have been unaware of what was already something of a truism: locating industry close to its raw material resource reduces the cost of production. The definitive consideration in Ward's dismissive judgement is the word, 'inefficient'. True enough, in comparison to industrial factory production, the Agaria craft techniques were demonstrably 'inefficient'. As such, the Agaria craft had ceased to be viable and could therefore be legitimately treated as an archaic survival devoid of legitimacy. All other considerations are mere details of no consequence. And errors of detail, particularly when they concern archaic survivals, are entirely excusable.

Forsyth's description of Gond women in the wild interior illustrates the same problematique at another level.[80] Dalton was acutely distressed by an account of the Juangs published by another Englishman named Strange. Juangs, also known as *Patuas*, were a small tribe of gentle forest dwellers in the hills of Orissa. Juang men and women wore dresses made of leaves instead of cloth. Till the mid-nineteenth century Juangs refused to take up any kind of cultivation and survived entirely on game and whatever they could gather in the forests. Strange's account bristled with severe judgements about their 'shameless ways and ugly appearance'.[81] Dalton castigated Strange's sketches of Juang life as 'very clever but very grotesque'. He found them to be false for 'grossly calumniating' a very shy and gentle 'race'.[82] In saying that Dalton was not being just kind or romantic.

Dalton felt Juang women would make 'good studies for a sculptor'. His account of the Juangs is tender and deeply considerate:

—whilst I conversed with the males on their customs, language and religion, the girls sat nestled together in a corner, for a long time silent and motionless as statues, but after an hour or two had elapsed the crouching nymphs showed signs of life and symptoms of uneasiness, and more attentively regarding them I found that great tears were dropping from downcast eyes like dew drops on the green leaves. On my tenderly seeking the cause of their distress, I was told the leaves were becoming dry, stiff, and uncomfortable, and if they were not allowed to go to the woods for a change, the consequences would be serious, and they certainly could not dance.[83]

Sensitive to the verve and rhythm of tribal dance and music, Dalton sharply remarked upon what he perceived as its virtual absence in the life of a 'Hindu peasant'. He also noticed that after conversion to Christianity Kol tribals abandoned their old tribal dances and songs. With that much of the zest and joy so character-istic of tribal life seemed also to wither away from their lives. Yet, Dalton was firmly convinced that conversion was the best that could happen to the Kols and other tribals.[84]

Perceptions marked by sharp divergence and distancing at the level of details—and details, whatever the framework which defines their placement, retain a certain inherent significance—seem to converge in their final judgement. Agaria craftsmanship may be recognised as an extraordinary skill. Tribal dances and music may be perceived as the vital fount of joy and spontaneity. But they are all, in the final analysis, fragments of a sensibility and mode of existence that have irrevocably exhausted their true worth and possibilities. And as such, marked out by History for eventual extinction.

The Agaria craft of iron smelting represents a most unusual case in this context. It consists of techniques and a technology that represent, as it were, the most advanced segment in both the pre-modern and the modern technological spectrum. But precisely for that reason, its continued presence in the modern context consti-tutes an intolerable disturbance. Other crafts, like the Garhwa craft in Bastar, also associated with archaic sensibilities and modes of livelihood, may be tolerated and even encouraged. The modern expectation seems to be that such crafts would be easily harnessed as harmless skills to brighten a little with their quaint and exotic artefacts the cheerless monotony of modern life. In modern cogni-tion, the Agaria craft signifies a different kind of presence. It signifies perhaps a disturbance and an unacceptable transgression of limits within which all things and sensibilities beyond the modern ambit have to be tamed and harnessed. But limits as they concern the modern mode of thinking and doing are seen as contingent and temporary, and therefore of no intrinsic significance.

Recognition of legitimate limits is seen in tribal sensibility as the precondition for order and human sanity. Limits and legitimacy are defined in terms of cosmic placement. Knowing one's true placement defines legitimacy and affirms order. Authority—as knowledge and as power—is legitimate in so far as it confirms and conforms to the true order of placement of Man and things.

At first glance this formulation only seems to confirm the modern categorisation of tribal sensibility as the repetitive play of mean possibilities within narrow and unchangeable limits. True, this mode of placement affirms certain limits as inherent and final. But that does not negate human imagination and effort. These limits are not marked out as the actual line beyond which human effort cannot proceed. They are invoked as the ultimate referent in reference to which the possibility of some human effort may be grasped. An extremely significant if somewhat ambivalent conse-quence of quite another kind also inheres in this mode of cosmic placement. Since all legitimate existence is subject to limits defined by correct placement, logically nothing can be absolutely opposed or absolutely superior. To clarify the logic of this mode of place-ment and comprehension consider the following excerpt from my conversation with a tribal Gunia in a little village in Bilaspur district:

Suresh: Your village has a school. There is a college in Bilaspur. Knowledge acquired in school or college is very different from your Gunia knowledge. Truth of that knowledge is ascertained by very different norms. Divine displeasure has no place in that. Would you say that such knowledge is also subject to limits? Could such knowledge, when it oversteps its limits, be the cause of insanity?

Gunia: Knowledge, all knowledge is subject to limits. Knowledge in excess of those limits can cause anyone to go mad. All things should be perfectly in between. The law in Nature and life is *mandras*. Every thing is fine so long as they are in *mandras*.

By *mandras* I mean each thing being in its place. In the entire cosmos, there is not a thing that does not have a place, all its own. And if each and every thing has its own place, then there are also limits. To transgress limits is to shake every thing from its place. Balance is disturbed. That is why every thing ought to be perfectly in-between. And that means to be in *mandras*.

Suresh: Scientific reason does not recognise your truth. It is the absolute opposite. Just as light and darkness. Like night and day, they are completely apart.

Science believes in continuous progress. What today seems beyond the control of Man, in the future is certain to be within Man's reach. What is impossible today may be possible tomorrow. Frontiers of knowledge keep expanding. For human life there are no final limits. For science, limits are strictly in the context of time and place. Knowledge and reason are boundless.

Gunia: Science does not recognise our truth. But that does not negate truth. And there are no things absolutely apart. Not even day and night. Or, light and darkness. We say, a little bit of darkness now. In that there is also a little light.

In the knowledge of science there is immense power. Its shadow is across all the world. But still, I would say it also has its limits.

Suresh: Belief in continuous progress has a basis. You do admit that in recent years a lot of things have been turned upside down. The old constraints have been broken. Today Patiya-pali also has a school. There is a radio. *Sarkar* has built roads and dug canals. Village *Gaontias* are no more. *Begar* has been abolished. Life in the village has changed a little. Is that all wrong?

Gunia: We think it is good the *Gaontias* are no more. Everyone should get enough food to fill their stomach. Everyone is entitled to live and live well. *Begar* was an evil. End of injustice is a good thing. School, water pumps, and roads are all very well.

Government has immense power. It can do what it likes. It can set up new trades and destroy old ones. If it wants, it can remove this village from here and build a dam. Before the might of the Government all of us have to bend.

Now you need a 'license' for every trade. I treat people very seriously ill. Suppose the illness gets worse, the patient dies and there is a police report. I would be in serious trouble. It has never happened. But the fear of it always remains. Could you tell me a way to obtain a 'Government license'?

All this I acknowledge. Yet, I must say there is a limit to the power of Government. There is a limit to the knowledge of science. Only we do not perceive it.

Suresh: You talk of final limits. How does one recognise them? Who would determine these limits?

You understand Gunia's knowledge. You believe that

there is a final limit for that knowledge. It may not be easy to know and recognise those limits. But you try to remain within those limits.

Those who understand the knowledge of science do not recognise the existence of limits. For them those final limits do not exist. If in their understanding final limits do not exist, then what sort of limits are they? Limits can only be if they are known and recognised.

Gunia: Science is moving ahead. It is moving very fast. Its power today is above all things. The entire world is in its grip. For us it is not possible to even truly know the extent of its power.

Those who know science do not recognise the existence of any final limits. We do not understand the knowledge of science. And we cannot understand it. We only know its power. Then how can we determine limits for science? They alone can determine the limits for their knowledge.

So long as those who know science do not recognise these limits, there are no limits for them. But final limits do exist. A time would come when even they would be forced to recognise these final limits. But until then they would keep moving ahead and beyond. Behind them would remain nothing. And when they would already be far, very far beyond, something would happen. But by then they would already have gone far beyond their final limits. Something terrible would jolt them. Mind would simply 'crack up'. At that point they would recognise their 'final limits'. But those 'final limits' would already be far behind. As to what would follow, no one knows!![85]

NOTES

1. See D.D. Kosambi, *The Culture and Civilisation of Ancient India in Historical Outline*, Vikas, New Delhi, 1976. On the eastward shift, also see Bridget Allchin and Raymond Allchin, *The Rise of Civilisation in India and Pakistan*, Select Book Service Syndicate, 1983, pp. 309–346.

Earliest traces of large human settlements and settled agriculture (club wheat Triticum Compactum) are in Ruetta Valley (7000 BC) and Mehargarh (5000 BC), pp. 95ff, and 105ff.

For the first large settlement complex in Mehargarh (Baluchistan) see Jean Francois Jarriage, 'Excavations at Mehargarh: Their Significance for Understanding the Background of the Harrappan Civilization' in G.L. Possehl, ed., *Harappan Civilization: A Contemporary Perspective*, Oxford & IBH, 1982, pp. 79–94.

2. For a measured comprehensive study of the Indus Valley, see, Allchin and Allchin, *Rise of Civilization*. Kosambi's study is of particular significance in that he seeks to place contemporary tribal survivals and their long presence in relation to the dominant historical rhythm: imperial consolidation, urbanisation, advance and diffusion of technology. Of course, for Kosambi technology as the pivot and mover in production furnishes the only form of true human significance. Changes in other forms, for instance religion, are categorised as primitive forms that signify in oblique and confused ways changes in production.

Kosambi in arguing for iron and steady extension of settled agriculture as determinants in the eastward locus of power and urbanisation touches upon an issue of enormous significance for my argument. Strangely Kosambi takes no notice of the tribal craft of iron smelting. Quite clearly this absence could not be due to lack of information. Rather, this absence is due to the way he reads significance. For the role of iron and settled agriculture as its concomitant see Kosambi, *Culture and Civilisation*, pp. 72–96, and 25–49.

3. See G.L. Possehl, ed., *Ancient Cities of the Indus*, Vikas, 1979. In particular B.K. Thappar, 'Kalibangan: A Harrapan Metropolis Beyond the Indus Valley', ibid. pp. 325–54. For the considerable pastoral presence in the Indus Valley period, see the meticulous report on the excavation of ash mounds in south India, F.R. Allchin, *Neolithic Cattle Keepers of South India*, Cambridge University Press, 1963.

4. Stuart Piggott, *Prehistoric India*, Pelican Books, 1961, pp. 13–14.

5. I was struck as I walked the lanes of Dokri, a dusty little village in the shadow of the ruins of Mohanjodaro, by the exact likeness of some of the bullock carts still in use to the clay carts housed in the Mohanjodaro museum (1987).

Allchin (*Rise of Civilization*, p. 177) notes remarkable craft continuity in house building: 'several of the basic types can be found widely among village houses in Pakistan and West India to this day.'

6. Allchin, *Rise of Civilization*, pp. 171–83.

7. Kosambi, *Culture and Civilisation*, plates 14 and 15.

8. Pathogens can breed only amidst certain demographic densities, which indicate basic shifts in Man–Nature equation. For instance, Levi-Strauss refers to the firm connection established between sickle cell anemia (drepnocythemia), a genetic disorder, and extension of agriculture. See Claude Levi-Strauss, *The View From Afar*, Basil Blackwell, 1985, pp. 16ff.

The connection between regular locomotion and the incidence of disease and epidemics has been widely noticed in the context of remote tribal regions. A characteristic instance:

Improved communications, while they have immensely facilitated internal trade, have undoubtedly spread disease. All Nagas assert definitively that since their country was taken over illness has increased. Not only specific diseases, such as venereal disease and tuberculosis been introduced, but epidemics spread more quickly.

J.P. Mills, *Census of India*, 1931, Vol. I, Part III B, p. 147.

9. Motte discovered (1766) that the effectiveness of his armed escort and horses collapsed as soon as he left the open Balasore plains and entered the zamindari of Boad.

Paths became 'quite impossible for wheel carriages' even though the tree cover was far from dense. Worse 'If any body of men refuses to make the mountaineers a present, they fell the largest trees, and lay them across the road, so as to obstruct the passage of horses; and this obliges the travellers to buy their assistance. . . .'

T. Motte, 'A Narrative of a Journey to the Diamond Mines at Sambhalpoor, in the Province of Orissa', in C.U. Wills, ed., *Early European Travellers in the Nagpur Territories*, Government Press, Nagpur, 1924, pp. 25ff.

10. For lucid and accurate details concerning geography and terrain, see *The Imperial Gazetteer of India*, Vol. 10, Clarendon Press, 1908, pp. 1–11.

11. Cotton has been important in pre-modern exchange and trade. Motte for instance noted, 'Coolo', situated on the edge of hilly country, is a 'large village' and the 'merchants of Berar, and the inland parts of Berar, bring cotton and other goods hither on bullocks, which return loaded with salt' to the interior hinterland, Motte, 'A Narrative', pp. 21ff.

12. For geographical details of Bastar and Kanker see E.A. de Brett, *Chhattisgarh Feudatory States Gazetteer*, Bombay, 1909, pp. 25ff.

13. *Imperial Gazetteer*, Vol. 10, p. 4.

14. *Ibid.*, pp. 4–5.

15. J. Forsyth, *The Highlands of Central India*, (London; 1889), Asian Publication Services, 1975, p. 5. Also see de Brett, *Chattisgarh*.

16. Forsyth, *Central India*, p. 4.

17. Concerning extension of the railway network see *Imperial Gazetteer*, Vol. 10, pp. 58–61.

18. In terms of area, Ladakh district in the state of Jammu and Kashmir is the largest.

Minor variations recur concerning the precise area of the Bastar principality. They indicate the rough character of survey operations in an area that remained untamed into this century. The *Imperial Gazetteer* records an area of 13,062 sq. miles for Bastar, *Imperial Gazetteer*, Vol. 10, Table III, p. 102. According to Grigson: 'according to the recently revised figures of Survey of India' the area of Bastar is, 13,725 sq. miles. W.V. Grigson, *The Maria Gonds of Bastar*, Oxford University Press, 1938, p. 3.

The area of Bastar district enumerated in the Census is: 39,114 sq. kms., of which only 53.6 sq. kms. is listed as urban. See *Census of India 1981*, Series II, Madhya Pradesh, Part II–B, Primary Census Abstract, Director of Census Operations, M.P.

19. The British acquired Bastar and Kanker as territories under the suzerainty of the Maratha ruler, Bhonsale (1818). But effective control over Bastar was extended only after the final disposition of the Maratha ruler in 1854. For an account of relations between the British, Bhonsale and the subordinate chiefs,

see Sir Richard Temple, *Report on the Zamindarees and Other Petty Chieftaincies in the Central Provinces*, 1863; and Richard Jenkins, *Report on the Territories of the Raja of Nagpore (1827)*, Government Press, Nagpur, 1923. For a comprehensive account of Bastar and its people, see Grigson, *Maria Gonds*.

20. *Census of India, 1981, Series-I, Paper 2 of 1984*, General Population and Population of Scheduled Castes and Scheduled Tribes, Registrar General and Census Commissioner, India, 1984, p.3, Statements 1 and 2.

 Ibid., note 13: 67.79 per cent of the Bastar inhabitants are listed as 'Scheduled Tribes' in the 1981 census. Census of India 1981, Series III Madhya Pradesh, Part-II B Primary Census Abstract, Director of Census Operations, Madhya Pradesh, Statement 8, pp. 8–9. According to Srinivas, various castes that predominate in different regions constitute the actual mediations that in practice translate the idea of what he terms 'sanskritization'—essentially an abstract idea of Brahminic purity and social conduct. See, M.N. Srinivas, *Caste in Modern India and Other Essays*, Asia Publishing House, 1952.

21. See Fernand Braudel, *The Mediterranean and the Mediterranean World in the Age of Philip II*, 2 vols., Fontana, 1978, Vol. 1, pp. 25–59 and 188–230.

22. The railway network was virtually non-existent till the recently built Vishakhapatnam link to Ballidilla to transport ore. In 1958 the ratio of surface roads was 5.2 to 100 per sq. miles of area, and no 'village roads'. U.N Dhebar, *Report of the Scheduled Areas and Scheduled Tribes Commission, 1960–61*, pp. 365ff, para 35.10, Table 71.

23. See Lt. Col. E. Clementi Smith, 'The Bastar Rebellion, 1910', *Man in India*, Vol. 27, 1947, pp. 239–53.

24. Prior to 1884, there were 'only footpaths' and a few 'narrow tracks for country carts of the solid *disc wheel types*'. Kedar Nath Thakur, *Bastar Bhushan*, Benares, 1908, p. 35.

25. Concerning *begar* and desertion of villages, see *ibid.*, pp. 39–40.

26. Smith, 'The Bastar Rebellion', p. 252.

27. Glasfurd's report had a formative influence on British policy in Bastar. See Captain C.L.R. Glasfurd, *Report on the Dependency of Bastar*, 1862, Foreign Department, General A., Pro. Feb/1863, No.151/56. The immediate cause of Captain Glasfurd's visit to Bastar was the persistent rumour of human sacrifices at the Danteshwari temple near Jugdalpur. The rumour proved baseless and was apparently instigated by the adjoining principality of Kalahandi. Bastar had a long-standing border dispute with Kalahandi.

 Captain Fenwick (1850) and Mr. Take (1855) were perhaps the first Europeans to visit Bastar. They travelled along the Kolab–Sabari river on the eastern border of Madhya Pradesh.

 Captain Elliot (1855) was the first important political officer to visit Bastar. Elliot's report is published as 'Selections from the Records of the Government of India in, Foreign Department, No. XXX, 1861'.

 Around this time, Captain Stewart, Explorer of Forests, also visited Bastar. A little later (1855-56) Lt. Goddard and Lt. Haig explored the Godavari Valley in pursuit of the abortive plan to 'open-up' Bastar by making Godavari river navigable.

28. Blunt's account of the hill country between Kaimur and the Godavari furnished the almost only available information to the colonial rulers till the mid-nineteenth century. See J.T. Blunt, 'Narrative of A Route From Chunarghur

to Yertnagoodum, In the Ellore Sircar', in Wills, *Early European Travellers*, pp. 91–174.

29. Motte's account of his journey (1766) to the Sambhalpur diamond mines in Orissa 'undertaken' at the direction of Lord Clive, Governor of Bengal, is a suggestive comment on the perceptions in the hinterlands concerning 'British Dominion' in India, and the Old Imperial idea symbolised by the Mughals. Motte's experience in this respect has the quality of an elaborately devised gesture. Hill chiefs through whose territories he had to pass handled Lord Clive's letter with 'indifference', that of the Maratha Subedar with 'contempt and hostility'; but that of the Mughal Emperor, by then a helpless exile under virtual British control, with 'exaggerated demonstration of respect and deference'.

Motte, it need hardly be emphasised, as a friend and confidant of Lord Clive had no reason to colour things in favour of the Mughal Emperor. The circumstance which necessitated the journey is itself a succinct comment on the character of the early British imperial enterprise in India.

Raja of Sambhalpur, unable to pay for the horses he had purchased, despatched his 'trusted servant' Surdar Khan with a diamond 'weighing carats sixteen and a half' to Calcutta. Surdar Khan was to sell the diamond and pay off the merchants who accompanied him the amount due on account of the horses purchased by the Raja. But once in Calcutta, in Motte's words;

> Mohunpersaud, a fellow of an infamous character, employed himself at this time in picking acquaintance with such strangers as came to that capital, making himself master of their business . . . . Surdar Khan fell into his hands, who introduced him to Lord Clive, the Governor, persuading him to deliver the diamond as a present from the rajah. The Patan merchants finding they were likely to be deprived of their chance of payment, assembled about his lordship's house, and made a clamour. Lord Clive knew not the cause of the complaint, while Surdar Khan and Mohunpersaud joined to persuade the poor merchants . . . .
>
> His Lordship then being at great loss for Means of remitting money to England, proposed to me to return with the Vakeel to the mines, and to endeavour to open the diamond trade. He offered to make it a joint concern. The proposal dazzled me . . . . (p. 1).

See, T. Motte, 'A Narrative', pp. 1–49.

30. Glasfurd, *Report*, para 31.
31. *Ibid.*, para 175.
32. *Loc. cit.*
33. *Loc. cit.*
34. *Ibid.*, paras 31–39.
35. *Ibid.*, para 172.
36. *Ibid.*, para 175.
37. *Loc. cit.*
38. Grigson, *Maria Gonds*, p. 13.
39. *Ibid.*, pp. 3–4.
40. *Loc. cit.* Glasfurd, *Report*, para 156.
41. Grigson, *Maria Gonds*, p. 4ff.

42. Glasfurd, *Report*, para 142.
43. As one moves away from the roads and railway line, houses reacquire their authentic integrity both in terms of materials used and aesthetic forms. As one moves closer to the modern communication grid, the first noticeable deterioration is in the materials used: left-over waste materials from modern industrial activity. And that is indicative of enclosements effected in Man–Nature equations.
44. As an example of the same vital impulse and its incredible dispersion at another level, consider the following note by Sir Monier Williams:

 . . . I met to my surprise with learned natives—not only in the cities and towns, but even in remote villages—able and willing to converse with me in Sanskrit, as well as in their own vernaculars, and to explain difficult points in their languages, literatures, religions and philosophies.

 Monier Williams, *Sanskrit–English Dictionary* (1891), Munshiram Manoharlal, 1976, p. VII.
45. Based on conversations with Shri Jayadev Baghel. For the origins and livelihood of Ghasias, see R.V. Russel and Hira Lal, *Tribes and Castes of Central India* (1916), Cosmo Publications, 1975, Vol. 3, pp. 27–31.
46. Baghel's narration evoked a sense of deep awe and submission as also an irresistible longing to touch and recast. See in this context the suggestive essay on contemporary tribal perception of the significance and power of writing by the painter J. Swaminathan, *The Magical Script*, Roopankar, Bharat Bhavan, Bhopal, 1983.

 For specimens of Garhwa craft and an excellent introduction to the present state of tribal arts and crafts, both as fact and possibility, see J. Swaminathan, *The Perceiving Fingers*, Bharat Bhavan, Bhopal, 1987. Also see, *Census of India, 1961* Vol. XII-Part VII-A, Superintendent of Census Operations, Orissa, pp. 65–132.

 For an account and record of tribal art and craft fifty years ago, see V. Elwin, *The Tribal Art of Middle India*, Oxford University Press, 1949.
47. Iron is used almost exclusively for certain implements: axe, arrow-heads, knives, etc. It is almost never used for what in modern demarcation would be termed aesthetic or ornamental purposes. See the excellent study of Verrier Elwin, *The Agaria*, Oxford University Press, 1941. On the matter-of-factness of Agaria craft and life, consider Elwin's observation '. . . work among them was difficult and sometimes depressing. They were not deliberately uninformative, but most of them had very little to say' (p. 14.).
48. Agaria proverb, cited, *ibid.*, p. 14.
49. Ibid., pp. 86–129.
50. *Ibid.*, p. XXI.
51. *Ibid.*, p. 33.
52. *Ibid.*, p. 2.
53. *Loc. cit.*
54. *Loc. cit.*
55. *Report of the Geological Survey of India*, Vol. 46, p. 99.
56. *Report of the Geological Survey of India*, Vol. 50, p. 284.
57. Elwin, *Agaria*, p. 10.
58. *Report of the Geological Survey of India*, Vol. 20, Pt. IV, p. 170.
59. Elwin, *Agaria*, p. 41.

60. *Loc. cit.*

61. *Ibid.*, p. 29.

62. *Ibid.*, p. 56.

63. *Report of the Geological Survey of India*, Vol. 46, p. 99.

64. Elwin, *Agaria*, p. 46.

65. *Ibid.*, p. 47.

66. See Bridget Allchin and Raymond Allchin, *The Rise of Civilization in India and Pakistan*, Select Book Service Syndicate, 1983, pp. 97ff.

67. D.L. Drake-Brockman, *Mirzapur Gazetteer*, 1911, p. 24.

68. Elwin, *Agaria*, p. XXV.

69. *Report of the Geological Survey of India*, Vol. 50, p. 284.

70. Elwin, *Agaria*, p. XXV.

71. R.S. Hole, 'The Iron Industry in the Central Provinces', (unpublished report), *Agricultural Ledger*, Vol. 5, No. 17, pp. 1–27, and Vol. 7, No. 14, pp. 146–60.

72. Cited in Elwin, *Agaria*, p. 15.

73. See Bipan Chandra, *The Rise and Growth of Economic Nationalism in India*, People's Publishing House, 1966.

74. Gandhi was acutely vigilant and sensitive to the modern fate of traditional crafts, and that makes his silence on the smothering of the Agaria tradition all the more glaring.

75. Elwin, *Agaria*, p. 32.

76. Hole, 'The Iron Industry'; Elwin, *Agaria*, p. XXVIII.

77. S.C. Roy, *The Asurs—Ancient and Modern*, *Journal of Bihar and Orissa Research Society*, Vol. XII, 1926. Also see K.K. Leuva, *The Asur—A study of Primitive Iron Smelters*, Bharatiya Adimjati Sevak Sangh, New Delhi, 1963. Also see, *Census of India, 1961*, Vol. XII-Part VII-A Superintendent of Census Operations, Orissa, pp. 1–64.

78. W.V. Grigson, 'The Aboriginal Problem in the C.P. & Berar', Nagpur, 1944.

79. H.C.E. Ward, *Report on the Land Revenue Settlement of the Mundlah District*, Bombay, 1870, p. 131.

80. Forsyth, *Central India*, p. 156.

81. Cited in V. Elwin, 'Notes On the Juang', *Man In India*, Vol. 28, Nos. 1 and 2, 1948, pp. 8–10.

82. E.T. Dalton, *Descriptive Ethnology of Bengal*, Calcutta, 1872, pp. 153ff.

83. Dalton, *Bengal*, p. 155.

84. E.T. Dalton, *The Kols of Chota Nagpur*, 1872, p. 41.

85. Record of my conversations with Bhattji, a tribal Gunia of Patiyapali village in Janjgir *tehsil* of Bilaspur district (M.P.), January 1982.

5. THE WORLD OF SHIFTING CULTIVATION

ABUJHAMAD: PENDA AS LIVING TRADITION

On my first visit to Bastar (January 1981) I came upon a little clay furnace on the way to Chote Dongar from Narayanpur, by the side of a forest track just being paved into a road. I knew a little about the Agaria craft. What struck me was the unusualness of the bellows. Firmly pegged into the ground they were being worked by feet. The little clay furnace fired by a neat smouldering heap of charcoal just as it was witnessed and recorded in Verrier Elwin's *Agaria* of forty years ago.[1]

The Agaria working the furnace was not very keen to talk. He said, he knew not why he still worked his clay furnace. Perhaps from old habit! Could it be just the involuntary play of instincts too deeply etched to be set aside? Or, was it the last re-enactment of an ancient memory about to be completely effaced?

The days of his craft, the Agaria whispered, were over. In words hauntingly reminiscent of the Gunia in Patiyapali, he said: 'Before the might of the Government who can dare stand. It can uproot and cast to the winds anyone and everyone. My craft is finished. How do I say where I come from? From no-where. And I go . . . .' He would speak no more. Abruptly he turned away from me to quicken the fire in his furnace. Then walked to the edge of the clearing and stood there a long while watching the trees on the Abujhamad hills sway on that windy cold afternoon. I desperately wanted to believe that what I had witnessed was not the last flicker of the Agaria furnace.[2]

The Abujhamad hills in Bastar represent an unusual survival that still retains the suggestive power to indicate some of the essential ingredients of the pre-modern rhythms of living that once prevailed in the Vindhyan highlands. What survives in Abujhamad is but a shrivelled fragment of what prior to the modern onslaught was the definitive substance of life and relationships. Its exceptional significance inheres not so much in the fragments of vanishing skills and artefacts, but in that as a living tradition it directs attention towards the quality and salience of the larger texture of which it was once a part.

Life in the Abujhamad hills, home of the Hill Madias, still tends to cling to a long superseded order of things. It is one of the few areas (about 600 sq. km.) in the country which has not been surveyed by either the Forest Department or the Department of Land Revenue. For the last sixty years the Hill Madia population has remained stable at around 13,000.[3] Direct intrusions from the modern world until barely thirty years ago could be counted, as it were, on one's fingertips. Hence the suggestive power of relatively untouched rhythms of life in these hills, as also the exceptional character of the cognitive distance between Madia sensibility and the modern world.

The widest clearing into Abujhamad is a gravelled forest road that runs from Narayanpur—a large village growing into a small town—for nearly 100 km. of hills and rapid streams up to the Nibra river. On the other side of the river is a *pucca* all-weather road and 'Colony Number 93', a refugee settlement under the Dandakaranya project.[4] The forest road is an old one, having been in existence for about seventy years.[5] But for four months in a year the innumerable hill streams on the way make vehicular traffic impossible. Around November–December every year, the Forest Department rigs up pretty little bamboo platforms of hefty timber across these streams. And each year, after the first monsoon showers (end June) they are swept away. Distance reacquires something of its old forbidding quality.

I am reminded of my fleeting acquaintance with distance as it would have been in times past. It was the month of October. Monsoon rains were just tapering off. The ground was still wet and the water in the numerous streams we forded cold and fiercely swift. Beyond the large Halba village of Sonpur the road seemed to dissolve into the forest. In large stretches it was entirely an expanse of dense vegetation and elephant grass, at places more than six feet high.

It was late in the evening. Just about another half-an-hour of daylight and a distance of eight kilometres to the village of Garpa. We thought of staying the night in Horadi, a pretty little clearing fairly close to the road. We knew it could not be more than a kilometre or so from where we were. Yet, we walked past Horadi, its nearest house a few steps from the road, without noticing the village. After fifty-five kilometers and ten hours of walking through the forest, wet and numb with fatigue, as we stepped across the little stream before Garpa, the darkness around us seemed suddenly less intense. We knew we were close to what could only be the work of Man: a clearing in the midst of a forest aggressively dense and lush after the monsoon.

Garpa is a neat looking cluster of houses spread out on an elevated plateau tapering eastward. Towards the west it is almost walled off by the still formidable Pangur Ghati. All around rise tall verdant hills teeming with wild animals—bears, wild boars and tigers—some of them not always friendly to Man. Dadangir Nala in the east flows close to the village and is the main source for drinking water. Natural drainage is excellent; and the village free of pools of stagnant water and dirty flies. For Abujhamad, Garpa is a large village. It comprises ten families.[6]

In the characteristic Madia fashion, houses are made of bare bamboo walls with a thatched roof and enclosed by sturdy bamboo fencing. In recent years, these enclosures have expanded into *baris*: the first beginnings towards regular tillage and settled cultivation. There are yet other signs of change in the offing. Garpa has a primary school. Until two years ago the school building was the only *pucca* tiled-concrete structure in the village. But in no time tiles came loose, the roof leaked, and the cement flooring, unable to withstand the daily tread of children's bare feet, was full of holes. The simple and much older thatch structure next door seemed far more functional and inviting.[7] It was being used as living quarters by the four teachers working in the school.[8]

Garpa also has a water hand pump. On my first visit it had been out of order for more than a year.[9] Six of the ten families in the village had bicycles. Young Juroo had just set up a little 'shop' in the village with the help of a government loan (1985). Three families owned bullock carts, also purchased with the help of government loans. But they are rarely used.[10] Doonga Sarpanch had travelled all the way to Raipur to buy himself a gun to 'scare off wild animals' from the *penda* during harvest time.[11]

Perhaps the most exciting modern acquisition in Garpa is the transistor.[12] A transistor in the hands of a Madia living in a little clearing in the midst of a forest acquires quite a magical presence. The *lohar* (blacksmith)[13] of Garpa had just returned from the *nagur* (town, in this case Narayanpur) with a brand new transistor set. All through the long winter night, the young man kept awake fondling and playing with that magic box. Enthralled to watch it come alive with strange voices, he swivelled the needle of the transistor set now to Peking, then to Moscow, and back again to the Voice of America.

In our little hut close by, we stayed awake through most of the night trying to figure out if the grunts of wild boars trying to crash through the *bari* fencing next door were still at a safe distance. I was struck by the anomalous inversion of distances which the voices from the transistor set, loud and very quaint in the moonless forest at midnight, seemed to represent. A slight flick of the hand, and voices thousands of miles apart could be summoned with the speed of lightning into this so remote and difficult to reach clearing in the forest. And I thought, how impossible the little distance which separated our hut from the *lohar's* house next door had become because of the grunts of wild boars. The young *lohar* of course noticed nothing of their grunts and struggle.

Garpa is just beginning to be more than a mere clearing in the forest. The presence of the forest is still visible in the minutest details of living and livelihood. For survival and sustenance the Madias continue to depend on hunting, food gathering, and the virtually unrestricted availability of hill slopes for slash and burn cultivation known as *penda*. Every year, in March–April, all the eight families set out to axe a fresh hill slope for their *penda*. Four to six weeks later when the timber is dry, it is burnt. Kosra seed, the staple crop of the *penda*, is dibbled on a thick spread of ash. That accomplished, Madias let the rains take over. Rains wash away a lot of seed. But, always, enough survives to give a reasonable harvest after five-six months.[14] Kosra is a hardy crop. Without much help from Man, it survives the aggressive profusion of other plants and vegetation on the *penda* after the rains. Harvests, even in years of bad monsoon, never fail completely. Last year (1984), the rains over Abujhamad were poor. The administration notified Abujhamad to be a drought-affected area. Still, the Madias managed a reasonable kosra harvest from their *pendas*. There was no mass hunger. No one died because of malnutrition. Abujhamad is one of the very few areas in the country entirely unblemished by destitutes condemned to beg and linger between life and death.[15]

Shifting cultivation has been condemned as inefficient, inherently wasteful and a threat to the rapidly diminishing area under forest cover. This condemnation represents an almost unanimous consensus. Colonial land revenue settlements and forest laws were consciously intended to curb and in swift stages eradicate shifting cultivation.[16] Forsyth thought shifting cultivation could not be seriously considered as a form of cultivation at all.[17] The Forest Regulations (1867) sought to completely prohibit the practice of shifting cultivation in the Central Provinces.[18] Its unhindered prevalence prior to colonial rule was seen as clear proof of the ignorance and indifference of 'native rulers' to forests as a productive resource. Baden Powell, one of the pioneers of colonial policy concerning forests and primordial social cohesions regarded as characteristic of the Indian situation, clarified that the freedom to 'slash and burn' at will could no longer be allowed. He conceded that the task was indeed a difficult one, and certain to arouse the resentment of adversely affected 'local interests'. But the imperative need was to uphold the interests of the entire 'public' realm, of which 'local interests' could hardly have any understanding.[19]

In the 1930s Verrier Elwin was fiercely attacked by A.V. Thakkar, a staunch nationalist passionately devoted to the cause of the tribals as he understood it, for defending shifting cultivation as a 'religious necessity' for the survival of Baiga tribals.[20]

The stern consensus against shifting cultivation remained basically unaffected by the end of colonial rule (1947). The only time when the National Commission on Agriculture (1976) took note of shifting cultivation was during its appraisal of the state and management of forests. Quite clearly the commission did not think that shifting cultivation could merit consideration as a particular form of cultivation and land use. In fact it was only noticed as a wasteful practice that depleted timber and other marketable forest resources. Hence the commission's plea that shifting cultivation be rigorously 'regulated' and rapidly 'replaced' by 'permanently settling shifting cultivators'.[21]

B.D. Sharma's recommendations which were based on close familiarity and extensive knowledge as a District Administrator in Bastar, were less drastic and distinctly more imaginative. Their characteristic significance, however, is in that they clarify the limits beyond which valid comprehension within the modern framework and the most genuine kind of anthropological sympathy become irreconcilable. B.D. Sharma is emphatic that for the inhabitants of Abujhamad shifting cultivation has been a 'traditional pursuit' and as such, it would be unfair and unrealistic to insist that they abandon it in a short period. The best course would be to 'slowly induce the community to meet its field requirements from settled cultivation and other needs from horticulture and cattle rearing'.[22]

Shifting cultivation is indeed inefficient and wasteful in the sense that crop yields per acre are considerably lower when compared to settled cultivation.[23] For basic sustenance it requires a larger area per person. But a threat to the forest it has never been. That momentous fact is irrefutably affirmed in a simple historical detail perversely disregarded: forests have survived best in regions of shifting cultivation.[24]

The modern sentiment against shifting cultivation bristles with righteous anger. It has come to signify the assertion of an inert human imagination forever bound to the immediate space and duration of survival. Hence its ineradicable tendency to posit local needs and absolutely localised interests as the only measure of worth and validation. Modern cognition concedes that such a sense of oneself and the human condition as a foreclosed fact and possibility perhaps did harness a useful salience so long as the long-term fluctuations of climate were the only connecting link between little communities dispersed all over the earth.[25] But in an age wherein distance and space has been transmuted into a more or less uninterrupted continuum of intricately connected human activity, the assertion of such a sense could only be at the expense of eroding and belittling the prospects of progress and well-being of the entire human species. The perception of shifting cultivation as inherently unacceptable has been conditioned by sweeping changes entirely beyond the world of shifting cultivation. To clarify the true meaning and implications of shifting cultivation, both as it has actually been and also as it could be, the structure of modern attention in relation to shifting cultivation merits consideration in some detail.

Shifting Cultivation and the Texture of Modern Attention

During the past 150 years or so, the recurrent mode of formulation concerning shifting cultivation has been some variant of the following: 'The problem of . . .; Forest Management and . . .; Increasing the Productivity of . . .; Carrying Capacity of Land and . . ., etc.[26] The cardinal presuppositions implicit in such formulations, however ostensibly varied their form, refer to a cognitive locus that is grounded in the world of settled agriculture (*kheti*) as it has been modified by modern technology. This brings to the fore a definitive question. What is the nature of the cognitive closure that inheres in formulations grounded in this locus?

First, an essential clarification concerning the serious and genuine rejection from within this cognitive locus of the stern fate prescribed for shifting cultivation. Grigson and Mills were among the first to recognise that some tribal communities could not be easily persuaded to abandon the practice of slash and burn cultivation. Mills also observed that in the north-east the prevalence of slash and burn cultivation had not caused soil erosion or any visible damage to forest cover.[27] Elwin's classic study of the Baigas was an impassioned plea for a sympathetic and tolerant consideration of the practice of shifting cultivation.[28]

Field studies in recent years have methodically exposed some of the flagrant misconceptions about shifting cultivation. Roy Burman, in a severe indictment of the pronouncements of the National Commission on Agriculture and Forest Policy as it affects tribal communities, has questioned the wisdom and justice of the prevalent sentiment against shifting cultivation.[29] Anthropological studies in recent years have come to be accented quite firmly in terms of 'sympathetic consideration' and 'harmonising', as far as possible, of the interests and feelings of tribal communities with the requirements of the modern age.

Such anthropological interventions have been of considerable significance in inducing a certain fluidity and have thereby somewhat softened the sense of righteous certainty against shifting cultivation. Hence the search, on the basis of steadily extended levels of information, for more sympathetic and imaginative ways to slowly 'wean away' tribals from shifting cultivation. The kind of closure that inheres in this cognitive terrain comes sharply to the fore in some of the more sympathetically informed anthropological interventions. Two instances would suffice to indicate the salience and implications of this closure.

The UNESCO sponsored study, *Swidden Cultivation in Asia*,[30] is very sympathetic to the needs and interests of communities engaged in shifting cultivation. It is extremely valuable in that it extends and deepens the range of reference. Yet, it lists the following in its 'research agenda': 'Testing Generalisations and Conducting Further Studies':

1. 'Burnt swidden destroys fertility, and brings about other harmful changes in the soil which inhibit higher productivity and promote higher weed growth.'
2. 'As swidden cultivation is labour intensive and family labour is the most important factor of production, there is a premium on large family size and hence swidden cultivation is deterrent to family planning.'[31]

Both these propositions are characteristic of a certain mode of formulation. Rising production per acre constitutes the decisive referent of worth and usefulness. And if that is not the case, it is assumed that soil fertility has been adversely affected. Absurd logic, if it can be called logic at all. Stable yields, one of the characteristic features of shifting cultivation, could be termed 'static'. The word static does convey absence of movement, and in modern cognition that signifies stagnation. But by no stretch of imagination could the word static or stagnant denote in this context a decline in soil fertility.

Perhaps what is most absurd and revealing in this formulation is the connection it posits between 'higher weed growth' and shifting cultivation. It shows utter incomprehension of the nature and basic facts of shifting cultivation. If it were so, shifting cultivation, which does not recognise the notion of weeds, would have quite simply disappeared within a few generations of its commencement. The second proposition is no less absurd. Dispersed and sparse demography has been universally remarked upon as a characteristic feature of shifting cultivation. It is not as if the authors of the 'research agenda' cited are unaware of this large fact. Indeed, their study amplifies, and on a richly varied continental scale, the implications of this fact.[32] Both these propositions exemplify the distance between perception and what one may see and record in great detail. The definitive concern in the propositions cited is to remain within what is accepted as the legitimate mode of formulation. Hence the representation of certain facts not as they happen to be, but as they should be.

Non-recognition of certain large facts associated with shifting cultivation could perhaps be posited as a serious issue from well within a cognitive locus grounded in the world of settled cultivation. True, that would not be easy and straightforward. The task would be more complicated, if one were to seek out the implications of such non-recognition. Still, it remains within the realm of what could be conceived as possible, from a vantage ground in the world of settled cultivation as it has been recast by the modern dynamic. What is entirely foreclosed, however, is any serious consideration of shifting cultivation as a possibility.

Shifting Cultivation as Possibility

To consider shifting cultivation as 'possibility' is not necessarily to confirm the large and seemingly definitive details associated with it. Instead, such consideration has to seek out terms and the sense of significance that approximate to a cognitive locus grounded in the world of shifting cultivation. Consideration of facts as inherence of certain kind of possibilities has necessarily to touch upon the world of inner sensibility and its translations in the complex of mediations and techniques. Translation ineluctably engenders a certain distance between the world of inner sensibility and the web of techniques, artefacts and relationships which express and sustain that sensibility. Therefore, it could well be that to affirm the sense of deep significance that inheres in shifting cultivation as possibility could mean negation of various details associated with it.

The basic complication in terms of modern cognition arises because of the imperative need to find placement for shifting cultivation as a contingent phase in the historical process.[33] To clarify its definitive implications, consider the following as contingent phases in the historical process, demarcated in terms of the Man–Nature equations they posit.

The ineradicable requirement of survival, be it animals or the human species, is food. Certain animals, like rats, otters, squirrels, do possess, somewhat like the human species, the skills to methodically collect and store their food requirements. Unlike humans, all of them acquire and use what could be termed harvesting skills within the more or less inflexible confines of a particular ecological niche. Like humans, they possess the capacity of locomotion and purposive movement. But locomotion and movement in their case is rigorously specialised and, therefore, effective only within a certain favourable niche. Their anatomical–physiological make-up, and the particular terrain in which they function as effective harvesters denote an analogous relationship.

Humans as harvesters display a very different kind of capacity. Their capacity for movement, due in no small measure to their non-specialised anatomy and physiological–mental make-up, belongs to a qualitatively different order. More crucial, humans as harvesters tend not just to select what they would eat but also, in however rudimentary a way, cultivate their preferred foods.

Consider in this context two analogous modes of human subsistence: 'transhumance' and 'pastoralism'.[34] Both survived well into historical times and share certain features in common. Clearly the most remarkable feature in the modern context is that both these modes of subsistence are linked to a capacity for regular and fairly rapid purposive movement across vast spaces. Viability of subsistence and the capacity of purposive movement are inseparably linked. Certain animals are selected as a resource for food and an enhanced capacity for movement. The animals—horses, cattle and sheep in the case of the pastoral mode, and reindeer in the case of transhumance—subsist on vegetation that grows on its own, untended in Nature. In both these modes, Nature supplies the food upon which animals chosen as useful by Man subsist. Man does not seek to select and cultivate the vegetation necessary for the survival of these animals. In this sense they could both be essentially termed extensions of harvesting modes of subsistence.[35]

In clear contrast to animal harvesters, in both these modes, humans seek to methodically consolidate their position at the apex of the food chain in Nature. This attempt is perhaps linked in deep and subtle ways to the human awareness of the unalterable eventuality of death. Man has perhaps always known that after death the human body must return to the food chain in Nature. Hence the awesome and profoundly disturbing self-sense of the human achievement: formidable and intrinsically beyond challenge and yet, its duration so gravely uncertain. It signifies an awareness, perhaps unique to Man, of a certain ineradicable tension between the human presence and Nature.[36]

At a more matter-of-fact level, both pastoralism and transhumance are inconceivable in the complete absence of the awareness and skills of cultivation. But the principle of cultivation is pursued very differently. In that difference is marked out the line of sharp divergence between these two modes. Communities that subsist on transhumance domesticate and breed reindeers. But the essential intent of this activity of selection and breeding (cultivation) is to harness animal power to be able to keep pace with the movement of reindeer herds moving at their natural pace. Man does not attempt to determine either the pace or the direction of movement. Reindeers lead, and Man simply follows the herd.

In the pastoral mode, the principle of cultivation (selection, domestication and breeding) is pursued at a strikingly different level. Animals are chosen and bred as providers of food, and as power for rapid movement. Animals so selected may move in herds across vast open spaces. But the direction and pace of their movement is determined by Man. In that specific sense they are fully domesticated. Pastoral herds, unlike the wild herds of the transhumance mode, are led and governed by Man. Animal power is harnessed not for the purpose of keeping pace with the herds of animals selected as providers of food, but to fully control the movement and habits of these animals.[37]

Certain aspects of the close likeness as also the sharp divergence between transhumance and pastoralism merit reiteration. Both could be characterised as essentially harvesting modes of subsistence. Domestication of plants is not essential to their viability. The principle of cultivation is applied primarily to control, albeit on different scales and levels, animals selected as providers of food, and power for faster movement. The sharp divergence arises from the different kinds of control sought over the lives of animal herds. In transhumance the principle of cultivation is used not to control the lives of reindeer herds but to be able to keep pace with their natural cycle of movement. As such it is a mode of subsistence which causes the least disturbance in Nature. In pastoralism the principle of cultivation is used to firmly control the lives of certain animals, and to secure for Man the capacity for movement at a pace which animals in a state of Nature cannot match. That inevitably caused abrupt and serious disturbances in the natural rhythm of vegetation and animals, as also in the lives of other human communities.[38]

Transhumance and pastoralism have been noticed in the world of settled cultivation for different reasons. This difference is instructive of the way attention is structured in the world of settled cultivation. Transhumance is seen to denote existential details of human life as it would have been over large parts of the world in the very early phase of Man's struggle to make Nature yield the bare minimum necessary for human survival. It evokes a certain anthropological resonance.[39] The smallness of its presence in historical times makes the task of placing transhumance as a stage in the historical process fairly straightforward.

Nomadic pastoralism represents another kind of reality. In periodic bursts of expansive energy, warriors from the pastoral hinterlands of Central Asia have threatened the more orderly and prosperous life of settled agrarian societies in both Europe and Asia.[40] Yet, it has been a mode that tends to cling to and feed upon settled agrarian societies in the manner of a parasite. Lattimore's classic study of the difficult and frequently violent relationship between the hinterland of nomadic pastoralism and settled agrarian societies outlines in intricate detail the recurring paradox in this relationship.[41] The capacity of pastoral nomads to accumulate surplus and nurture the crafts and skills of civilisation is severely confined. Political authority is inherently unstable and fragmented. But pastoralism has known the use of iron and horse to harness decisive armed power. Hence the paradox of repeated nomadic conquests of settled agrarian societies, and always in the end the triumph of settled agriculture over nomadic pastoralism.

Shifting cultivation signifies a profoundly subtle inversion of the theme basic to transhumance: human presence so modulated as to cause the least disturbance in Nature. Somewhat like transhumance and pastoralism, shifting cultivation is inseparable from a cycle of regular movement. But the duration of this cycle is differently constituted. Unlike the cycle of movement in transhumance and pastoralism, movement in shifting cultivation is from year to year. Sites of cultivation and dwelling remain stable and fixed for at least a year. Some animals—mostly pigs, chickens and dogs—are domesticated. But domesticated animals play no role whatsoever in sustaining shifting cultivation, either as providers of manure or as draught animals.[42] Shifting cultivation is marked by the complete absence of the use of animal power to quicken the pace of human movement. The principle of cultivation is applied primarily to plants. And as in transhumance, plants selected for their value as food are left to subsist untended in the midst of Nature.[43]

Perception of shifting cultivation in the modern world has been influenced by two connected historical details. One, in Europe nothing like shifting cultivation seems to have ever been practiced. The European term 'swidden', often used to denote shifting cultivation, refers to quite another kind of activity. The word swidden (dialectically, swizzen) is related to the Old Norse practice of setting large tracts of virgin forests on fire to clear land for tillage and regular cultivation.[44] In sharp contrast, shifting cultivators set fire to small forest patches and in an effectively controlled way.[45] Two, shifting cultivation came to be noticed as a practice confined to the remote hinterland of lands conquered and colonised by Europe. Areas of shifting cultivation were thus seen to signify an existential situation frozen, as it were, at the bottom end of the historical scale. The sheer inaccessibility of these areas, and the fact that shifting cultivators had never intruded into the world of settled cultivation, came to be the basis for the belief that it represents a form of subsistence that had existed in more or less complete isolation. The modern perception of shifting cultivation has been that of an impediment which blocks and complicates the effective use of forest and other natural resources in the hinterland.[46]

To comprehend the distinctive salience of shifting cultivation and the implications of the Man–Nature dialectic it sustains, it is necessary to indicate the nature of the modern impingement in the remote hinterlands of the colonial periphery. Regions harnessed to the grid of modern production as its periphery are perceived primarily as a resource for certain raw materials. This sense is immensely intensified in relation to the hinterland regions of shifting cultivation. The human presence is seen to be so weak as to be devoid of the capacity to bend Nature to the needs of Man. In fact, the only thing that is of use and benefit to the modern world is the virtually untouched wealth of Nature: most notably timber and mineral deposits.[47] Efficient mass production of goods and services in the modern world has made itself felt in these regions in the development of specialised sectors or enclaves to the relentless ruin of all other forms of natural and human life.[48]

These specialised sectors—notably timber felling and mining—imbued as they have been with an irresistible vigour, represent in fact only the sharp brute edge of a more general process. It is a process which at its most unrestrained has aptly been characterised as the 'casting of Neo-Europe'.[49] Conquest of things has been the definitive impulse in the modern quest. Wherever this impulse could come fully into its own, the landscape and all that the inhabitants of these regions had known as the essential wherewithal of survival, was fragmented and recast according to requirements that had nothing to do with the past of these lands.[50] The modern onslaught has been of a kind unknown and unthinkable in all the human past so full of brutal inflictions. Its colossal sweep and grim force is powerfully encapsulated in a Maori proverb cited by the geologist Julius Von Haast (1858):

> As the white man's rat has driven away the native rat so the European fly drives away our own, and the clover kills our fern, so will the Maoris disappear before the white man himself.[51]

Nature itself seemed to sharpen the ferocity of this intrusion. Joseph Dalton Hooker (1853) characterised it as the 'double anomaly' of Australia providing a more congenial environment for certain 'English plants than England', and of certain English plants 'better suited' to Australia than those native plants which have 'given way before English intruders'.[52] Darwin was convinced that even though the 'most skilful naturalist' could not have 'foreseen' so amazing an outcome, it clearly signified that the natural products of Great Britain 'stand much higher in the scale' of evolution.[53]

Recasting of Nature is a phenomenon characteristic of the modern age since its inception. The unrestrained raw brutality that inheres in this most potent impulse of the modern age is at its most stark precisely in regions where communities attuned to the older Man–Nature equations were decimated or reduced to utter insignificance. Not even the colossal magnitude of the landscape in America could quite contain and modulate its disruptive consequences.

In the words of that foremost witness of our times, Levi-Strauss, 'In the inhabited regions of America there are only two alternatives: either nature has been so ruthlessly mastered that it has been turned into an open air factory', as in most of North America; or the 'territory has been sufficiently inhabited by man for him to have time to lay it waste but not long enough for slow and continuous cohabitation to have raised it to the dignity of a landscape', as in most of South America. Nature here is 'devoid of any real freshness' and exists as 'degraded rather than wild'. Regions 'as large as provinces' after a brief span of intense activity were abandoned a 'battered landscape'.[54] During the mid-nineteenth century the 'mineiros' having 'abandoned their exhausted mines' lit the 'agricultural blaze' in the state of Sao Paulo in Brazil. Vast virgin tracts were cleared for cultivation, but after a few years, 'the land became exhausted and was washed away by the ruins from round the coffee shrubs. The plantations were then moved farther afield, where the ground was still virgin and fertile. That careful and reciprocal relationship between Man and the earth which, in the Old World, established the age-old bond where one fashioned the other has never existed here, where the ground has been violated and destroyed'.[55]

As a counterpoint, consider another kind of instance: 'several thousand Coahuila Indians never exhausted the natural resources of a desert region in South California, in which today only a handful of white families manage to subsist. They lived in a land of plenty. . . .'[56]

Shifting Cultivation as Universal Impulse

Shifting cultivation denotes the working out of an impulse which could be said to be akin to the mode of livelihood alluded to by Levi-Strauss in the case of Coahuila Indians. Such closeness in the sensibility of human communities so far apart and quite definitely unaware of each other affirms universality in a sense that is as far removed from the modern conception of universality as two human conceptions can be. It is in this sense that Coomaraswamy invokes universality in a paper of formidable scholarly density. The anthropologist's preoccupation, argues Coomaraswamy, with 'peculiarities of primitive people' entirely neglects the possibility that 'local origins' may denote variations and fragments of the deep self-sense common to 'primitive peoples' and 'sophisticated communities'.[57] Universality in this sense does not entail the logic of limitless extension and progressive incorporation of the other.

Variations Within the Framework of
Shifting Cultivation

Shifting cultivation is known by different names in different parts of India. The most widely prevalent name (from the north-east to Bihar) is *jhum*. In parts of Nagaland it is called *tekonglu*. Across the border, in Burma it is called *toungia*. Among the Rang in Tripura it is known as *hooknismang*. Close to Bastar, it is identified as *podu*, *gudia* or *dongrachas* among the Khonds and Koyas of Orissa. Saoras call it *bagada*. Among some of the Khonds of Orissa it is known as *rama*. The Khutia Khonds know it by yet another name, *barenga*. Hill Bhuiyans of northern Orissa speak of shifting cultivation as *komanchas*. Baigas of Madhya Pradesh, one of the last communities to stubbornly cling to that immemorial way of life, call it *bewar*. Korkus of the Melaghat forest know it as *dahiya*. Shifting cultivators in the far south (Tamil Nadu and Karnataka) refer to it as *kumari*. This term is also prevalent in parts of Maharashtra. Among the Soloza of Karnataka it is referred to as *podu*, a term in fairly extensive use among tribal communities in Orissa and Andhra Pradesh. In the hill areas of Rajasthan in the west, it is known as *daikast*. Madias of Abujhamad in Bastar, one of few communities to continue the practice of shifting cultivation in its immemorial form, refer to it as *penda*.[58]

The prevalence of different names for the practice of shifting cultivation denotes the range of variations in the details of its practice among different communities. Names for shifting cultivation may differ among communities living in close proximity. For instance, some Khonds refer to it as *rama*, while another kindred branch of Khutia Khonds refer to it as *barenga*. And the same term, for instance the word *podu*, may be in use as far apart as Orissa and Karnataka.

Variations in the details of shifting cultivation could be characterised as of two kinds. One, variations that essentially relate to the use or absence of certain tools and techniques (digging sticks, hoe, dibbling seed or implanting seeds in little dug-up holes) in areas not markedly affected by techniques and consideration definitive to *kheti* or settled agriculture (mainly weeding, ploughing and monoculture).[59] Two, variations that are primarily the consequence of influences from the world of *kheti*. Such variations are generally related to the nature of the terrain. In the hilly tracts variations of detail are likely to be of the first kind. The second kind are mostly found in forest tracts comprising low hills or well-wooded level plains.

Variations of the second kind denote a fluid mediation between techniques used in settled and shifting cultivation. *Dahi* or *dahiya*, practiced until recently in large parts of Orissa and Madhya Pradesh, refers precisely to such a variation. A *dahiya* patch is prepared for shifting cultivation by spreading and burning brushwood and branches of trees cut from nearby forests. As on a *penda*, ash from burnt vegetation is used to manure crops. Unlike *penda* cultivation, *dahiya* is practiced invariably on more or less level ground. Sowing techniques could be exactly as they are on *penda* slopes (dibbling or otherwise broadcasting seed in a bed of burnt ash), or they could be somewhat like techniques used in *kheti* (digging, ploughing, generally overturning the soil). Seeds sown on a *dahiya* patch could be as in *penda*, a mix of different crops, or as in *kheti*, different crops could be sown in more or less separate strips. In some cases weeding would also be practiced. But generally the tending of crops sown would be minimal and marked by an absence of irrigation. The crops sown (*kodoṅ, kosra, media*) would be of the hardy *penda* variety.[60]

During the last hundred years or so, most of the lands under *dahiya* have imperceptibly been transformed into fields of dry settled farming. But the ostensibly *kheti* form of farming in such situations continues to be linked to forests. Without the flow each year of decayed biomass from forests, *kheti* on such lands would cease to be viable.[61]

Another significant variation concerns the modulation of certain practices akin to those used in *kheti* as a specialised form of shifting cultivation. Such variations are exceedingly significant in that they vividly indicate the inherent fluidity of boundaries in the world of *penda*. Baiga tribals in Madhya Pradesh subsist primarily on the cultivated slopes of *bewar*. Forest clearings on gentle slopes of low hills and level ground, which in the first year would be cultivated as *bewar*, are cultivated in the following year or years like a patch of *dahiya*.[62] Hill Bhuiyans of Orissa refer to shifting cultivation as *komanchas*, which is demarcated as *birbihuin* for the first year of cultivation, as *jala* for the second year, and as *nala* in the third year.[63] Such modulation could also be in the reverse direction. *Ponam*, for instance, refers to the practice of clearing gentle forest slopes or flat forest lands for rice cultivation by peasants engaged in regular settled cultivation in the Ernad taluk of Malabar. Such clearings would be cultivated for a year or two and then relinquished back to the forest.[64]

In Bastar, the word *dahi* or *parka* is used by the Halbas to refer to the practice of spreading brushwood and branches of trees on level but unembanked fields. Among the Halbas this practice is restricted to lands not considered fit for regular tillage. Another Halba term, *marhan* denotes forested flat lands cleared for shifting cultivation.[65] The Halbas in Abujhamad represent the presence of *kheti* deep in the midst of the most untouched region of shifting cultivation. Hill Madias of Abujhamad and the Dandamis of southern Bastar have subsisted primarily on *penda*. After the first crop has been harvested on a freshly cleared patch of forest, they would cultivate the same patch for another year or so in a *dahi*-like way. Such clearings would be either on level land or on the gentle slopes of low hills. Among the Hill Madias this practice is known as *dippa* and among the Dandamis as *erka*. After two or at the most three years *erka* or *dippa* clearings would be relinquished back to the forest.[66]

The divide between *dippa* or *erka*, and *perka* or *dahi*, has been rather fluid. An exhausted *dippa* or *erka* clearing would frequently regress into the *perka* or *dahi* form. Wherever surrounding forests were thinned out or altogether cut down, even *perka* cultivation would cease to be viable. Cultivation on such lands could only continue as a rudimentary form of settled dry farming.[67]

But in the pre-modern context, *erka* or *dippa* signified a fairly stable modulation of techniques associated with *kheti* within the framework of *penda*. The main crop would be *mandia* (eluesine coracoma), also known as *gurra* or *kutki*, which ripens at the same time (early December) as the *kutki* sown on *penda* slopes. In a context oriented to the requirements of *penda*, *dippa* and *erka* could be said to signify the presence of a 'nursery', just a little tended and still chaotic, in the midst of wilderness.[68]

Shifting Cultivation as a Promixity to Nature

To speak of variation, be it in terms of variety in the details of shifting cultivation or in terms of fluid mediations between settled and shifting cultivation, raises certain questions. What, for instance, constitutes the definitive substance and form of shifting cultivation?

Could this form be posited in a sense that cannot conceivably be construed either as a case of regression from proper settled agriculture, or as a rudimentary beginning towards some form of settled agriculture? Is it possible to conceive the emergence and survival of shifting cultivation in the complete absence of settled agriculture?

In a bare technical sense shifting cultivation could be regarded as a specific resolution of the problem of pursuing cultivation in a hilly terrain. Another kind of response to the same problem is known as 'terraced cultivation'. It is a practice widely prevalent in many hilly parts of India and similar regions all over the world.[69] In the highlands of central India terraced cultivation is practiced among the Saaras tribals living in the remote hill tracts of Orissa.[70] Terraced cultivation is universally recognised as a proper form of settled cultivation.

Strictly in a technical sense shifting cultivation could be demarcated as a stable form in reference to: terrain, techniques and choice of crops. It can only be practiced in little clearings in the midst of a forest. Viability of shifting cultivation is inseparable from the survival of vigorous natural forest vegetation. Such clearings have invariably been on the slopes of hills. But the definitive feature of the terrain in which shifting cultivation is viable is not the slope of a hill but the close proximity of forests and their undisturbed natural vigour.[71] Techniques characteristic of shifting cultivation are modulated as much to nurture cultivation as to preserve the variety and vigour of forest vegetation.[72]

The patch of land selected is cleared by cutting down the large trees and smaller plants which are then left on the ground to dry under the hot summer sun. Before the onset of rains the clearings are set on fire and the ash carefully spread over the entire patch. This entire process is carefully controlled. Some trees are always left standing to allow for quick regeneration of forest vegetation after the clearing has been harvested. Soil and the bed of ash is left undisturbed. Seeds are merely scattered on the ground.[73] Weeding is unknown either as a concept or as a practice.[74]

Crops are never irrigated. Crops characteristic of shifting cultivation are of the very stable and hardy variety. Entirely untended by Man they can hold their own ground against the wild forest vegetation. Their capacity to resist pests and survive on whatever rain water the ground can soak is as good as that of wild vegetation in Nature. Seeds of different crops are sown together in the same patch. But care is taken to see that the mix of crops seeded do not ripen at the same time.[75]

Clearly the intent and nature of assumptions implicit in these techniques arise from considerations that belong to an order very different from that of settled cultivation. To reiterate the basic considerations definitive to settled and shifting forms of cultivation: whereas in settled agriculture Man seeks an irreversible consolidation from which Nature is sought to be banished forever, in shifting cultivation Man seeks with sensitive care and deliberation a survival space so modulated as to nurture an organic proximity to Nature.

The origins and emergence of shifting cultivation are exceedingly uncertain. On the basis of archaeological evidence, according to T.C. Sharma, its beginnings in India could be traced back several thousand years. But the historical duration of this practice in no way affects the statement about the human presence and Nature implicit in shifting cultivation.

Two kinds of details are crucial for understanding the fact and possibility of shifting cultivation as it has been in India. First, a fact that is strictly technical in nature and intrinsic to shifting cultivation as it has been known and practiced. In that form, shifting cultivation is simply inconceivable in the absence of iron. The surprising fact is that, whereas extensive settled agriculture of a fairly intensive kind has been practiced in India as elsewhere long before iron tools came into use, shifting cultivation simply cannot sustain without the use of an iron axe to clear a forest patch each year. Smelting and forging iron has been the traditional occupation of Agaria tribals of central India. Iron, in the context of pre-modern tribal–non-tribal interaction, represents an unusual tribal mediation in the world of settled agriculture.[76]

The other crucial fact is that shifting cultivation in India has existed for several thousand years in a relationship of proximity with settled agriculture. This relationship could be located at several levels. In a general and sweeping sense, the Gangetic Doab in the north and the plains in the south and west comprise the primary locus of settled agriculture. The highlands of central India, in that sense, could be said to comprise the primary locus of shifting cultivation.

This relationship of proximity was textured somewhat like a concentric web. Within the tribal contiguity of shifting cultivation, the plains of Chhattisgarh and the Narbada Valley sustained on a substantial scale the continuous presence of settled rice agriculture.[77] In Bastar, still perhaps the least touched part of the tribal contiguity in central India, regular paddy cultivation and irrigation tanks made of solid brick and lime are known to have existed for close to a thousand years in the plains and valleys around Jugdalpur.[78] In the still wild and untamed hills of shifting cultivation in Abujhamad, the Halba village of Sonpur has, for several hundred years, been a little enclave of settled agriculture.[79]

Shifting cultivation could be quite accurately characterised as a practice peculiar to tribal communities. But like the spatial referents just outlined, this demarcation has been very fluid. In many parts of India, shifting cultivation has also been the traditional occupation of 'non-tribal' groups like some Kunbis and Thakurs in Gujarat and Maharashtra, Jogis and Dholis in Rajasthan, and Jogis, Gandas and Rauts in Madhya Pradesh.[80]

Nursery and Forest as Fluid Boundaries

Penda cultivation in the hills of Abujhamad is of exceptional significance not merely because the practice of shifting cultivation still survives in its old immemorial form. Its true significance inheres in that *penda* in Abujhamad still persists as a mode of livelihood. It invokes the inherent and intensely suffused fluidity of boundaries: in Nature, between Man and Nature, as also between proximate human groups vigorously distinct from each other.

Penda on the Abujhamad hill slopes is emblemetic of the delicate play of human distancing from Nature. Its resilience is anchored in an ambivalent orientation. *Penda* is a clearing that simulates the forest and Nature. Teak and cashew plantations that now dot the Sonpur–Garpa forest roadside mark out, instead, irreversible boundaries of a conquest consolidated in the midst of the forest. Row upon row of neat straight lines of cashew or teak, cleansed and sanitised of all undesirable undergrowth, etch out an almost permanent geometry onto an apparently wild landscape. It is an enclave of monoculture at war with chaotic wilderness. A forest plantation requires constant tending. Its capacity for self-renewal is at best limited. *Penda* denotes a different kind of presence. Sharp, near geometrical contours of a landscape transfigured by human activity—so universal and ineradicable a consequence of human activity—dissolve with the ripening *kosra* harvest.[81] A *penda* clearing, unlike an abandoned *kheti* field invariably full of *birsam* weeds and useless grass, never regresses into cluster of weeds or degraded forest.

Penda has been practised in Abujhamad for countless generations, but perhaps never in complete isolation. Sonpur, a large Halba village in a pretty little valley watered by the Kukur river, is right in the middle of Abujhamad. An old village, it has been in existence for at least 300 years. The Halbas[82] of Sonpur have always practised settled cultivation. Paddy is their staple crop. They have never been known to cultivate a *penda*. Yet, no more than half-an-hour's walk from Sonpur, the Madias of Sergapali continue as of old to tend their *pendas*. In those lovely months after the *penda* harvest has been gathered, as the last rays of light melt in the expanse of wild green ushering in the long winter night while the horizon over the Garpa hills is still faintly aglow, the vibrant music of Madia drums and songs is distinct and clear in Sonpur.

The Halbas of Sonpur have their own pale version of *Madia Ghotuls*[83] in the *natchgudi*. It is lifeless and neglected. Just once a year, at the time of the grand harvest festival of *medai* does the *natchgudi* really come to life. The *medai* in the Halba village of Sonpur is the largest gathering of Madias anywhere in Abujhamad. As the time fixed for *medai* approaches (March–April), Madias from the hills all around begin to trickle into Sonpur. They come in little groups, mostly of young boys and girls, having walked in some cases for days through the forest.[84] Most of them have an earlier acquaintance with a Halba or Ganda[85] family in the village, and if there is still room they camp in their *bari*. As the sunlight begins to flicker and fade, fires are lit in *baris* or just anywhere. Around the warm glow of fires and *sulphi*, arrowheads glint and dancing bells jingle to the vibrant rhythms of Madia music. Music and rhythms, that all these evenings had been distant voices from across the hills, become for a few days the rhythm of Sonpur.

On the day of *medai*, from early morning the Halba *pujari* of the Sonpur *devagudi*[86] begins to brace himself with leaf-cupfuls of *mahua* and *sulphi*.[87] The *medai* begins with an elaborate ritual of worship and sacrificial offerings to the Kudantola.[88] His face flushed, steps not very steady, the Halba *pujari* ambles down the little mound on which his hut stands, and in deliberate half-steps walks to the shrine of Kudantola across the street. Kudantola, the *pujari* assured me, is the most powerful deity in all of *mad*. As the older *mad* sister of the more famous Danteshwari of *Dantewada*,[89] her stature is much higher. *Mungraj* of Paralkot, he conceded, is another powerful deity in *mad*. But Kudantola's stature is unique. She chose to be in *mad* because Danteshwari in her pride was disrespectful to Kudantola. And so it is that she always has her back turned to Danteshwari.

Worship and sacrifice to Kudantola duly performed, the Halba *pujari* takes a back seat. As the *Anga Dev*[90] is carried in procession from the *devagudi* through the *medai hat* and village streets, *sirhas*[91] take over. *Sirhas* in their person mediate between the mysterious unknown, the will and whims of powerful deities, and the everyday details of life that sustain the world of Man. It is an institution of clearly Madia origin. But that swaying circle of the elect around the *Anga Dev* is open to all; Halbas, Gandas, Rauts, Gonds and anyone else who would dare to be in touch with the powerful deities of *mad*.[92] For a few exhausting hours, their bodies, slashed and lacerated with dusty iron thongs, are not their own. They speak—a shrill, quivering swishing sound crystallising suddenly into a distinct linguistic message—but the voice and speech is not their own. The message may not always be to the liking of the awed listeners. They know, however, that it is given to no one among them to defy or disregard that voice. But its malignant consequences for the details and rhythm of everyday life may need to be curbed and even exorcised by appropriate ritual and sacrifice. No such ritual and sacrifice was indicated by the voices that spoke through the *sirhas* on the *medai* (1985). Everything was in its place, in order. As the formidable *sirhas* and others in the circle of the elect around the *Anga Dev* slumped or sat on the dusty ground, their occult fervour now settling visibly into taut intense equanimity, people from the crowd of onlookers begin to drift into the circle of the elect with little offerings to seek their blessings, or just to be close to them for a brief while. All distances, meticulously retained on other days and occasions, seem to melt.[93] It is a fraternity, for the moment all-encompassing and very intense, of the possessed.

Late in the afternoon, *Anga Dev* is duly escorted back to the *devagudi*. From then on there is no circle of the elect. Instead, as evening comes, in the flickering light of innumerable fires, circles form and dissolve all through that night of joyous abandon over-flowing with *sulphi*, music and dancing. Next morning they all leave with their drums and dancing bells, and a few colourful trinkets and other purchases from the *medai hat*.[94] They walk out of Sonpur with their inseparable *tangiyas*, and bows and arrows. So it has been after every harvest. Madias return to their *penda* slopes and the Halbas to their paddy fields.

Kheti and *penda* in Abujhamad to this day are visibly two distinct modes of livelihood. They have co-existed for centuries in close proximity, and never as worlds completely apart. Being and coming together inevitably meant interaction. In co-existing as close proximities neither the modes of livelihood, nor the textures of social life they sustained, remained what they would have been as worlds apart. Change in this framework of interaction amplified, as it were, the distinctness of the other. New dimensions were elaborated in terms of elements intrinsic to the original texture of a particular sensibility and livelihood.[95]

Selective appropriation of certain elements from settled cultivation subsisted invariably as a kind of subform; a new variation on the old rhythms of both settled and shifting cultivation.[96] Cultivation of *dippa* in Garpa, as in most other villages of *mad*, denotes the presence of this kind of variation in a fairly stable form. Along with the *penda*, the Madias of Garpa also clear and cultivate another patch called *dippa*. Unlike the *penda*, a *dippa* clearing is almost always on a gentle slope or flat level ground. *Dippa* clearing is much smaller than a *penda*, and is located close to the village. *Dippa* is never ploughed. But, unlike the *penda*, a *dippa* is worked over with a hoe or a digging stick to prepare the soil for sowing.[97] *Mandia*, the staple *dippa* crop, is tended and kept relatively free from weeds and other vegetation. The same patch is used for *dippa* cultivation for two or three years in succession.

Bari is another interesting adaptation which extends deep into the *mad* hinterland.[98] It comprises a fenced bamboo enclosure around the dwelling site. The area enclosed as *bari* varies enormously. In its rudimentary form the *bari* could be characterised as a segment of the *penda* close to the house. A few relevant details concerning crops cultivated in a *penda* would help to mark out the underlying continuity. *Kosra* is the staple crop of the *penda*. A typical *penda* slope is a rich profusion of several other crops sown along with *kosra*. Seeds of various crops are dibbled at random on the same patch of ground. Stumps of large trees are left undisturbed, and around them are tended creepers of beans and other vegetables. If the *penda* slope happens to be favoured by some little *nullah* flowing across, the stream is embanked with stone boulders and earth.[99] The rich silt cover thus created upstream is used for cultivating local varieties of melon and other vegetables. Very like the *penda*, the *bari* in its rudimentary form is a rich profusion of different plants growing close together: a miniature forest in the midst of a clearing.

The largest and best tended *bari* in Garpa is the creation of a fellow by the name of Butlu. For the last ten years or so he has been living in Garpa and works as a peon in the village school. In the context of Garpa, Butlu—originally from a village near Narayanpur—is an exceptionally progressive cultivator. His *bari* is large (about six-seven acres) and is well equipped with a *dhekuli*[100] to draw water for his paddy and maize crops. Another well tended *bari* is of some interest for another reason.

Suku's family is originally from Wadependa, a village deep in the hinterland. It is a good two days' walk from the Sonpur–Banda forest track. The practice of weeding and ploughing is unknown in Wadependa. *Baris* in Wadependa are small and continue to be cultivated as of old; a simulated miniature forest in the midst of a clearing made by Man. In 1983 the *penda* harvest in this village, was exceptionally plentiful. So they all decided not to cultivate the *penda* the following year and, instead, let that year of plenty be a long memorable period of festivity and dancing.

Something, but only something, of that immemorial resilience and spirit of abandon survives even in Garpa. The Garpa Patel is an eccentric character in a peculiarly Madia way. I first met him while Narendra and I were walking past his house one evening to stand on the edge of the forest and watch the sun set. There he stood, with his blazing intense eyes in a frayed black coat without buttons, which nevertheless seemed strangely to blend in that forest clearing with his loin-cloth.[101] He wanted medicines for his sick wife. A man of few words, and as I found out not inclined to do much else either. That year, his *penda* had yielded nothing. Though he went like everyone else in the village every day to his *penda*, all he did was to go up and down the *sulphi* tree on his *penda.* Yet, his family never went hungry. Every family in the village contributed to provide enough grain to see the family through till the next harvest.[102]

As an adaptation within a texture of livelihood grounded in the *penda, bari* represents an unstable form. Quite rapidly in recent years, *bari* has come to denote a practice in transition towards settled cultivation.[103] Certain factors intrinsic to the *bari* favour such transformation. *Bari* in its conception denotes an extension of the house. It demarcates a virtually permanent boundary between the forest and a Man-made clearing. It encloses a ground that is relatively more open than a *penda* clearing. To begin with, the area enclosed is not too large. The very marginal character of the *bari* facilitates experimentation with new techniques like weeding, and cultivation of new crops.[104] But all these factors do not entirely explain, at least in the context of Abujhamad, the increasingly rapid transformation in recent years of the *bari* into a transitional practice towards *kheti* and settled agriculture.

This shift in the function of the *bari* into a rudimentary beginning towards *kheti* is the consequence of the impingement of powerful impulses that arise from far beyond the world of the *bari* and *penda.* As the reach of the modern market extends deeper into the backward hinterland, experiments with new techniques and plants in the *bari* come to be decisively oriented to the requirements of the modern market.[105] An old woman walking for five hours to sell just a few handfuls of tomatoes and exactly two papayas at the Sonpur *hat* is characteristic of a pattern that is becoming even more frequent in *hats* all over Bastar. In Abujhamad the first things to be tended largely for the market are raised in the *baris.* In recent years government schemes of liberal loans and other incentives to encourage the spread of *kheti* in Abujhamad have quickened market forces to a new vigour and intensity.

In tribal perception the government represents a strange presence: tangibly of this world, yet so remote and distant as to be beyond comprehension. Government schemes and announcements are read as the signs of the time. From this distant and abstract arbiter of destiny, they expect protection and justice.[106] But it is an expectation tinged with a keen awareness of the irresistible nature of its power. Hence the acute sense that the days of the *penda* are in any case numbered, and the best that is given to anyone to do is to prepare for its inevitable replacement by *kheti.*

In the recent as also the distant past, *kheti* has taken the place of *penda* in Bastar. Murias in the foothills and valleys around the Abujhamad hills were already practicing a rudimentary form of *kheti* at the time of Glasfurd's journey into Bastar (1861–62).[107] The older name for Murias is 'Jhoria Madias'. They are originally from the Abujhamad hills. For the Murias migration from Abujhamad and adoption of *kheti* came to be uniquely invigorating. Muria cultural life centred around *Ghotuls* blossomed to a new creative cultural vigour.[108]

Muria's adoption of *kheti* and the contemporary transition from *penda* to *kheti* in Abujhamad are rooted in two distinct and qualitatively distanced historical textures of interaction and validation. The pace and intensity of change, though important, does not constitute the definitive element in demarcating the qualitative distance between these two apparently similar processes. The definitive referents of the transition in recent years towards *kheti* in Abujhamad are: clear demarcation of the 'individual' from the 'community', and of Man from Nature.

The traditional texture of living and livelihood was worked out as a complex of proximities, never entirely free of a certain tension, between Man and Nature, and between communities. Notions of relevance and effectiveness during the pre-modern Muria transition to *kheti* were oriented as much to the requirements of the community as to that of Nature. Relevance and effectiveness in the contemporary transition to *kheti* in Abujhamad translate primarily as the individual's capacity and achievement to stay ahead and above other Men and Nature. It denotes a pattern in which dissolution of community cohesions as a fact of everyday living is accompanied by its resurrection as reified ethnic–cultural memory: a potent instrument for political mobilisation and power.

Penda on the slopes of Abujhamad is the last, and that too not for long, of the little that is left of the world of shifting cultivation which sustained the tribal contiguity as a salient element in the texture of Indian civilisation. Within this texture varied and distinct cohesions and modes of livelihood could persist for thousands of years precisely because assertion of any and every kind was modulated by a sense of ineradicable limits.

Shifting cultivation, in affirming the fleeting nature of the human presence on earth, does not seek to degrade or reduce the stature of Man. In fact, it is intensely alive to a deep concern with the survival and fate of the human species. It seeks for human life an almost timeless span of survival. But it does so by elaborating human activity as a homologue to Nature. To clarify the significance of its achievement as also the possibilities which inhere in it, one fact would suffice. Communities that lived on shifting cultivation have never known mass hunger and famine. This was possible because, in the words of Geertz: '. . . the systemic congruity between the biotic community man artificially establishes on his swidden plot and that which exists there in stable climax independent of his interference . . . . Any form of agriculture represents an effort to alter a given ecosystem in such a way as to increase the flow of energy to man: but a wet rice terrace accomplishes this through a bold reworking of the natural landscape; a swidden through an uncanny imitation of it . . . .'[109]

Notes

1. See Verrier Elwin, *The Agaria*, Oxford University Press, 1941.
2. Sarat Chandra Roy in his foreword to Elwin's, *Agaria* had spoken of his faith that so long as Agaria myths remain alive, the 'primitive smelting industry cannot altogether die'. *Ibid.*, p. IX. Myths have survived but only as memory, and the ancient Agaria craft is no longer a living tradition.

   I saw a furnace being worked by an Agaria family from Balaghat district as an exhibit at the Indian Science Congress, Delhi (6–10 January 1986). The Agaria working the exhibit furnace was certain that for the last ten or fifteen years no furnace had been worked in his area.
3. See W.V. Grigson, *The Maria Gonds of Bastar*, Oxford University Press, 1938. On the basis of census enumerations (1931) and detailed personal investigations Grigson estimated the Hill Maria (Spelling used by Grigson for Madia) (Abujhamad) population 'just over 12,000', p. 50.

   According to the estimate of the Socio-Economic Survey (1971) the population of Abujhamad was around 13,000. An average family size 5.4 persons per family in Orcha. *Report of the Socio-Economic Survey of Abujhamad*, Tribal Research Institute, Chindwara, Madhya Pradesh, 1963, p. 136, Appendix A, and pp. 97–98.
4. The Dandakaranya project was undertaken to settle refugees from East Pakistan in the 1960s. R.C.V.P. Naronha, a senior civil servant with close

personal knowledge of conditions in Abujhamad protested in vain against the proposal. It meant the loss of land and livelihood resources without any compensation to local communities.

5. Grigson, *Maria Gonds*, pp. 17–18 and 24–30. Forest roads were built as 'feeder links' to the main Raipur–Jagdalpur road, which Grigson reported as 'motorable' throughout the year by 1930s.

6. In the 1963 survey, the population of Garpa is listed as 13 persons, indicating a sharp increase over the last two decades. In 1985 the population was 52 persons. *Survey of Abujhamad*, p. 137, Appendix A.

7. This state of things represents a recurrent pattern. Houses built by the Public Works Department, one of the insane and arrogant schemes for tribal development, are never used by tribals, except occasionally to house domestic pigs.

8. All the four teachers were non-Madias.

9. This is a recurring feature in tribal areas. Unlike the school compound, the area around the handpump is invariably in neglect. This indifference is significant. The aesthetic and functional implications of certain new technologies simply fail to register for a long time. Consider in this context the invariably filthy plastic utensils in both tribal and peasant villages and the sparkling cleanliness of earthen pots and wooden utensils in tribal villages.

10. Until fairly recently, cattle have not been a part of the *penda* mode of livelihood. Government loans for purchase of carts and bullocks are a part of the grand design to 'wean away' the Madias from *penda*.

11. In terms of actual use the gun is akin to the various noise-making devices used by the Madias to protect *penda* harvests from wild animals.

12. Glasfurd had noted a similar fascination for beads and colourful trinkets, see C.L.R. Glasfurd, *Report On the Dependency of Bustar*, 1863, Foreign Dept. Gen. A. Pro. Feb/1863, No. 151/156, para 87.

    In Grigson's time beads from Czechoslovakia were selling in the *hats* of Bastar. To this day that kind of preference persists. Between a bicycle and a transistor, Madias would invariably prefer the transistor.

13. Bastar blacksmiths are dispersed, a few families in a village or cluster of villages, all over Bastar. Madia–*lohar* relationships are characterised by a sharp sense of meticulous distancing. *Lohar* boys and girls are admitted to the Ghotul but marriage with a *lohar* is taboo. Verrier Elwin in *Madia Murder and Suicide*, recounts a case of murder of a *lohar* girl by two Madias who had made her pregnant. But for the fact that she was a *lohar*, it would not have caused any hardship or shame to any of the persons concerned. All that would have happened, in the event of the concerned man refusing to marry the woman, would be that the girl would have been asked to name the father of her child. And the child would have inherited the name as also the right to a share in the father's property.

    Recently, a Madia girl of Garpa eloped with a *lohar* boy. But they dare not return to the village.

    Despite the name *lohar*, they are clearly of Madia origin. In the words of Grigson:

... of Madia stock, speaking the Madia language, indistinguishable physically, having the same phrateries and clans, and following the same customs. Enquiry showed in every case that some of the blacksmiths either had themselves once been cultivators. In some cases they had obtained cultivator's daughters . . . yet, for some reason the aboriginals everywhere look down on the smith, and as soon as Madia takes to this occupation he must live with his fellow smiths either in a separate village or hamlet, or segregated in a separate part of the village. Grigson, *Maria Gonds*, p. 175.

14. For details concerning techniques of cultivation, the *penda* calendar, crops sown and harvest yields in Abujhamad see Grigson, *Maria Gonds*, pp. 125–50, and Sardindu Bose, *Carrying Capacity of Land Under Shifting Cultivation*, Asiatic Society, Calcutta, 1967, pp. 55–87.

15. Jugdalpur now has a few destitutes whose only sustenance is what they can beg at the bus stand or in the bazaar. Kondagaon is still free from destitutes.

    Singrauli region furnishes a striking illustration of the terrible cost of 'development'. The number of helpless destitutes increases as one moves towards the road, and into areas where industry and development have had a longer presence.

16. Delegitimisation of shifting cultivation was accomplished first by asserting the 'sovereign right' of the state to all 'land not owned or occupied in proprietary right' which required uninterrupted and exclusive use and control of that land. See *Explanatory Notes On Forest Law*, Government of India, Calcutta, 1926, pp. 10ff.

    Lucie-Smith estimated that the State had effectively appropriated around 50 per cent of the hitherto 'common resource' from forests and wastes. See C.B. Lucie-Smith, *Report On the Land Revenue Settlement of Chanda District, 1870*, note 54, para 303.

    Regarding the tax to discourage *penda* in its last enclave in Abujhamad, see *Survey of Abujhamad*, pp. 47ff, pp. 52ff.

17. J. Forsyth, *The Highlands of Central India*, (London, 1889), Asian Publication Services, 1975, p. 105.

18. Shifting cultivation was tolerated simply because its immediate abolition was not feasible. But the laws were consistent and emphatic that it was not to be treated as a 'forest right'. Forest Settlement Officers were not empowered to 'grant rights to shifting cultivation.' At best they could record their 'opinion in the matter.' Shifting cultivation was to be 'deemed a privilege subject to control, restriction and abolition' by the Government. *Explanatory Notes*, p. 32.

19. See *Report On the Proceedings of Forest Conference Year 1873–74*, pp. 4ff. The rights of usage extinguished by Forest Laws affected not just the practice of shifting cultivation but the very basis of livelihood and survival. Some of the colonial officers recognised its annihilating sweep: '. . . the ultimate extinction of all private rights in or over forest or waste land and their absorption by Government.' Thus extinguishing 'large mass of native prescriptions and usages' and 'immemorial private and communal property'. See *Earlier Indian Forest Legislations*, Note by the Governor, 9 February, 1879, and Note by Sir W. Robinson, 3 February 1878.

20. See V. Elwin, *The Baiga,* Oxford University Press, 1939, pp. 100–31.

21. *Report of the National Commission on Agriculture,* Vol. 9, Ministry of Agriculture and Irrigation, New Delhi, 1976. Randhawa's monumental *A History of Agriculture* devotes less than two pages to shifting cultivation. See M.S. Randhawa, *A History of Agriculture in India,* Indian Council of Agricultural Research, New Delhi, 1980, Vol. I, pp. 220–21.

22. See, B.D. Sharma, *Development of Small Tribal Communities—A Theoretical Frame,* Ministry of Home Affairs, Occasional Papers No.6, New Delhi, 1978, pp. 21ff, and 38ff.

23. For comparison of yields see Sardindu Bose, *Shifting Cultivation.*

24. Shifting cultivation in fact nurtures the soil of hill slopes. See the exceedingly well considered but virtually unheard argument, D.C. Kaith, *Shifting Cultivation Practices in India,* Indian Council of Agricultural Research, New Delhi, Review Series, No. 24, 1958.

25. For a statement concerning universality as a deep inheritance etched in the human condition see Ananda Coomaraswamy, 'Spiritual Paternity and the Puppet Complex—A Study in Anthropological Methodology', *Psychiatry— Journal of the Biology and Pathology of Interpersonal Relations,* Vol. 8, No.3, August 1945, pp. 287–97.

26. Kinder formations would begin with the word development and or of . . . . Whatever the syntax and choice of words, modern formations are predicated on the certainty that something has to be done to shifting cultivation from the outside and towards an end that lies beyond the world of shifting cultivation.

27. See J.P. Mills, 'A Brief Note On Agriculture In the Dirang Dzong Area', *Man In India,* March 1946, Vol. 26, No. 1, pp. 8–11.

28. Elwin, *Baiga.*

29. B.K. Roy Burman, *The Development of Forestry in Harmony with Interests of Tribals,* T.I.F.R., Bombay, 1979 (unpublished).

30. *Swidden Cultivation In Asia,* 3 vols., UNESCO Regional Office for Education in Asia and the Pacific, Bangkok, 1983.

31. *Ibid.,* pp. 47ff.

32. *Ibid.,* Vol. 3.

33. Apart from the fact that the possibility of such placement remains uncertain, preoccupation with the problem of placement of shifting cultivation in a schema of evolution tends to foreclose its consideration as a distinctive statement on the human presence, and its place in Nature.

34. See, *Pastoral Production and Society,* Proceedings of the International Meeting on Nomadic Pastoralism, Paris, 1–3 December 1976, Cambridge, 1979.

35. See Walter Goldschmid, 'A General Model for Pastoral Social Systems', in *ibid.,* pp. 15–28.

36. Perhaps the inherent tension between Man and Nature is rooted in the awareness, unique in its intensity and clear foreknowledge to the human species, of death. Perhaps upon that awareness is also predicated the sense of past and future as constitutive of human identity.

37. See Phillip Burnham, 'Spatial Mobility and Political Centralisation in Pastoral Societies', in *Pastoral Production,* pp. 349–60.

38. See Owen Lattimore, 'Herdsmen, Farmers, Urban Culture', in *Pastoral Production*, pp. 479–90.

39. Transhumance is generally subsumed in Anthropological–Historical writing within the rubric of hunting-foodgathering as the earliest form of organised human activity, at a bare remove from hunting-foodgathering among animals.

40. Owen Lattimore, *Studies in Frontier History—Collected Papers 1929–58*, Oxford University Press, London, 1962, pp. 85–118, and pp. 514–41.

41. Owen Lattimore, *Inner Asian Frontiers of China*, Beacon Press, 1962, pp. 255–336.

42. The referent is shifting cultivation unaffected by settled cultivation techniques: *penda* as still practiced in Abujhamad.

43. Except for one difference of detail: *penda* crops around harvest time have to be guarded by humans, and the ground has to be prepared afresh every year.

44. The only exception concerns certain parts of Finland. See special issue on Swidden Cultivation of the Finnish Anthropological Society, 'Suomen Antropologi' 4/1987, Vol. XII.

45. Rarely do fires get out of hand. Were it not so, shifting cultivation would have ceased to be viable in a few generations.

46. See *op. cit.* Forest conference year 1873–74, and *op. cit.*, Commissioner on Agriculture, Vol. IX.

47. See *op. cit.*, Forest Conference 1873–74, p. 31ff and *op. cit.*, Earlier Forest Legislation.

48. See for instance the study of the devastating implications of mining in Bastar, Ram Sharan Joshi, 'Impact of Industrialization on Tribals: A Case Study of Bailadilla (Bastar)', in K.S. Singh, ed., *Economies of the Tribes and Their Transformation*, Concept Publishing, 1982, pp. 369–80.

49. Until the early nineteenth century there were billions of 'passenger pigeons', a native American bird, and no 'house sparrows and starlings' of Europe (not wild, but urban–rural Europe). 'As the European frontiersman advanced, with torch and axe and livestock, North America became more and more suitable for sparrows and starlings, and less and less so for passenger pigeons, which apparently could not sustain reproduction in the scattered flocks to which the Europeanised landscape reduced them . . . .' Worse, Europeans acquired a taste for them as food, just as their livestock acquired a taste for 'native grasses' which proved simply too 'tender and unaccustomed' to reproduce and survive under such 'stress'. Today, 'millions of sparrows and starlings live in North America, as in all Neo-Europes, and no passenger pigeons whatsoever.'

Alfred W. Crosby, *Ecological Imperialism—The Biological Expansion of Europe* (900–1900), Cambridge University Press, 1986, pp. 292–93. Also see Charles S. Elton, *The Ecology of Invasions by Plants and Animals*, Chapman and Hall, 1972.

Forsyth, an adventurous officer of the early imperial phase, was distressed that the tribal hinterland in central India had neither been left entirely alone nor quite humanised according to the measure of Europe: 'The abandoned *dahiya* clearings are speedily covered again with jungle . . . composed of a variety of low and very densely growing bamboo . . . which together form in a year or two a cover almost impenetrable by Man or beast'. But in such dense thickets 'no timber tree can ever force its way into daylight', Forsyth, *Central India*, pp. 104ff.

The makers of colonial Forest Laws drew pointed attention to the legal implications of Man–Nature interaction so markedly different from those of Europe. It was easy in Europe to demarcate 'tables showing the age or size of trees' to render them safe against grazing. But in India 'such rules are not always applicable', since 'forest growth is so varied', *Explanatory Notes*, pp. 26ff.

50. It has been an enterprise in which only the select among humans as much as plants and animals are allowed to thrive and prosper. Of course in this complex of breaking-up and reconstitution, the chosen among the human groups are firmly placed at the apex of all other forms of life.

51. Crosby, *Ecological Imperialism*, p. 267.

52. *Ibid.*, p. 145.

53. Charles Darwin, *The Origin of Species*, Mentor Book, 1962, p. 332.

54. Claude Levi-Strauss, *Tristes Tropiques*, Penguin, 1984, p. 117.

55. *Ibid.*, pp. 111–15.

56. Claude Levi-Strauss, *The Savage Mind*, Weidenfeld and Nicolson, 1972, p. 5.

57. Coomaraswamy, 'Spiritual Paternity'.

58. I take the detailed description of *penda* practices recorded by Grigson sixty years ago as the referent for shifting cultivation as a distinct and stable form. Refer Grigson, *Maria Gonds*, pp. 125–50.

Two other accounts record the practice of shifting cultivation, around the same time, and in a form very little touched by considerations crucial to *kheti*. See S.C. Roy, *The Hill Bhuiyas of Orissa*, Man In India Office, Ranchi, 1935. And V. Elwin, 'Notes on Juang', *Man In India*, Vol. 28, No.182, pp. 7–146.

59. Of course there are enormous variations within the *kheti* form. Certain techniques like irrigation, manuring and weeding in fact may not even be practiced in the enclaves of *kheti* within the tribal contiguity. The crucial consideration is that they are accepted as legitimate and desirable for *kheti* yields.

60. Significantly crops sown on *penda*, even in areas most affected by *kheti* have not changed. See *Survey of Abujhamad*, pp. 83ff. For detailed listing of *penda* crops see Bose, *Shifting Cultivation*, pp. 70ff, 84ff, and 103ff.

61. This connection is clearly perceived by cultivators within the tribal contiguity. Use of manure is sparse and infrequent.

62. Elwin, *Baiga*, pp. 106ff.

63. Roy, *Hill Bhuiyas*, pp. 69ff. And *Swidden Cultivation*, pp. 17ff.

64. *Op. cit.*, *Swidden Cultivation*, p. 18.

65. Grigson, *Maria Gonds*, pp. 126ff.

66. *Ibid.*, pp. 120ff.

67. *Survey of Abujhamad*, pp. 76ff.

68. Comparison with *bari* is instructive. Both *bari* and *dippa* or *erka* require more intensive human tending. But *bari*, unlike a *dippa* patch represents a more or less permanent clearing. Hence perhaps the fact that new exotic crops are first grown in a *bari*.

69. Terraced cultivation is the norm amongst the agrarian communities in the Himalayan hills. Some of the north-eastern tribes like the Angami, Chakasang also practice terraced cultivation.

70. Saoras (Orissa), practice both shifting and terraced cultivation, *op. cit.*, *Swidden Cultivation*, p. 41ff.

71. Shifting cultivation was practiced until recently on more or less level terrain by Koyas and Soaras in Orissa, and Kamars around Dhamtari in Bastar. See S.C.

Dube, 'Economic Life of the Kamars', *Man In India*, Vol. 27, 1947, pp. 146–61.

72. *Penda* is inconceivable except in the midst of forests in full vigour. For evidence concerning swift regeneration see Elwin, *Baiga*, pp. 124ff.

73. An important variation is the use of a digging stick to make holes for seeding.

74. In a characteristic *penda* clearing weeding is unnecessary since the natural resilience of crops cultivated is adequate to ensure healthy survival.

75. Important if crops are to be harvested. In this as in other techniques, the implicit determinant seems to be the principle of least disturbance.

76. In Latin America shifting cultivation is known to have been practiced using stone axes. But two features concerning the use of iron stand out in the context of shifting cultivation in central India. The long tribal tradition of iron smelting and its extensive dispersion deep in the tribal hinterland. In instructive contrast to the tradition of brass casting, which is invariably located around fluid zones (valleys and relatively plain countryside) where the world of *penda* and *kheti* converge, iron smelting has always thrived dispersed deep within the tribal hinterland.

77. See J.W. Chisholm, *Report on the Land Revenue Settlement of Bilaspore District*, 1868, paras 141–45.

78. See Glasfurd, *Report*, para 139. And de Brett., *Chattisgarh Feudatory States Gazetteer*, Bombay, 1909, para 221-23.

79. See Grigson, *Maria Gonds*, p. 26, and Glasfurd, *Report*, para 109.

80. *Swidden Cultivation*, p. 18.

81. The contours of a *penda* do demarcate lines but they never align straight for long. They tend to meander. No attempt is made to retain demarcations between the forest and *penda* clearing beyond the cycle of sowing and harvesting.

82. Halbas are clearly of mixed descent. Since the militia soldiers known as *paiks* (a term now used in Orissa to denote all outsiders and officials) had to grow their own food, the first Halba settlements grew around the mud forts. Children from their marriages with local tribal women in time came to form a distinct social group. In the state of Kanker adjoining Bastar, Halbas enjoyed considerable influence. See Kedar Nath Thakur *Bastar Bhusan*, Benares, 1908, pp. 86–125.

83. See V. Elwin, *The Muria and Their Ghotul*, Oxford University Press, 1947.

84. *Ibid.*, pp. 213ff.

85. See R.V. Russel and Hira Lal, *Tribes and Castes of Central India*, (1916), Cosmo Publications, 1975, Volume 3, pp. 182–200, 14–17.

86. See Grigson, *Maria Gonds*, pp. 208–221.

87. In Abujhamad, *sulphi* trees are never planted. They grow wild, and there are always a few near about a *penda*. A fringe benefit of wild propagation is the distinct flavour of the drink tapped from each tree.

88. See Grigson, *Maria Gonds*, pp. 198ff.

89. *Ibid.*, pp. 7–11. See, *Dashera of Bastar*, Tribal Research and Development Institute, Bhopal, 1988.

90. The *pat devs* are two logs joined together in a square shaft-like frame. They mediate between the cult of Danteshwari and the spirits who are supposed to

be exclusive to the hills and forests in Bastar. *Pat devs* are worshipped alike by the Madia tribals and other communities in Bastar.

91. Elwin, *Muria*, pp. 179ff and V. Elwin, *The Religion of An Indian Tribe*, Oxford University Press, 1955, pp. 460–83.

92. For the way regional locus gets woven into ritual and worship, see Grigson, *Maria Gonds*, pp. 193–207.

93. These distances are evident at several levels in the minute details of everyday life. To take a characteristic instance in Garpa, Patiram the *Kotwar* is the only Ganda resident. His house, unlike any other in Garpa, is carefully plastered with mud and brightened with a dab of paint in the Chhattisgarhi fashion. Patiram's wife is the only woman who wears a sari. Her brother had mobilised the village to excavate a tank in which he drowned while trying to save a neighbour's child. After that the tank has been abandoned.

Last year when Patiram's house needed a fresh cover of thatch, people in the village helped. The task would have been quite impossible for him alone. Yet the Ganda family is kept at a certain distance and treated with a certain degree of contempt.

94. Madia's fascination for beads is indeed remarkable. Glasfurd pointedly noted this fact. Between fascination for beads and transistors or tape recorders in recent years, there is a continuity. Not very different perhaps from an earlier pattern, wherein between beads, mirrors, and clothes; the Madia invariably preferred beads and mirrors.

95. Several such forms, that represented transitory or fairly stable mediating forms between shifting and settled cultivation were prevalent in various parts of India. For the Bastar region, see Grigson, *Maria Gonds*, pp. 125–50.

For the Central Provinces, see, W.V. Grigson, *The Aboriginal Problem in the Central Provinces and Berar*, Government Press, Nagpur, 1944. For references to similar forms of agriculture, see, *Report on the Proceedings of the Forest Conference, 1973–74*, pp. 8ff.

96. *Bari* in the world of *penda*, and the living mode of Rauts (cattle herders) is typical.

97. In *podu* cultivation, the Durwas in the Tulsi hills in Orissa use ploughs even on slopes to scratch the ground before sowing. Elwin refers to identical practices in Keonjhar during the 1930s.

98. See *Survey of Abujhamad*.

99. Grigson, *Maria Gonds*, pp. 146ff and pp. 149–50.

100. *Dhekuli* is powered by human muscles. Animal power is never used to work a *Dhekuli*.

101. Madia fascination for the black coat dates at least since the time of Grigson.

102. The harvest in Abujhamad during 1984–85 suffered because of insufficient rains. But it did not seem to cause excessive hardship. Consider in this context the following extract concerning years of bad harvest in the Bastar of hundred years ago:

> Even a partial failure of crops affected the people but little, since the wild aborigines, who form about two-thirds of the population are accustomed to live on forest produce and hunting. Prior to 1884 no records of any famine are forthcoming. The distress of 1896–97 did not affect the state

much, though it sent a number of Chattisgarhis into Bastar in search of relief.

Op. cit., de Brett, *Gazetteer*, para 52.

103. *Survey of Abujhamad.*

104. In Grigson's time *baris* in Abujhamad were rare. Perhaps the most remarkable achievement of the *bari* as a sub-form within the 'penda mode of livelihood' is the cultivation of tobacco. The village of Maspur near Garpa has considerable reputation for producing good tobacco. It is still grown largely for household consumption and barter with neighbouring villages.

Madia like all tribals have a tremendous fascination for tobacco. A Madia folk tale has an endearing story about the origin of the plant. Long ago, a girl, not very pretty, could not find a boy to marry her, and so the *Devs* consoled her with the boon: 'in your next life you shall be the desire of the world'.

105. The market in the context of Abujhamad is the periodic *hat* held at various places.

106. The degree of legitimacy enjoyed by the modern nation-state in the hinterland is truly extraordinary. It co-exists with another contrary sense of the irresistible sweep of its power to uproot and destroy.

107. Glasfurd, *Report.*

108. Elwin, *Muria.*

109. Clifford Geertz, *Agricultural Involution—The Process of Ecological Change in Indonesia*, University of California Press, 1968, p. 16.

6. POLITICAL AUTHORITY AND THE TRIBAL CONTIGUITY

Until barely thirty years ago, Bastar, the hub of the tribal contiguity, remained far removed from impulses precipitated in regions of intense settled cultivation to control and reorder the relationships between Man and things. Regions proximate to this hub have been in relatively longer and more intimate touch with impulses originating from regions of settled cultivation. But responses to these impulses in the eastern and the western proximities[1] of Bastar have been of a different order.

The eastern proximity, comprising the hill tracts of present-day Orissa has, for over 2,000 years, known something of the world of settled cultivation. Cattle grazers, itinerant artisans and Banjara traders, mendicants and pilgrims, as also footloose adventurers from the lands of settled agriculture in search of fortune have traversed those lush wooded hills year after year.[2] Scattered enclaves of settled cultivation endured in the midst of slopes of shifting cultivation. Local communities have always exercised decisive control over narrow passes which traders, pilgrims and soldiers had to traverse. Yet, the eastern proximity never nurtured a political authority that sought to steadily extend the area under its control.

In sharp contrast, the Garha tribal kingdom[3] in the western proximity made a determined bid to extend and consolidate control over the entire region. Rulers of Garha, in the words of Abul Fazl, were regarded since 'old times' as being of 'high rank'.[4] But recognition of social pre-eminence, however general and of long standing, meant very little in terms of actual political control. The rulers of Garha remained one among several ruling chiefs of the region. They could extract 'nothing beyond reverence'[5] from the rulers of neighbouring principalities. Some time in the mid-fifteenth century, the Garh ruler Kharji, through sheer 'ability and contrivance', began to consolidate a position of political supremacy by securing *peshkash* from other rulers of the region around present-day Jabalpur.[6]

By the first quarter of the sixteenth century, Garha had evidently come to be reckoned as a factor of consequence in the calculation of the several powers contending for control of passes and routes that connected the Deccan plateau to the vast plains of north India.[7] That inevitably involved the Garha rulers in a politics of shifting alliances and armed combat with local rulers and the imperial power in Delhi. Sangram Shah (1510–40), during whose long and eventful reign Garha emerged as the foremost power in central India, was quick to seize the opportunity to 'gain the good will' of the Delhi Sultan Ibrahim Lodi by handing over the Sultan's rebel brother Jalaluddin (1517).[8]

Imperial Control and Regional Self-Assertion

Historical antecedents of the relationship between imperial control and the viability of a regional power centre of consequence in central India indicate a complex pattern. Haihaiya rulers were the first to establish political supremacy (eighth to twelfth century) as a regional power over most of central India. Except for brief periods, their political control never extended beyond central India.[9] In the absence of an entrenched sub-continental imperial power, Haihaiya rulers never needed to take into account the demands and expectations of a more powerful polity. Effective Haihaiya control as supreme overlords of the region lasted for close to 300 years. That simple fact suggests remarkable success in modulating local resistance and harnessing local sustenance for a large regional polity. A detail of some significance in this context is that it is as difficult to determine the precise moment at which Haihaiya supremacy ceased to be effective as it is to demarcate the time of its beginning. Its end seems to have come about through slow loss of control and gradual fragmentation. Cadet branches of the Haihaiya dynasty continued in fact to rule in Ratanpur and Raipur until the eighteenth century.[10]

The historical situation in which Garha and Rewa emerged as regional centres of power is marked by incessant struggles, never quite concluded, to establish imperial control over the entire subcontinent. At least ten military expeditions of the Turkish rulers of Delhi marched through the Garha territories between 1294 and 1344 on their way to the Deccan.[11] This area escaped direct conquest since, as a forest wilderness supporting at best scattered tracts indifferently cultivated, it was not reckoned to be of much worth. From an imperial vantage, its importance was essentially as a passage to the cultivated tracts and the settled peasantry of the Deccan. Unlike the Garha territories, the Deccan held out a clear promise of considerable surplus that could be regularly extracted. The imperial effort, therefore, was to secure acquiescence and support of local chiefs for the safe passage of armies on the march. It is likely that the Garha chiefs used this opportunity to strike advantageous bargains.[12]

Two definitive factors made possible the eventual emergence of Garha and Rewa as powers of regional consequence during the fifteenth-sixteenth centuries. Turkish conquest of the Gangetic plains in the north had decisively smashed entrenched power configurations with a regional or subcontinental salience. Several ruling Rajput clans retreated to the less accessible forest tracts of central India and established new kingdoms. But the Turkish conquest failed to establish an enduring basis of acceptance and support for their rule. Dynasties replaced each other in quick succession. Whatever basis of support the new Turkish rulers had succeeded in creating was rudely broken by the invasions of Timur towards the close of the fourteenth century. Hence the situation, during the fifteenth-sixteenth centuries, of fierce efforts at consolidating imperial control and intense political fluidity.[13]

Garha occupied a strategic space dominated by hills and forests. Certain details concerning the inherent salience of hills and forests require close consideration in this context. Hills impede the movement of Man and things. They impose stiff limits on the reach and effectiveness of intrusions and influences from beyond the hills.

They demarcate a historical space wherein rhythms of living and livelihood often at sharp variance with those in the adjoining plains may persist, as it were, mute and barely noticed. Hence the deep significance of Braudel's remark that while the formidable might of the Roman empire could assert across vast distances along the Mediterranean coastline, its reach across the barrier of hills remained weak and uncertain.[14] More than a thousand years later, high up on the mountains, practices and beliefs stigmatised as dangerously tainted by Islam continued long after such things had been banished from the plains by the Christian reconquest of Spain.[15]

Armed Conquest and Erosion of Limits

Limits imposed by hills and forests were never constant or immutable. The very fact of human presence tends always in some measure to modify them. They could and indeed did shift in substantial ways long before the onset of modern transformation. But the pre-modern capacity to alter such limits in the vast tribal contiguity of central India was vigorously modulated by precepts and practices that defined Man's relationship to Nature within the world enclosed by hills and forests. Armed conquest, never without consequence in quickening the reach of changes far into the hinterland, could accomplish very little on its own to alter these limits. Rather, the feasibility of armed conquest itself depended upon prior erosion and shift of limits.

Settled cultivation denotes the vital grid that set in motion changes which over a long period altered the substance and operation of these limits. For at least a thousand years before Garha's rise to political pre-eminence, settled cultivation had been practised within the tribal contiguity. But two facts distinctive of settled cultivation within the tribal contiguity meant that even as limits were eroded and altered, their assertive power was revitalised at another level. One, settled cultivation subsisted essentially as an enclave in the midst of slopes of shifting cultivation. Two, it did not embody the logic of limitless extension.

Quite like shifting cultivation, tracts of settled cultivation remained scattered. They could be fairly continuous and considerable as in Chhattisgarh and along the Narbada Valley, or isolated and small as in the numerous remote valleys in the hills. But whatever their magnitude and location, settled cultivation endured within limits that remained more or less stable over long periods. Undemarcated spaces mediated between fields of settled and shifting cultivation. Boundaries, both as geographic space and as cognitive social demarcations, remained fluid.

Mediating spaces as fluid boundaries signify the resilience and reelaboration of limits. Erosion and shift of limits was not a linear thrust steadily extending the reach and power of the plains of settled cultivation. Limits shifted in enduring and significant ways not so much along the divide between the tribal contiguity and plains of settled cultivation, but around widely dispersed enclaves of settled cultivation deep within the tribal contiguity. Hence the vigour of sharply distinct modes of livelihood within a texture of proximities, and the continual modulation of influences from the powerful world beyond the tribal contiguity to the requirements of its own distinctive rhythm.

The emergence of the tribal kingdom of Garha as a regional polity encapsulates the complex and never entirely stable equation between erosion of limits and their revitalisation at another very different level. To clarify the working of this equation, constituted as it was of impulses which in their point of beginning and original orientation were sharply opposed, consider the implications of the absence through the fifteenth-sixteenth centuries of any serious attempt at direct conquest of the Garha region. This absence could not as C.U. Wills suggests, be simply due to the fact that the empire of the Khiljis and Tughlaks remained for ever embattled and burdened by an excess of armed enterprise.[16] Clearly that did not prevent the despatch of no less than ten military expeditions to the Deccan over a period of just fifty years. All these expeditions marched through the Garha territories. This absence is due, instead, to historical constraints of quite another kind.

The bare simplicity of Abul Fazl's explanation of the rise of Garha invokes rhythms distinctively of the region. For a very long time, records Abul Fazl, rulers of Garha had commanded 'reverence' from other rulers in the region. Yet, until the time of Kharji (mid-fifteenth century) they remained powerless to translate 'reverence' into political control. Implicit in this fact is the resilience of a distance between reverence and the capacity to coerce disproportionately large share of the local surplus. Reverence so situated is akin to an elevated ritual space. To this day something of that sense and reality remains manifest and vivid in the everyday rhythms of tribal living. What then is the meaning and implication of Kharji's 'ability' and 'contrivance' as marking the decisive turn in the political fortunes of Garha? For instance, does it signify, as Wills has argued, the first stage in the assertion of 'foreign Hindu' influence?

Wills' explanation has the merit of firm certainty. Its neat demarcations are instructive of the basic difficulty that afflicts even the most meticulously informed attempt at making sense, in terms of modern cognition, of the vital reach and salience of pre-modern identities. He is emphatic that the Garha kingdom marks the assertion of what are clearly 'alien Hindu' influences.[17] Sharp demarcations between 'tribal' and 'Hindu' in his explanation subsist untouched with another recurrent assertion: the 'political vacuum' created by the collapse of Rajput Hindu power and the utter disarray within the ranks of Islam in the aftermath of Timur's invasion provided the tribal Garha chiefs a unique opportunity to establish a powerful kingdom.[18] 'Tribal' and 'Hindu', posited as antagonistic identities in a relationship of incessant combat in the first assertion, are transposed in the second assertion as integral constituents of a single process: Garha polity as comprising tribal mediation and Hindu assertion. Neat demarcations engender a cognitive closure. The two assertions remain closed to each other. The sense of inherent significance, that endures for centuries despite the near absence of power to coerce and command, is thus consigned to the realm of natural facts. Hence the assertion that since 'Nature abhors political vacuum', Garha chiefs succeeded in establishing a powerful kingdom.[19]

The emergence of Garha as a polity of regional consequence signifies in fact a remarkable process of translating 'reverence' into political control. In this process of translation, Kharji's 'ability' and 'contrivance' were noticed as crucial by Abul Fazl precisely because they came into play within a texture of relationships that negates neat demarcations. For, however flawed and imperfect, translations simply do not happen in situations defined by impermeable demarcations. It involved sustained modulation of the power of the world of settled cultivation at two levels.

First, the configuration of settled cultivation within the tribal contiguity. Its physical contours were marked by extensive dispersal bounded in each instance by vast undemarcated spaces. Its social analogue comprised communities with fluid boundaries. Their self-sense and everyday rhythms were oriented to both the existential territorial space (village, region) and some shared memory of origin (clan, jati, cluster of clans-jatis). Skills and capacities nurtured within this web of proximities, even though elaborated in most cases within particular social segments, could nevertheless be harnessed to secure and enhance the quality of the shared existential space.[20] This level constituted the formative basic ground from whence emerged the capacity to modulate at the second level.

Second, the salience of imperial control. The strategic significance of the region compelled serious notice. Viability of direct conquest depended, however, upon the certainty of regular and substantial yields of revenue. The fluid configuration of settled cultivation within the tribal contiguity exerted severe constraints on the ability of even the most brutal ruler to collect revenue with any degree of regularity. The fact that local rulers could without much exertion harass and disrupt the movement of soldiers on their way to the Deccan meant that the region could not be dealt with as if virtually empty of human presence. Hence the confined reach of imperial control, which in the pre-modern situation could never seek anything more than nominal submission and nominal tribute.

Conquests, be they of the modern or pre-modern kind, never happen in the absence of evident and certain prospect of gain. Such gain could be in the form of plunder of accumulated wealth. Or, it could be in the form of regular extraction of local surplus as revenue. At the bare minimum, such extraction had to be sufficient to meet the costs of conquest. During the fifteenth-sixteenth centuries, the Garha region could yield very little by way of regular revenue or tribute. The strategic location of the region and the ability of local chiefs to disrupt imperial control of the Deccan helped to keep alive a level of political fluidity in which the enormous power of imperial mobilisation could be confined and modulated to enhance regional self-assertion. The substantial but dispersed nature of settled cultivation within the tribal contiguity made the crucial difference. Proximity as the definitive referent made possible eventual consolidation of a regional polity as an effective device of local self-assertion. But effective modulation of the imperial salience was beset by an ineradicable irony. Effective

182 • Tribal Identity and the Modern World

modulation, in harnessing sustenance for Garha to emerge as a regional polity, created conditions in which prospect of gains came to be real and very tempting.

By mid-sixteenth century, the process of political consolidation initiated by Kharji had traversed its full cycle. Modulation of the imperial salience had come to acquire a certain visibility. References in contemporary imperial records to Garha and its ruler Sangram Shah begin to convey definiteness of actual events.[21] It no longer made good imperial sense to treat the ruler of Garha as a mere petty chief of wild tracts somewhere along the line of imperial advance. The suzerain control of Garha extended over an area of about 60,000 square miles, bounded by Malwa to the north-west, Baghelkhand to the north-east, Chhattisgarh to the south-east, Chanda to the south, and Berar to the south-west.[22] Garha could mobilise thousands as infantry and a considerable force of cavalry.[23] Sangram Shah was an active participant in several battles fought among different powers of the region for territorial gains and political supremacy.

The capacity to mobilise for the battlefield reflected the vitality of certain basic shifts within the tribal contiguity. Enclaves of settled cultivation had multiplied. Around them had emerged relatively more populous clusters of habitation comprising in many instances migrant peasant and craft communities from across the plains of settled cultivation.[24] The most crucial shift concerns perhaps the ability of the Garha kingdom to enlist the services of diverse communities: notably Pathans, Brahmins and Rajputs from ancient clans.[25] An inscription (1514) of the early years of Sangram Shah's reign identifies him as *Maharaj Shriraj*.[26] Sangram Shah is still remembered as the builder of fifty-two forts and numerous irrigation tanks.[27] More than 300 years later, while surveying the varied surviving fragments in memory and in ruins of brick and mortar of the stupendous exertions of Haihaiyas and the Raj Gonds, Hira Lal noticed that the local term *putari* for gold coinage was identical with the name used for gold coins minted during the reign of Sangram Shah.[28] The prestige that the Garha rulers had come to command acquired a decisive edge. Sangram Shah's son and successor Dalpat Shah married Durgavati, the daughter of a Chandel Rajput Chief.[29] Sangram Shah's achievement dazzled folk imagination. Hence the persistence in folk memory of an event that may or may not have taken place: the unchallenged journey of the royal horse let loose by Sangram Shah through the entire length and breadth of the land.[30]

But the very vitality of these shifts also eroded the protective barrier of imperial indifference. That happened not because of a perceived shift towards enhanced and regular yields of revenue. It was the lure of accumulated treasure and wealth, projected in contemporary accounts to fancy proportions, which eventually tempted the Mughal *subedar* Asaf Khan to launch an expedition of conquest (1564).[31]

For the imperial forces the conquest of Garha was not exactly a military walk-over. In fact the conquest was seen as an achievement of some significance. Asaf Khan had to exert hard to overcome fierce resistance put up by the soldiers of Garha led in person by Durgavati. The value of treasure seized was reckoned as sufficient to justify the expense and effort of a large expedition. Abul Fazl's account of the conquest, though marked by an imperious moral certainty, is meticulous in acknowledging not only the determination and valour displayed by Durgavati on the battlefield, but also her skills and sagacity as a ruler.[32]

Armed conquest, complete and decisive on the battlefield, could do precious little to alter the deeply entrenched limits which defined the nature and reach of political authority. The prime concern of imperial officers sent to adminster the newly conquered territories was therefore confined to extracting tribute. Even tribute, once treasure and elephants accumulated over a century or more had been harvested, was subject to the law of diminishing returns. Local chiefs continued to rule as of old.[33] By the first decade of the seventeenth century imperial conquest began to shrivel. Garha reacquired something of its former power and influence. And in Deogarh another powerful Gond dynasty established suzerain control over a large area.[34]

Singrauli, the northern extremity of the tribal contiguity, has been geographically the closest to influences emanating from that vast plain of settled cultivation, the Gangetic Doab. It comprises parts of the districts of Sidhi in Madhya Pradesh and Mirzapur in Uttar Pradesh. The modern fate which has overtaken the region of Singrauli in recent years furnishes an instructive instance of what the implications of extending the process of modern transformation have been for tribal communities.[35] Singrauli, prior to the modern onslaught, exemplifies a different order of possibilities. It is always been no more than a few days' walk from the ancient pilgrimage centre of Varanasi and the mighty fortress of Chunar. Still, the Chandel Rajput chiefs of Mahoba failed to dislodge the Kharwar tribal ruler of Singrauli.

The region derives its name from the Kharwar tribal kingdom of Singrauli. A bare outline of the political fortunes of the Kharwar dynasty is suggestive of the resilience and autonomy of tribal social cohesions prior to the modern colonial impingement. In the last decade of the twelfth century (1190), Chandel Rajputs, displaced from Mohaba by the legendary Prithviraj Chauhan, overthrew the tribal king Buland Shah. A hundred years later, the Kharwars regained control of their kingdom. They were ousted for the second time by the Chandel ruler Orandeo (1310). Once again, the Kharwars regained possession of their kingdom (1450). After another conflict the Kharwars finally vanquished the Chandels in 1560.[36] The resilience of tribal social cohesions through centuries of fierce political struggle is worth serious notice. Tribal social cohesions could never have survived were it not for the fact that pre-modern political economy allowed for the co-existence of diverse modes of livelihood. Implicit in the enduring vigour of diverse modes of livelihood and cohesion existing for centuries in close proximity is the working of an equation between the political and social realm wherein difference and distance sustained an intricately nuanced structure of coherence.

Power as Control and as Dependence

In sharp contrast, the process of change unleashed by colonial rule sought coherence in the progressive negation of distance and difference. But long after British rule had come to be firmly entrenched as supreme across the subcontinent, its capacity to recast primal equations between Man and Nature in regions like Bastar remained uncertain and fragmented. To the intrepid officers sent to open up this remote wilderness, Bastar in the mid-nineteenth century appeared a land still untouched and virtually closed to the world beyond its hills.[37] Glasfurd and before him Elliot voiced their sense of grave apprehension that the conquest and opening up under colonial rule may well be overtaken by what had so far been the immemorial fate of conquests in Bastar. Armed might alone would never suffice. For the colonial experiment to endure, it was imperative that the basis of livelihood be recast.[38]

In his reflections on the nature of power and armed conflict in human societies, Tolstoy remarks that power in its root sense signifies a deep structure of dependence.[39] In speaking of power in this sense, Tolstoy was alluding to the irony and paradox of power, whatever be its magnitude, as control and as tacit consent. Both Elliot and Glasfurd knew the firm details of whatever had survived in Bastar of past impingements of the world beyond the hills.[40] The resilience, despite these intrusions, of primal changelessness so very striking in Bastar was to them a grave reminder of the magnitude of their task. They were determined, in a way that simply could never have been thought possible in the long past of armed combats much more fierce, not to allow the continued sway of primeval forces which in the past could tame and limit armed political conquests; and to modulate what had arrived as strange and threatening alien presence to the requirements of distinctive local rhythms of life and livelihood.

Powerful kingdoms and empires in the past did indeed seek to extend their control over the tribal contiguity. But the maximum that pre-modern conquest could exact was nominal submission. Such submission meant the toleration of an enclosed fort-like structure, made invariably in the more remote tracts of mud and timber, and a nominal annual tribute. The fluid divide between resistance and retreat, submission and defiance, in such situations is vividly invoked in the matter-of-fact details recorded by Blunt (1795) of the Maratha military expeditions to subdue refractory chiefs in Sirguja hills.[41]

The countryside seemed 'very poor' and movement 'exceedingly difficult' for Man and cattle alike. Narrow paths meandering through forests were 'rarely frequented', and often 'entirely overgrown with bushes'.[42] And this, in the best dry part of the cold weather. A brief shower of rain could make movement of any kind virtually impossible. Despite the appearance of extreme poverty, Blunt was assured of a 'sufficient supply' of dry grain.[43] The difficulty was not the availability of grain but the villagers. Most of them had 'fled with their property into the hills and woods' to escape 'plunder' at the hands of the Maratha army.[44] As Blunt walked for two long days, he noticed just one 'hut' and that also 'deserted'. When he arrived at the next village (Nutwege), he found the inhabitants busy 'packing up their property and hurrying away' to the woods.[45] The ruler of this not so small principality of 'Corrair' (Koria), 'besieged' as he was at that time, in his 'little mud fort' at his capital Sonehut, seemed equally helpless.[46]

The principal objective of the military expedition was to secure recognition of Maratha supremacy in the region. Marathas sought this recognition as legitimate successors to the Haihaiya (Rajput) dynasty and the Gond rulers of Garha (tribal dynasty).[47] The 'mud fort' of the refractory chief located upon an 'eminence' comprised just about 'forty huts'. Soldiers of the Maratha suzerain power were encamped 'about a mile to the west'.[48] When Blunt arrived on the scene the 'battle' had just been concluded.

On both sides, barely 400 soldiers were involved in the conflict. The total number of casualties was exactly five killed and a few more injured. The entire battle seemed to be a series of exhausting marches and counter-marches over difficult terrain. Villages were deserted *en masse* with the inhabitants carrying their stores of grain and driving their cattle to the safety of the forest.[49] Like the British imperial expedition nearly a century-and-a-half later in the hills of Abujhamad, the worst the Marathas could do was to set fire to abandoned huts in deserted villages.[50]

The details of the peace treaty are an instructive comment on the limits of what could be exacted from the defeated. The vanquished chief, Ram Gurreb Singh, recognised 'after much contention' the Maratha claim to levy a tribute of Rs. 200 per annum. He had refused to pay anything at all for the last five years. But all that the Marathas actually succeeded in collecting were 'five small horses, three bullocks, and a female buffalo'.[51] The local ruling chief was as powerless as the Maratha *subedar* in garnering more than a nominal share of surplus from the countryside. Blunt's remark that the Marathas well knew that 'the Rajah had it not in his power to pay one rupee'[52] is characteristic of a general situation.

The Mughal conquest of Garha was swift and decisive on the battlefield. Yet, effective control proved exceedingly elusive. Within two years of conquest, the emperor had to despatch Mahdi Qasim Khan to reassert Mughal control over Garha. The entire territory came 'into his hands without much exertion'. But in less than a year, overcome by 'depression' at his inability 'to manage' these vast and wild tracts, Qasim Khan quietly fled from Garha.[53] A succession of Mughal governors over the next twenty-five years failed to enforce a system of regular revenue collection. After 1590 even the attempt to exercise direct control over Garha seems to have been given up.[54] As Garha reacquired some of its old power and influence, and as the Gond Chief Jatba succeeded in extending his control from the hills around Deogarh to the Nagpur plains the imperial effort came to be directed essentially at co-opting the rulers of Garha and Deogarh as *marzabans* (border lords) of the Mughal realm.[55]

The first harvest of plunder after the initial conquest seems to have been substantial indeed. According to Abul Fazl, an 'incalculable amount of gold and silver' including 'one hundred *degs* of Allaudin *asharfis*' fell into the hands of the Mughal commander Asaf Khan.[56] A striking and perhaps instructive feature of his account is that the only precise and firm figures are of 'two hundred elephants' presented to the emperor.[57] Whatever the exact worth of treasure seized by the Mughal commander, the significant fact is that it represented an accumulation made by the Garha rulers over a period of 150 years or more. Subsequent attempts at squeezing Garha rulers yielded nothing of great value. Invariably tribute remained unpaid. The emperor had to be content with a few elephants offered as *nazar*, and occasional personal homage by the ruling chief.[58]

Towards the end of the sixteenth century, Jatba of Deogarh succeeded in consolidating a new power centre of consequence in territories formerly controlled by Garha. With the loosening of control over the Deccan during Jehangir's reign (1605–27), the Deogarh chief stopped paying tribute to the Mughals altogether. Deogarh even extended its authority over tracts which the Mughals regarded as a part of their domain.[59] To put an end to such flagrant infringement of Mughal prestige, Shahjahan despatched a military expedition (1637).[60] This expedition, like most other imperial expeditions, resulted in complete triumph on the battlefield. The Deogarh chief surrendered the fort of Nagpur and 'offered' to the Mughal commander 'in the form of presents one lakh and fifty thousand rupees' and all his 'elephants, male and female, numbering one hundred and seventy'. He also promised not to ever 'waver from his old path of obedience and loyalty', and pay 'every three years' a tribute of four lakh rupees to the imperial treasury.[61]

Victory on the battlefield, swift and complete as it was, could do nothing to enhance the capacity of the Deogarh ruler to collect from the local populace what he was expected to pay to the imperial treasury. So another imperial expedition marched into Deogarh (1648) only to discover that there was nothing left to plunder or seize.[62] Subdued perhaps by this experience, the Mughals reduced the tribute to one lakh rupees per year. But even the reduced amount proved beyond the grasp of the Deogarh ruler. In a desperate bid to realise unpaid dues, the Deogarh chief was detained for six months in Buhranpur.[63] Still the tribute remained unpaid.

After the ample takings of the first conquest, repeated imperial attempts to squeeze ruling chiefs in the tribal contiguity proved uniformly barren. This failure was not due to any lack of determination or skill in exacting from local chiefs the maximum possible. Aurangzeb, known for his exceptional energy and severity, discovered at first hand as the *subedar* of the Deccan the compelling nature of constraints upon the extent of plunder the rulers could collect from the vast hinterland of hills and forests. The failure to pay tribute, argued Aurangzeb, did not represent unwillingness to pay. Rather, it represented helplessness and utter inability to pay. The 'present zamindar' of Deogarh, he informed Shahjahan, lives in 'straitened circumstances' of 'great misery'. Armed force would be of no use in realising arrears of tribute. It could only result in the 'ruin of his territory'. Conquest would be an 'easy matter'. But the conquered territory, Aurangzeb knew, 'could not be easily held or controlled'. Even if it were possible to somehow hold on to the conquest, 'the whole of the surplus (*siwai*) revenue derived from it will have to be spent in its administration every year'.[64] So the utmost the Mughal *subedar* could do for the emperor was to seize from the local chief a few elephants every few years.[65]

Distance as the Measure of Tacit Consent

Constraints within which political authority based within the tribal contiguity could assert were perhaps far more unrelenting and inflexible. Anam Dev's conquest of Bastar[66] in the early fifteenth century meant perhaps far more restricted exercise of power than was true of Mughal power in Garha and Deogarh during sixteenth-seventeenth centuries, or of Maratha supremacy in the hills around

Chhattisgarh in the late eighteenth century. Distance signified, as it were, the measure of tacit consent indispensable to the survival of political authority. Pre-colonial political authority in regions like Bastar could survive only on the condition that it recognised the autonomous realm of local social cohesions as a legitimate presence. The structure and conduct of political authority had to conform, as in fact it did, to a pattern defined by equations between political authority and social cohesions which no ruler could substantially alter.

The supreme ruling chief stood at the head of what may be characterised as a confederation of chiefs controlling varying extents of territory and owing allegiance to him. This confederation of chiefs governed with the help of autonomous tribal councils or *panchayats*. At no level, from the 'Raja' to the *sarpanch* or 'Pargana Manjhi,' could any individual usurp arbitrary powers with impunity.[67]

Kingdoms were divided into *garhs* (literally forts) or *chaurasies* (literally eighty-four). The total number of *garhs* or *chaurasies* in a kingdom was notionally fixed at thirty-six or eighteen. Both these numbers—eighty-four villages to a *garh* and, thirty-six or eighteen *garhs* to a kingdom—represent a conventional ideal figure.[68] The relationship between the ideal figure and actual reality is somewhat akin to the relationship between the ideal norm of a four-fold *varna* hierarchy and the historical fact of numerous *jatis*. As actual practice, a *chaurasi* may in fact never comprise eighty-four villages; and the actual number of *garhs* in a kingdom may only rarely conform to the ideal number, thirty-six.

The *chaurasi* or *garh* was divided into *barhons* (literally twelve) or *taluq*, or *pargana*. The number twelve, as the other two numbers, also represents a conventional ideal figure. The extent of territory under a local chief could vary anywhere from a village to a *pargana* or a *garh*. But whatever his standing, the local chief could only govern with the help and advice of *panchayats*, or *pargana* councils comprising village headmen.[69] The villages, *barhons*, *chaurasies* or *garhs*, were linked in loose subordination to the supreme chief at its apex. The vigorous and assertive democratic ethos of tribal life and *pargana panchayats* kept in constant check the exercise of authority at all levels. Clan cohesions, particularly in areas like Bastar, reinforced the assertive power of tribal sentiments and customs.

The vigorous presence of tribal social cohesions was not just an inconvenient fact impossible to ignore for the ruler; it constituted rather the very basis of legitimacy for political authority. A revealing and by no means exceptional instance of their decisive role as arbiters of political legitimacy: 'the usurper' to the Sambhalpur throne while 'parleying with the exiled Raja' suggested that a 'Panchayat should be held to settle their rival claims'.[70]

Another remarkable illustration of the self-assured exercise of authority by large regional assemblies or *panchayats* is furnished by an inscription from Bastar. It records a notification of the 'elders of the great assemblies and the agriculture class in meetings assembled' to denounce and register their emphatic disapproval of certain exactions by the chief's followers on the occasion of his accession to the *gaddi*.[71]

At the other end of the subcontinent, and at a time when ancient textures had already begun to wither, Macmurdo witnessed something quite similar while travelling (early nineteenth century) in the more remote parts of Gujarat. Some of Macmurdo's soldiers were arrested and put on trial by the village *panchayat* for cutting a tree earmarked for making cartwheels. The local ruler was present at the trial, but simply as one among several *sarpanches*. The panchayat's judgement was unique. Macmurdo was told that the soldiers were guilty of a crime for which they would not forgive even their ruling chief. But since they were strangers, and as such unaware of local usage and customs, the *panchayat* had decided to forgive them.[72] Rarely if ever, in the age of progress that has since steadily swept across the entire subcontinent—mediated by colonial rule and now by an independent national government—would the ordinary inhabitants of the hinterland summon such profound audacity as to forgive transgression of soldiers and officers of the supreme power.

The significance of this incident cannot be fully comprehended entirely in terms of actual physical constraints on the power of the ruler at that time and place. Of course, they are vital and important. What merits deeper attention is the structure of cognition and legitimacy. The *panchayat's* judgement is also an implicit statement as to what constitutes the legitimate ambit of political authority. That referent constitutes the abiding substance which gives spontaneous reality to possibilities available in a particular social–cultural texture. Even as the vital founts of this mode of cognition and validation were steadily smothered, its assertive power persisted, albeit in fragments. Clifford Geertz, in a context as far apart in time and space as is possible for two historical situations sharing a similar tradition of validation, records a strikingly similar instance in the island of Bali in the mid-twentieth century.[73]

To return to the metaphor of distance in the pre-modern context, the distance between ruling chiefs in the tribal contiguity and their subjects was in inverse proportion to the distance from the world beyond the hills. The surplus that ruling chiefs could appropriate was very limited. Tracts cultivated directly for the upkeep of a chief's household were never too extensive. From subordinate chiefs who accepted their supremacy, they could rarely exact anything more than 'occasional service' and an annual tribute of a 'jar of butter or one or two bamboo walking sticks or the like'.[74] A characteristic instance of the nominal nature of tribute which subordinate chiefs could effectively claim is furnished in the precise rendering of Montgomerie (1829). The Chief of Harrai ruled over an extensive territory comprising three *ilaqas* (tracts) consisting of twenty-six taluks. His *takoli* (tribute) according to long established usage consisted of 'Chironji (nuts) three *seers*, honey ten *seers*'.[75]

Quite like the rulers of Bastar, powerful regional rulers like the Gond rulers of Garha and Deogarh and the Haihaiya Rajput rulers of Ratanpur, merely 'stood at the head of a number of petty rajahs and chiefs'.[76] The 'principles of their rule', noted Agnew (1820), 'precluded anything in the nature of revenue'. Lands under their direct management were no more than what was 'necessary for their own comforts and dignity'. The numerous 'petty lords' in their domain 'followed the same system'. Direct exercise of 'judicial authority' was confined to 'important cases'. On all 'common occasions' the chief executive authority in revenue as well as other matters was exercised by the 'head of each talooq or village'.[77]

Consider in this context the description of the house of the ruler of Bastar in 1861: 'the Raja resides in Jugdulpoor', the town consists of '400 to 500 huts of the most inferior description' and the Raja's residence consists of 'thatched sheds differing only from that of his subjects in size'.[78]

Distance, at least in measurable physical terms, between chiefs or patriarchs of tribes and their subjects was even less perceptible. A meticulous description that survives of a Khond patriarch in the eastern proximity of Bastar is categorical in marking out absence of distances within the community:

The patriarch or the Abbaya of a Khond tribe . . . is in no respect raised above the community. He has no separate residence or stronghold, no retainers, no property save his ancestral fields by the cultivation of which he lives. . . . He transacts no affairs without the assistance and sanction of the *Ahhayas* or of the assembled society. He leads in war. . . . At home he is protector of public order and the arbiter of private wrongs.[79]

Proximity as the Locus of Legitimacy

In the more remote hill regions, equations that defined living and governance continued to conform to this immemorial rhythm until the mid-nineteenth century. Macpherson, charged with the mission of bringing to an end the *meriah* sacrifice (human sacrifice) practiced by Khonds in the zamindaris of Boad and Gomsur (1841), encountered a texture of relationships quite unlike anything he had known.[80] The foremost feature in the situation of 'primitive people' in India, Macpherson noted, was that such communities were dispersed wherever there were hills. In their mode of living, beliefs and language they represented 'every stage of assimilation'. In the remote hills, the 'primitive people' remained 'virtually independent' and more or less 'completely cut-off' from the world outside.[81]

The word 'Khond' denotes a hill or the inhabitant of a hill. As often in the case of communities small and large, it is a name given by others. In this case, the 'Hindus'. Macpherson's surmise is that the word is probably a variation of the Sanskrit name *pulinda*.[82] The Khond word for 'Hindus' is *sassi*, or plain-dwellers. Khonds, despite their extreme isolation, have, for a very long time, maintained some links with inhabitants of the plains and their world of *kheti*.[83]

'Conquest' of Khond lands began as early as the ninth century. They were steadily 'displaced' from the 'sub-alpine and maritime tracts' south of the river Mahanadi.[84] Displacement, though continuous, was slow and intensely fragmented at each level. But the distinctive and perhaps the most significant feature of this conquest has been that it was 'principally by private enterprise', rather than by organised mobilisation of a 'national' character.[85] It took three centuries or more for this process of displacement to extend up to the 'Ghauts' or hills.

Conquest inevitably entailed the intrusion of settled agriculture.

But this intrusion in the pre-modern context subsisted as an enclave of *kheti* within limits that remained fairly stable over long periods. In a strictly technical sense, the intrusion of *kheti* was sought to be quite systematically organised. According to the records of the zamindari of Goomsur and Boad, each conquering Rajput chief assigned lands on a tenure to his soldiers called *paiks*;[86] a term still used in Orissa and Bastar to denote an outsider. According to established usage, the zamindari was divided into twelve (*barhon*) sub-chiefships. But the actual pace and effectiveness of this process acquires a different kind of focus in certain other details recorded by Macpherson. Despite the long duration of 'conquest' stretching over a millennium and perhaps more, the average size of villages around Boad in the 'Hindu' countryside below the *ghats* remained ten households to a village. In the remote hills inhabited only by Khonds, the average size was eight households to a village.[87]

Most Khond tribals retreated deep into the hills. But a small community of Khonds known as 'Benniah Khonds'—an appellation shared with a 'Hindu' caste—retained or acquired lands in tracts below the *ghats*.[88] That happened, according to Macpherson, during the 'long period of intercourse' with Rajput 'conquerors' who chose for their own reasons to grant them 'land tenures' in lieu of service as *paiks*.[89]

The zamindari of Boad and Goomsur, situated on the banks of the Mahanadi, controlled the valley through which passed the 'lucrative traffic' of pilgrims to Jagannath and merchants between the Bengal coast, the Deccan, and central India. Fairly early in the Khond–Rajput relationship a 'firm compact' was established between the Rajput zamindars of Boad and Goomsur and the independent confederation of Khond tribes living in the hills.[90] Support of the Khond confederation came in fact to be decisive for keeping control over the valley.

Relations between the tribal community and the zamindar were mediated by the Chief *Abhaya*. But in no sense could he function as an autocrat. All his decisions and dealings with the zamindar were closely 'controlled' by a 'council composed of the Heads of its branches'. Such councils were themselves responsible to 'Abbayas of Villages', who in their turn were assisted and rigorously scrutinised by the 'elders of their hamlets'.[91]

Certain *Abhayas* or patriarchs of the confederacy might in practice command immense prestige and reverence. Whatever their personal standing, they could not undertake anything of public significance without the consent and participation of other *Abhayas*. Their control over surplus generated by the community was in no sense greater than that of other members of the community. According to Macpherson:

> The Patriarch or the Abbaya—is simply the Head of a family—the first among equals—in no respect raised above the community, whose interests, associations, traditions and manner of life he shares—no one ministers to his wants—no separate residence or stronghold, no retainers, no property save his ancestral fields, by the cultivation of which he lives. He receives neither tribute nor aid, save perhaps an occasional harvest offering of good will.[92]

The zamindar was accorded all the forms and symbols due to a supreme ruler. As for control over surplus, the zamindar could claim no more than a nominal tribute of some harvest offering, and the right to summon assistance in situations of armed hostilities with other zamindars. But in each instance it was the prerogative of the tribal council to decide if the request was legitimate and proper. Besides, the zamindar expressly recognised the right of any tribal segment to dissolve its allegiance to the suzerain ruler.[93]

Anam Dev's 'conquest' of Bastar could not have been very different in character from the 'conquest' of Goomsur and Boad. Quite like the 'conquest' of Boad and Goomsur, establishment of Anam Dev's rule in Bastar was by no means an unopposed eventless occupation of a backward hinterland just waiting to be conquered. Anam Dev had to fight hard and long to subdue the chiefs of Paralkot, Bhairamgarh and Barsur.[94] Anam Dev's early years in Bastar were apparently spent in skirmishes and camping in the forest. The name Bastar itself is supposed to have been derived from *bans* (bamboo), under whose protective shade Anam Dev is said to have often rested in the forest.[95]

Considerations of sheer survival in situations like Bastar compelled political authority to come to terms with the decisive presence of tribal social cohesions. Bastar offered at best meagre sustenance for protracted military operations in any significant sense. The ability of a ruler to appropriate surplus from the countryside, if anything, would have been far more severely restricted than in the situation which prevailed 500 years later in the mid-nineteenth century. At the time the British assumed control over Bastar the revenue assessment, Glasfurd pointedly noted, was exceedingly 'light, averaging from half a rupee to a rupee and a quarter' per plough, and 'four annas to a rupee' per axe.[96] Besides, the shifting nature of village settlements dispersed as they still were in the midst of wild hills and dense forests, made it a 'difficult matter indeed to collect land revenue with regularity'.[97] In the year 1855 the total revenue of the 'Bastar Dependency' in cash and kind was estimated to be Rs. 30,000.[98]

In situations like Bastar large armed formations simply could not be kept together for any length of time. Like other ordinary mortals, soldiers in the service of the Bastar ruler had to grow their own food.[99] *Penda* and the freedom of the forest provided an assured though hard livelihood and very few could be lured to serve as soldiers in the King's army.[100] Settled cultivation had been known and practised at least since the tenth-eleventh centuries. But it remained confined almost entirely to little clearings around Barsur and a few other places. Boundaries between 'forest' and '*kheti*' remained fluid.[101] Soldiers, fortifications and *kheti* fields have all left marks of their long presence in Bastar. These marks are of human effort modulated in profound humility to Nature as the measure and fount of life as it has been and could be. Lucie-Smith, while on a mission (1860) to map the advance of a human effort that seeks to recast Nature fully in the measure of Man, was thrilled by the sheer grandeur of a landscape seemingly untouched: 'the fortified rock of Bairamgarh, in a wild expanse of hill and forest unbroken by a single clearing'.[102]

Human settlements were of a small size and thinly spread in the midst of forests and hills. Jugdalpur represented the high point of demographic concentration in Bastar. But its population in 1861–62 could not have been more than 500. In 1891 the density of population of Bastar was still twenty-two to a square mile.[103] By 1931 it had risen to thirty-four. The demographic profile of Bastar had begun to shift in significant ways. But still, 'except Jagdalpur' with a population of 10,128 (1931), the 'other headquarters' retained the character of villages. Of the 2,442 villages in Bastar, only 'five had populations between 2,000 and 2,500'. Another forty-two settlements had populations between '1,000 and 2,000'.[104]

The demographic profile of remote and to this day little touched

Abujhamad represents perhaps a closer approximation to the situation that characterised most of Bastar till the mid-nineteenth century. In forty years—between 1891 to 1931—the population of Bastar increased by about 69 per cent. In the next fifty years the population more than doubled.[105] The demographic profile of Abujhamad during the latter period—1931 to 1981—represents a striking contrast to the general trend of rapid increase in population. In this context, the fact that Abujhamad was the only large area in Bastar where *penda* or shifting cultivation continued to be the principal source of livelihood is of crucial significance. In 1931, Grigson estimated the population of Abujhamad to be around 12,000.[106] According to figures collected by Abujhamad Project Administration the total population in 1983 was around 14,000.[107]

The Logic of Modern Demarcations

The foremost modern instinct would be to read in this more or less static demographic profile, so characteristic of the pre-modern tribal contiguity, clear evidence of a short and nasty life span racked by hunger and disease. True, livelihood was hard and things they could consume and own very few. But basic sustenance was assured for all.

Until 1887 there were no legal restrictions on the free appropriation of forest produce.[108] The Chhattisgarh Fuedatory States Gazetteer is categorical that prior to '1884 no records of any famine are forthcoming'[109] for Bastar. Movement, be it of Man or beast, was full of hardship. And distance, always a forbidding constraint. But that also meant 'immunity from the ravages of epidemics'.[110]

Distinctness, as distance within this texture, cannot be meaningfully grasped as a measure of the relative capacity of a particular cohesion to control and appropriate available surplus. Hence perhaps the fact, at best exceptional in modern contexts, that distinctness as distance and distanciation was not perceived as hostile or threatening. True, in certain contexts, distinctness signified hierarchical segmentation. For example, the chief, the *gaita* or *gunia* were accorded a manifestly elevated placement. Certain functions, regarded as vital to the sanity and survival of the prevalent social order, remained their exclusive prerogative. This quality of distance and elevated placement essentially refers not to privileged access to surplus but to a prime ritual space.[111] To clarify the basic difficulty—in terms of modern sensibility—consider the paradox implicit in this statement. The formative terrain—control over surplus—of which rituals and symbols associated with the exercise of power are essentially an expression, is virtually absent. Yet rituals and symbols that affirm and elevate the exercise of power as the mediation of an exalted primal space persists with undiminished vigour.

It is emblemitic of the ceaseless striving towards a poised recognition of distances in space and time as the pre-condition for order and survival. Everyday details in this civilisational texture sought to modulate distances as fluid demarcations. Social cohesion as proximities and as locus of legitimacy and power textured interaction and living marked by a near absence of distance within.

Unfettered access to nature furnishes the vital clue to the manifest capacity of tribal social cohesions to survive as distinct entities, despite a long and not always peaceful history of interaction with powerful centres of political authority. Definitive shifts and changes in the pattern of interaction between tribal social cohesions and political authority began with the gradual consolidation of the modern colonial state during the mid-nineteenth century. In these changes one can read the critical details of what the extension of the 'historical process' associated with the industrial revolution in Europe has meant for the tribal contiguity. As the effective reach of the modern colonial state began to extend deeper into the hinterland, access to nature came to be progressively restricted. This marked a shift, utterly unlike others which had preceded it. Choices available to communities even in the remotest hinterland came to be ever more rigorously foreclosed in favour of the requirements of the colonial state and the world political economy. Singrauli, the northern extremity of the tribal contiguity, encapsulates the blinding force and brutality of what the modern fate entails for tribal communities.

Survival of the poorest in Singrauli, as everywhere else in the tribal contiguity, had been linked to virtually unrestricted access to the natural produce of forests, village commons, and other fairly large spaces beyond the effective control of either the state or private capital.[112] Survival quite often meant severe hardships and strenuous effort. Occasionally it also involved doing *begar* for the local chief. In extreme situations, the most vulnerable also submitted to labour under conditions of bondage on the lands of the locally powerful.[113] But the untamed forest was a never failing assurance against hunger and oppression. Settlement Officer Conybeare was emphatic that the famine of 1865, was the first such occurrence in living memory in the region of Singrauli.[114]

To consolidate profitable political control, the colonial administration had to overcome certain basic impediments inherent in regions of shifting cultivation like Singrauli. The principal impediment was the virtual absence of a regular source of revenue. Unlike the level plains of settled cultivation, the highlands of shifting cultivation prior to the colonial intervention never paid regular revenue. The maximum that political control in such regions could secure was nominal annual tribute. But if the colonial state were to adequately discharge its self-assumed function of extending the modern dynamic of progress to the farthest corners of the earth, this situation had to be altered.

Land revenue settlements enforced by the British were conceived as a device for consolidating a firm nucleus of proprietory rights in zones of settled cultivation.[115] As a first step, the hereditary collectors of revenue or tribute were designated as proprietors of land. These new proprietors were accorded a privileged position so as to encourage the extension of the area under settled cultivation, sufficient at least to defray the cost of local administration. In the initial phase the colonial rulers could not impose too heavy a tax for the simple reason that the peasantry would desert lands so taxed. But settlement records, meticulous and precise so far as it concerned enclaves of settled cultivation, simply took no notice of those engaged in 'intermittent' and 'shifting cultivation'.[116] Most of them were tribals. In terms of the new legal definition ordained by colonial rule, they ceased to have any legal–legitimate existence. They had become 'non-persons'.

Land revenue settlements also initiated the process of appropriating vast stretches of land as 'reserved forests' and 'government lands'.[117] Its consequences have been simply annihilating for more than 90 per cent of people in regions like Singrauli. Their survival and livelihood depended on these lands. From time immemorial these people had lived on a complex combination of gathering forest produce, cattle grazing, craft skills and intermittent or shifting cultivation. Under the colonial dispensation this mode of livelihood ceased to have legitimate existence. They were tolerated because forest lands which sustained them were not within the immediate effective reach of the administration. Besides, the penetration of market forces in such regions had to be slow and very gradual. Lands theoretically appropriated by the colonial state were not immediately required for systematic exploitation by industrial enterprise and the modern market. Early linkages that were forged between these hinterlands and the colonial metropolis and its mediating centres, the presidency towns (Calcutta, Madras and Bombay), were entirely for procurement of certain forest produce. These procurements (timber, lac, silk, etc.) did not however immediately deprive tribal communities of their livelihood. In the initial phase, the notion of absolute ownership and rights of usage did not come into open conflict.[118] But this marks the first phase of an irreversible process which now threatens to render the livelihood of the poorest ever more precarious.

It has generally been assumed that as the effective reach of the process of modern development penetrates into the rural–tribal hinterland, better conditions of life and livelihood would become available to people in these regions. But far from that being the case, a powerful impulse embedded in the process of modern transformation has tended to adversely transform the life-situation of the poorest in these regions. Labour of the increasingly impoverished, commonly designated as the 'unorganised sector', is being harnessed on an expanding scale in the service of the modern organised sector of the economy.

For the Singrauli region, demands created by the development of an advanced industrial sector have unleashed devastating consequences. The Rihand Dam (1961) marks the beginning of a direct industrial presence in this region. Its sheer magnitude quite overwhelmed a people barely accustomed to the use of bullock carts. Around 514 square kilometres were inundated by the reservoir. Inhabitants of 146 villages were cast adrift to an uncertain future. That was in 1961.[119] Jawaharlal Nehru himself inaugurated the dam.

In those moments of numbing uncertainty Nehru's presence was a comforting assurance. People felt that their suffering would not be in vain. Their instinctive sense of nobility was stirred when Nehru spoke of the 'Nation' and 'Development'. They believed in his promise of a future of plenty to be shared by all. Believing in the promise of irrigated fields and plentiful harvests, they half accepted the trauma of displacement. So often have the survivors of Rihand Dam told us that they accepted their sufferings as sacrifice for the sake of the 'nation'. But now, after twenty-five bitter years of being adrift, their livelihood ever more precarious, they ask: 'Are we the only ones chosen to sacrifice for the nation?'[120]

It is not easy to fully comprehend the literal truths embodied in this statement. Even the more sympathetic among us may suspect in this query a tinge of rhetoric. A cursory look at what happened to those who were displaced by Rihand would reveal the cruel enormity of their suffering. Nearly a lakh people were displaced by the dam. Entire villages and families were uprooted and dispersed. Those who could demonstrate a firm legal claim to lands they cultivated were given meagre compensation. Those with holdings below three acres were not deemed eligible for any kind of compensation.

The vast majority in these areas earned its livelihood from small cultivated patches, designated 'forest land', *varg char* or *shaskiya zameen*, and gathering forest produce.[121] These people were altogether excluded from the framework of compensation and legal reckoning. In the final phase of eviction people were literally flushed out of their homes and villages. While announcements were being made asking the people to evacuate, water was released from the reservoir to flood the villages.

The fortunate few who were given land as compensation began the difficult task of clearing and levelling. Almost without exception, lands given as compensation were the worst and least valuable rocky hill slopes. In a few years they were again uprooted. This time the hills were required for mining rich layers of coal seams buried beneath. For most of the affected people this was the second massive displacement in ten years.[122]

Even that marked just the beginning of an almost continual process of displacement and dispersion. Planners in Delhi had decided that it would be best to set up a massive complex of super thermal power stations close to sources of coal and plentiful supply of water from Rihand for cooling. Inevitably, this massive investment spawned a varied range of other industries. Each time a new industry is set up, hundreds of families are uprooted from their ancestral lands. In the span of a single generation, communities and families have been displaced as many as four to six times.[123]

Penetration of market forces into the rural–tribal hinterlands has progressively diminished the bargaining power of rural workers and artisan communities. A wide range of skills and crafts, vital to the earlier economy of the region, are being smothered out of existence by industrial competition. In the small town bazaars of this area one hardly finds anything of local manufacture. In fact most traditional skills are no longer recognised as legitimate skills. For most people the only choice is to enter the new industrial world as 'unskilled' workers. Bands of homeless destitutes grow visibly larger and more crushed, as one approaches the main road and the railway line.[124]

Each year lakhs of displaced people migrate in search of survival. An entire rhythm of life is being torn asunder. Folk songs affirm the deep sense of loss felt by the victims. That remains perhaps their only assertion to keep alive memory and a sense of belonging. It signifies their refusal to be lumpenised. Loss of memory signifies the final and irrevocable leap into lumpenisation.

Suffering and injustice can never be measured. The tragedy which continues to unfold in predominantly tribal regions like Singrauli needs to be understood. The process initiated by colonial intervention so defined the situation that our modern cognition is predisposed to overlook the well-being and livelihood of most of the inhabitants in regions like Singrauli. The destruction of their livelihood is thus presented as almost akin to an unavoidable natural calamity. Such a view absolves the perpetrators of such horrendous destruction of any sense of guilt.

Prior to the colonial onslaught two distinct modes of livelihood had persisted for centuries in a relationship of 'approximation': *kheti* in the valleys and riverlines, and *penda* on the hill slopes. Cattle grazing and gathering forest produce in the unbounded, undemarcated spaces constituted a complex mediation between these two modes. Boundaries that demarcated 'tribals' from 'non-tribals' and the diverse communities living in close proximity remained exceedingly fluid.

The irresistible sweep of the sophisticated infrastructure of mining in the hills and power generation and other industries in the valleys has diminished the viability of livelihood both in the hills and valleys. Access to the produce of the formerly undemar-cated spaces—forests and other lands—has been firmly foreclosed. Choices available in the Man–Nature relationship even in the remotest hinterland have been ruthlessly restricted in accordance with the requirements of modern industry and progress. Boundaries that demarcate 'tribals' from 'non-tribals' have tended to become more rigid and inflexible.

Changed patterns of land-use and the systematic harnessing of all natural resources for the continual enhancement of industrial production have had devastating implications for the livelihood and survival of the poorest. Regions and communities which were seen at the moment of their first encounter with the modern world as stagnant on the brink of survival, have been condemned to a half-life utterly at the mercy of the modern world.

True, life and livelihood of tribal communities in the hinterland in the past was always devoid of luxuries. But prior to the modern onslaught the rhythm of life in the remotest hamlet was vibrant to a profound sense of its own music and intrinsic worth. Lands and people like Kalahandi (Orissa), which after a century of progress are today in the grip of famine, had perhaps never known famine and mass hunger.

Cultural sensibilities and modes of livelihood subsist in a relationship of intimate distance. Destruction of modes of livelihood are also moments of deep anguish. The sense of one's self and the world are traumatically shaken. It is imperative that the modern sensibility learns to own in adequate measure the destructive consequences inherent in the modern process. Ecological devastation in our context, unlike the west, has also to be comprehended as a question of livelihood and survival.

Tribal survival in the modern world would be possible and meaningful only if it is recognised as a presence with its own intrinsic worth, and not merely as a quaint and interesting illustration of the logic of progress. That perhaps may in some measure also furnish a corrective to the selfish and ultimately suicidal self-centredness of modern civilisation.

NOTES

1. The terms 'eastern' and 'western' proximities refer to the hills and plain country in present-day Orissa, and the hills and plain country of Narbada Valley and Chhattisgarh towards the north and west.

2. For the Banjara trade see, R.V. Russel and Hira Lal, *Tribes and Castes of the Central Provinces of India* (1918), Cosmo Publications, 1975, Vol. 2, pp. 162–91. Also see notes on Ahirs (cattle herders) Aghori, Bairagi (mendicants) and Bania and Bhat, pp. 18–37, 13–17, 93–104, 111–61, and 257–70. For the pilgrim route and institution of Jagannath temple, see, A. Eschmann, H. Kulke and G.C. Tripathi, *The Cult of Jagannath and the Regional Tradition of Orissa*, Manohar Publishers, 1979. And, Prabhat Mukherjee, *History of the Jagannath Temple in the 19th Century*, Firma KLM, 1977. For certain illuminating details of Mahaprabhu Chaitanya's journey to Jagannath see, S.C. Roy, *The Mundas And Their Country* (1912), Asia Publishing House, 1970, pp. 97ff.

3. Garha refers to the Gond kingdom established some time in the mid-fifteenth century with its capital at Katanga (Garha Katanga in Mughal records) and in the later period with its capital in Mandla.

   See C.U. Wills, *The Raj Gond Mahrajas of the Satpura Hills*, Government Printing Press, Nagpur, 1925.

   Hira Lal, *Madhya Pradesh ka Itihas* (Hindi), Kashi Nagri Pracharni Sabha, 1942, pp. 85–105.

4. *Akbarnama*, Bibliothica Indica, Calcutta, 1886, Vol. II, pp. 324–25.

5. *Loc. cit.*

6. *Loc. cit.*

7. Wills, *Raj Gond*, pp. 34ff.

8. *Ibid.*, p. 45.

9. See Hira Lal, *Itihas*, pp. 30–55.

10. Wills, *Raj Gond*, paras 79 and 80.

11. *Ibid.*, p. 30.

12. The 100 *degs* of Allaudin *asharfi's* seized by the Mughals (1564) probably indicate gifts or payments (demarcation between them being fluid indeed) made to the Garha chiefs to secure safe passage for Khilji expeditions. *Ibid.*, p. 66.

    For the general tenor of relationships between the Mughal and subordinate chiefs in the outlying regions see A.R. Khan, *Chieftains in the Mughal Empire—During the Reign of Akbar*, I.I.A.S., Simla, 1977, in particular pp. 129–40.

13. See Wills, *Raj Gond*, paras 34, 35, 36 and 37. Also see R.C. Majumdar. ed., *The Delhi Sultanate*, Bharatiya Vidya Bhavan, Bombay, 1967, pp. 116–24 (on the invasion of Timur).

14. Fernand Braudel, *The Mediterranean and the Mediterranean World in the Age of Phillip II*, 2 vols., Fontana, 1978, Vol. 2, pp. 770ff.

15. *Ibid.*, pp. 785ff.

16. For Wills argument: the Garha kingdom as the 'inevitable consequence of a political vacuum'; see Wills, *Raj Gond*, paras 34 and 9.

17. *Ibid.*, paras 5, 6, 7 and 8.

18. *Ibid.*, para 34.

19. *Ibid.*, para 39.

20. The cult of *Nar Tullar*, the village goddess, common to both tribal and non-tribal communities to this day, is symbolic of the primal common space. See Grigson, *Maria Gonds*, pp. 193–207. For an account of the working of regional assemblies in Bastar, pp. 284–98. Also see V. Elwin, *The Religion of an Indian Tribe*, Oxford University Press, 1955, pp. 530–56.

21. In imperial records, rulers before Sangram Shah remain shadowy figures: persons and events remembered in folk traditions and fabricated genealogies. That invokes of course significance at another level: texture of folk memory untouched by the modern impingement or medieval imperial influences. For instance, the story of Yado Rai, a Rajput adventurer and the founder of Garha kingdom, being chosen as the husband by the only daughter of the Gond chief in a *swayamvar* like ceremony, *op. cit.*, Wills, *Raj Gond*, pp. 11–24.

    Concerning folk memory and the Ramnagar inscription (1667 AD, first published 1825, genealogy beginning with Yado Rai, 627 AD), which Wills convincingly refutes as 'fable and fabrication', see the first attempt at a history of Garha kingdom: W. Sleeman, 'History of Garha Mandla Rajas', *Journal of the Asiatic Society of Bengal*, Vol. VI, Part II, 1837, pp. 621–48.

22. According to Abul Fazl, Garha Katanga in the sixteenth century comprised territory '150 *kos* or 340 miles east to west' and '80 *kos* or 180 miles north to south'. A description Wills acknowledges as 'fairly accurate'. For Wills's estimate see, Wills, *Raj Gond*, paras 92 and 93.

23. For Abul Fazl's considerably inflated figures of Garha cavalry (20,000) at the time of Asaf Khan's conquest (1564) see *ibid.*, para 50; for figures of actual mobilisation on the battlefield see *ibid.*, para 52.

24. Detailed enumeration by Captain Gordon (1820–21) of the range of skills and professions practiced in the district of Nagpur, referred to as the *Gond Qila* in records of Shahjahan's reign, are indicative of a long process of slow dispersal of new crafts and skills along with extension of settled agriculture. See Richard Jenkins, *Report On the Territories of the Raja of Nagpur (1827)*, Government Press, Nagpur, 1923.

    'Artisan, mechanics and manufacturers' belonged to '29 castes' comprising 77,668 males of an estimated total male population of 249,844. pp. 13–14.

    For the town of Nagpur, twenty-nine trades are listed. Among them weavers and spinners are most numerous, followed by builders and stone masons, carpenters and blacksmiths, p. 44.

    Quite in consonance with the prevalent ethos within the tribal contiguity, Jenkins noted:

    > A peasant or mechanic, of the lowest order, will sit down of his own accord, tell his story without ceremony, and converse more like an equal than an inferior . . . p. 28.

25. Wills, *Raj Gond*, paras 40 and 46.
26. *Ibid.*, para 43.
27. W.H., Sleeman, *Rambles and Recollections of An Indian Official*, J. Hatchard, *1844*, pp. 644ff, and 14ff.
28. Hira Lal, *Inscriptions in the Central Provinces and Berar*, Government Press, Nagpur, 1924, p. i ff.
29. Wills, *Raj Gond*, paras 48 and 49.

30. *Op. cit.*, Sleeman, pp. 14ff.
31. *Akbarnama*, Vol. 2, pp. 327ff.
32. *Loc. cit.*
33. Wills, *Raj Gond*, para 66.
34. *Ibid.*, pp. 123–36.
35. Rihand dam (1961) followed by large-scale coal mining and thermal power generation (1970s) have completely transformed the landscape, demography and the rhythm of human living in a region which had just about known the use of bullock carts. Enormous investments have been made and an impressive high-tech modern infrastructure erected in this region. But for local communities, mostly tribal, this has meant continual dispersion and devastation.

    See *Vikas ki Keemat* (Hindi), SETU, Ahmedabad, 1985. And S.K. Grover, 'Quality Parameters of Coal and Singrauli Coalfield', *Urja*, March 1982, pp. 155–76.
36. See H.C.A. Conybear, 'Report On Land Revenue Settlement of Mirzapur District—Note On Pargana Dudhi of Mirzapur District', 1879 (unpublished report), paras 33 to 53.
37. C.L.R. Glasfurd, *Report On the Dependency of Bustar*, 1863, Foreign Department, Gen. A. Pro. Feb/1863, No. 151/156.

    Also, *Report On the Zamindarees and Other Petty Chieftaincies in the Central Provinces*, Nagpur, 1863.
38. See Glasfurd, *Report*, para 175.
39. Nicola Chiaromonte, *The Paradox of History*, University of Pennsylvania Press, 1985, pp. 17–50.
40. C. Elliot, *Report On the Bastar and Kharonde Dependencies of Raepore District (1855)*, in *Selections From Records*, Foreign Department, No. XXX of 1861.
41. Blunt's account of the hill country between Kaimur and the Godavari furnished the almost only available information to colonial rulers till the mid-nineteenth century. See Captain J.T. Blunt, 'Narrative of a Route from Chunarghur to Yertnagoodum, in the Ellore Circar, in *Early European Travellers in the Nagpur Territories*, reprinted from old records (Nagpur, 1924), pp. 91–174.
42. *Ibid.*, p. 106.
43. *Ibid.*, p. 102.
44. *Ibid.*, pp. 104ff.
45. *Ibid.*, p. 108.
46. *Ibid.*, pp. 109ff. Corrair or Koria was a fairly large chiefship with an area of 1,631 sq. miles, but only 250 villages, see *Imperial Gazetteer of India*, Vol. 10, Clarendon Press, 1908, Table III, p. 102.
47. *Ibid.*, pp. 110ff. *Tilak* at the coronation ceremony had to be offered by the former Gond rulers, Jenkins, *Report*, p. 75.
48. Blunt, 'Narrative', p. 110.
49. *Ibid.*, pp. 99ff, 100ff, 109ff.
50. Cf. E. Clementi Smith, 'The Bastar Rebellion, 1910', *Man In India*, Vol. 27, 1947, pp. 239–53.
51. Blunt, 'Narrative', pp. 110–11.
52. *Loc. cit.* On the nature and extent of tribute under Bhonsale rule see Jenkins, *Report*, pp. 131–42.
53. Wills, *Raj Gond*, para 59.

54. *Ibid.*, paras 65ff.
55. *Ibid.*, para 66.
56. *Akbarnama*, pp. 328ff.
57. *Loc. cit.*
58. Wills, *Raj Gond*, paras 110 and 111. Under the Marathas, Jenkins, *Report*, pp. 137ff.
59. Wills, *Raj Gond*, para 105.
60. *Ibid.*, para 111.
61. *Loc. cit.*
62. *Ibid.*, para 114.
63. *Loc. cit.*
64. *Ibid.*, pp. 146–50.
65. *Loc. cit.*
66. According to the local tradition cited in *Bastar Bhusan*, Anam Dev is said to have entered Bastar with 2,000 soldiers. To sustain such a large body of men for any length of time on the revenue collected would have been impossible. In 1855, Elliot reported the Bastar revenue as being Rs. 30,000. In 1830, the Raja had been compelled to part with the Sihawa tract in lieu of the annual tribute of Rs. 5,000 the Marathas had levied. *Bastar Bhusan* takes pointed note of instances of the King's servants being beaten up in the interior on suspicion of rude or improper behaviour. Hence the fact of early enclaves of settled cultivation in the hinterland began as settlements of *paik* militias.
67. Grigson, *Maria Gonds*, pp. 284–98. Jenkins, *Report*, pp. 264–80.
68. C.U. Wills, 'The Territorial System of the Rajput Kingdoms of Medieval Chattisgarh', J.A.S.B., New Series, Vol. 15, 1919, pp. 197–262.

John Beames referring to Tod's remark in the *Annals* on the significance and prevalence of these other numbers in India, see John Beames, *History, Folklore of the Races of the North-Western Provinces of India*, 2 vols. (1869), Reprint, Gian Publications, 1980.

John Beames, referring to Tod's remark in the *Annals* that *chaurasies* are comparable to the 'Saxon Hundreds', argues that unlike the 'Saxon Hundreds', *chaurasies* originally always contained eighty-four villages, 'even though it may have dwindled down to ten or twelve villages, of which every originally component village' local tradition may not be able to identify. (Vol. 2, p. 84).

Beames cites nearly a hundred instances of *chaurasies* prevalent in north and central India. A few examples 'in Deoli, . . . in Etawah, there is a chaurasi of Trilokchandi Bai's Rajputs'.

'The Pargannah of Kuraoili, in Mainpuri, constitutes a chaurasi of Rathor Rajputs'.

'In Pargannah Kantit, of Zillah Mirzapur, there is a chaurasi of Gharwar Rajputs'.

'From Allahabad to Karra there is a chaurasi of Johya Rajputs'.

'. . . a Chaurasi of Rangars in Pargannah Kata of Saharanpur'.

'. . . Chaurasi of Chauhan Rajputs in Bhopal'. (Vol. 2, p. 53).

'Garu Kota in Damoh of Sangor is a Bundela Chaurasi. In the same Pargannah the Deswal Ahirs had half a Chaurasi . . . a Taluka Chaurasi to the north of the Son (Soane) in Azori Barhar of Mirzapur . . . the Bunaphar Rajputs have a Chaurasi in Garha Mandla'. (Vol. 2, pp. 52–53).

Beames also cites numerous instances of the prevalence of the larger terri-torial and clan divisions of 360, which number, . . . bears an intimate relation to the Chaurasi, and is based on the same principle of computation . . . for territorial subdivisions there is no intermediate number between 84 and 360 (Vol. 2, p. 55).

Concerning the cosmological and mythological significance of *chaurasi*:

> . . . the emblemetical figure of Surya, the Indian Sun. He is represented with 12 spokes of his wheel indicating, as the Bhagwata expressly says, the number of months, and sitting under a canopy formed by the 7 heads of the Coluber Naga. He is also represented driving 7 steeds and also has 12 titles, form or manifestations which denote his distinct powers . . . . The allegorical import of this Chaurasi is so evident that we need go no further to assign the causes for the selection of this mutiple of 7 and 12 to represent territorial subdivisions in India; no numbers being considered more appropriate for the purpose than those which bear reference to the motion of the Earth, the revolving seasons, and the succession of seed time and harvest (Vol. 2, pp. 74–75).

69. Wills, *Territorial System*, pp. 202ff.
70. Wills, *Territorial System*, pp. 224–25, p. 249.
71. Hira Lal, *Inscriptions*, No. 213.
72. See James Macmurdo, *Journal of a Route Through Peninsula of Guzaraut in the year 1809 and 1810*, in Suresh Chandra Ghosh, ed., *The Peninsula of Gujarat in the Early Nineteenth Century*, Sterling, 1977, p. 124.
73. The King of Bali, in response to the plea of a villager, sought to have the *panchayat's* judgement reversed. The *panchayat* simply told him, 'slowly, obliquely, and even more deferentially, to go fly a kite'. See Clifford Geertz, *Local Knowledge: Further Essays in Interpretive Anthropology*, Basic Books, 1983, pp. 176–81.
74. R.V. Russel, *Report of the Land Revenue Settlement of Damoh Disrict*, 1866, para 36.
75. Wills, *Raj Gond*, p. 189.
76. J.W. Chisholm, 'Report of the Land Revenue Settlement of Bilaspur District', 1868 (unpublished report), para 64.
77. P. Vans Agnew, 'A Report on the Subah or Province of Chattisgarh', 1820 (unpublished report), p.10.
78. Glasfurd, *Report*, para 139.
79. S.C. Macpherson, *Report Upon the Khonds of the District of Ganjam and Cuttack*, Madras, 1863, pp. 17ff.
    Also see Bailey's study of their contemporary situation, F. Bailey, *Tribe, Caste and Nation*, Manchester University Press, 1960.
80. *Ibid.*, pp. 92ff.
81. *Ibid.*, para 36, p. 19.
82. *Ibid.*, para 42, p. 20.
83. *Ibid.*, pp. 20ff.
84. *Ibid.*, para 41, p. 19.
85. *Loc. cit.*
86. *Ibid.*, pp. 20–21.

87. *Ibid.*, para 31, p. 18.
88. *Ibid.*, para 50, p. 21.
89. *Ibid.*, pp. 19–20.
90. *Ibid.*, pp. 20–27.
91. *Ibid.*, pp. 32-38.
92. *Ibid.*, p. 30.
93. *Ibid.*, p. 22.
94. Grigson, *Maria Gonds*, p. 10.
95. Kedarnath Thakur, *Bastar Bhusan* (1908), Itihas Deepan, Ratanpur, 1982.
96. Glasfurd, *Report*, para 172.
97. *Loc. cit.*
98. *Ibid.*, Appendix IX.
99. Thakur, *Bastar Bhusan*.
100. Even now in Garpa, a relatively exposed village of Abujhamad, it is impossible to hire wage labour. Last year in order to construct a new school building the administration had to bring labourers from Narayanpur.
101. See Chisholm, *Report*, note 41, para 7.
102. C.B. Lucie-Smith, 'Report on the Land Revenue Settlement of Chanda District', 1870 (unpublished report), para 56.
103. Grigson, *Maria Gonds*, p. 37.
104. Grigson, *Maria Gonds*, p. 32.
105. The 1981 census lists 67.79 per cent of Bastar inhabitants as 'scheduled tribes', Census of India 1981, Series III Madhya Pradesh, Part III B Primary Census Abstract, Director of Census Operations, Madhya Pradesh, Statement 8, pp. 8–9.
106. Grigson, *Maria Gonds*, p. 28.
107. Personal communication.
108. *Op. cit.*, de Brett; para 50.
109. *Ibid.*, para 52.
110. Glasfurd, *Report*, para 66.
111. Macpherson, *Report*, pp. 30ff.
112. Lucie-Smith, *Report* and *Op. cit.*, Chisholm.
113. Jenkins, *Report*, pp. 32–34.
114. *Op. cit.*, Conybear, *Report*, para 61.
115. Lucie-Smith, *Report*, and Chisholm, *Report*.
116. Explanatory Notes on Forest Law, Government of India, Nagpur, 1926, pp. 18–32.
117. *Ibid.*, pp. 12ff.
118. *Ibid.*, pp. 7ff.
119. *Vikas ki Keemat*, pp. 99ff
120. *Ibid.*
121. Logical consequence of redemarcating rights and obligations in terms of individual proprietory rights, in an area where the definitive referent had been not proprietory rights but customary rights of usage. Cultivators working little plots on land variously characterised as *varg char, shaskiya zameen*, 'forest land' are mostly descendants of shifting cultivators who made a precarious transition to some form of settled cultivation during the last hundred years.
122. Grover, 'Quality Parameters', pp. 155–76.

123. See *Vikas ki Keemat—Singrauli Mein Visthapam Ki Samsya*, Setu, Ahmedabad, 1985.
124. The cultural analogue to this impoverishment is strikingly manifest in the enhanced quality of houses built with local materials and traditional crafts.

Select Bibliography

Bailey, F. *Tribe, Caste and Nation,* Manchester University Press, 1960.

Beames, John. *History, Folklore of the Races of North-Western Provinces of India,* 2 vols (1869), Gian Publications, 1980.

Bose, Sardindu. *Carrying Capacity of Land Under Shifting Cultivation,* Asiatic Society, 1967.

Brandis, D. and **A. Smythies** (eds.). *Proceedings of the Forest Conference* (October 1875, Simla), Calcutta, 1876.

Cassirer, Ernest. *Language and Myth,* Dover Publications, New York, 1953.

Census of India, 1981, Series II, Madhya Pradesh, Part II.B, Primary Census Abstract, Director of Census Operation, M.P.

Census of India, Series-I, Paper 2 of 1984, Registrar General and Census Commissioner, India, 1984.

Chisholm, J.W. *Report on the Land Revenue Settlement of Bilaspore,* 1868.

Constituent Assembly of India, Government of India Press, New Delhi, Vol. 7, 1949.

Conybear, H.C.A. *Report on the Land Revenue Settlement of Mirzapur District,* 1879.

Coomaraswamy, A.K. *What is Civilization and Other Essays,* OUP, Delhi, 1989.

Crosby, Alfred W. *Ecological Imperialism—The Biological Expansion of Europe 900–1900,* Cambridge University Press, 1986.

Dalton, E.T. *Descriptive Ethnology of Bengal,* Calcutta, 1872.

———. *The Kols of Chota Nagpur,* 1872.

de Brett, E.A. *Chhattisgarh Feudatory States Gazetteer,* Bombay, 1909.

Drake-Brockman, D.L. *Mirzapur Gazetteer, 1911.*

Elliot, Captain. *Report on the Bastar and Kharonde Dependencies of Raepore District,* Selection from records, Foreign Department, No. XXX of 1861.

Elwin, Verrier. *The Baiga,* Oxford University Press, London, 1939.

———. *The Muria and their Ghotul,* Oxford University Press, Bombay, 1947.

———. *The Agaria,* Oxford University Press, 1949.

———. *The Tribal Art of Middle India,* Oxford University Press, 1949.

———. *The Religion of an Indian Tribe.* Oxford University Press, Bombay, 1955.

Eschmann, A., H. Kulke and **G.C. Tripathi.** *The Cult of Jagannath and the Regional Tradition of Orissa,* Manohar Publishers, New Delhi, 1979.

Forsyth, J. *The Highlands of Central India,* London, 1871.

Fukuoka, M. *One Straw Revolution—An Introduction to Natural Farming,* Friends Rural Centre, Rasulia, Hoshangabad, 1985.

Geertz, Clifford. *Agricultural Involution—The Process of Agricultural Change in Indonesia,* University of California Press, 1969.

Glasfurd, C.L.R. *Report on the Dependency of Bastar, 1982,* Foreign Department, General A., Pro. Feb/1863, Nos. 151–156.

Grigson, W.V. *The Maria Gonds of Bastar,* Oxford University Press, Bombay, 1938.

————. *The Aboriginal Problem in the C.P. and Berar,* Nagpur, 1944.

Hamilton, Walter. *East India Gazetteer,* London, 1828.

Lal, Hira. *Inscriptions in the Central Provinces and Berar,* Nagpur, 1924.

The Imperial Gazetteer of India, Vol. X, Clarendon Press, Oxford, 1908.

Jenkins, Richard. *Report on the Territories of the Raja of Nagpur (1827),* Nagpur, 1923.

Latham, R.G. *Ethnology in India,* 1859.

Lattimore, Owen. *Inner Asian Frontiers of China,* Beacon Press, Boston, 1962.

Luice-Smith, C.B. *Report on the Land Revenue Settlement of Chanda District,* 1870.

Macpherson, S.C. *Report Upon the Khonds of the District of Ganjam and Cuttack,* Madras, 1863.

Maine, Henry. *Ancient Law,* London, 1861.

Pastoral Production and Society. Proceedings of the International Ministry on Nomadic Pastoralism, Paris, December 1–3, 1976, Cambridge, 1979.

Report of the Commissioner of Scheduled Castes and Scheduled Tribes, New Delhi.

Report of the National Commission on Agriculture, Vol. IX, Ministry of Agriculture and Irrigation, New Delhi, 1976.

Report of Socio-Economic Survey of Abujhamad, Tribal Research Institute, Chindwara, Madhya Pradesh, 1963.

Roy, S.C., *The Hill Bhuiyas of Orissa,* Ranchi, 1935.

————. *Mundas and their Country (1912),* Asia Publishing House, New Delhi, 1970.

Russel, R.V. and **Hira Lal.** *Tribes and Castes of Central India (1916),* 4 vols., Cosmo Publications, Delhi, 1975.

Swaminathan, J. *The Perceiving Fingers,* Bharat Bhavan, Bhopal, 1987.

Swidden Cultivation In Asia, 3 vols., UNESCO Regional Office of Education in Asia and Pacific, Bangkok, 1983.

Temple, Sir Richard. *Report on the Zamindarees and Other Petty Chieftaincies in the Central Provinces,* Nagpore, 1863.

Thakkar, A.V. *The Problem of Aborigines in India,* Gokhale Institute of Politics and Economics, Poona, 1946.

Thakur, Kedarnath. *Bastar Bhusan,* Benares, 1908.

Vans Agnew, P. *A Report on the Subah or Province of Chhattisgarh, 1820.*

Ward, H.C.E. *Report on the Land Revenue Settlement of the Mundlah District,* Bombay, 1870.

Wills, C.U. *Early European Travellers in the Nagpur Territories,* Nagpur, 1924.

————. *The Raj Gond Maharajas of the Satpura Hills,* Nagpur, 1925.

Index

Abujhamad, location of, 140–41; as living rhythm of shifting cultivation, 140ff, 159ff, 173 n102, 174 n104, 196; quality of distance in, 140–41; Sonpur as a proximity of *kehti* to *penda,* 160ff; *sirhas,* 160ff; *patdevas,* 161ff; Garpa, 141, 142, 162ff, 173 n93; bari, 141, 142, 163ff; *medai,* 160ff; Kudantola, 161ff; Halbas, 159, 160, 172 n82

Abul Fazl, 179, 180, 183, 187, 199

Administration of things', 21, 26–27, 39; and freedom, 24, 40–41

Agarias, 119–27; in modern perception, 129; the last survivals, 124ff, 139–40; as tribal mediation, 119–27, 158, 172 n76; as possibility, 123, 125ff; absence in national discourse, 126, 127; techniques of iron smelting, 122–24

approximation, the concept of, 85–87, 95–97, 158

autonomy, cultural referents, 51 n39; as principle of self-governance, 30–31; in modern discourse, 29–34, 48 n27; nature of, 30, 48 n26

Bastar, Anam Dev, 116, 194ff; Barsur ruins, 115, 117ff; pre-modern revenue system, 114; the hub of tribal contiguity, 109–10; and political authority, 184–88; Garhwas of, 95, 104, 118–19, 137 n46; history of, 115ff; location of, 109–10; Nagvansi rulers of, 116–17

Blunt, J.T., 112, 185ff

Bose P.N., 120, 121

Braudel, Fernand, 19–20, 110, 178

Cassirer, Ernest, 72

centre–periphery, 13, 22, 33, 85

change, as organic process, 23; as progress, 23–25, 61, 62; and legitimacy of distinctness, 96–97, 116ff, 137 n44

Christianity, heresy and its modern analouges, 25; the pagan Graeco–Roman past, 37, 41 n11, /45 n15

class, as social homologue of technology, 32, 33, 48 n28; as principle

of modern cohesion, 32; and
the modern universal, 34
cognitive closures, the concept of, 31,
46 n18; in modern discourse,
28, 74–75, 127–29; as structure
of attention, 27–28, 72–75
colonial, rule, 24, 66–68; discourse,
68–70
colonialism, as instrument of unification and progress, 55–56,
65–71; and tribal identity,
58–59, 78 n7; natives as victims of, 70–71, 82 n31
Coomaraswamy, A.K., 153
culture, cultural diversity, 11, 19ff, 35;
as fragmented survival, 87–88,
104, 137 n43

development, as statement of human
presence and nature, 21ff
distance, as measure of space and history, 110ff, 178; as measure of
social consent, 188–92; as
measure of proximity to nature,
113; the modern universal and
the conquest of, 46 n19, 110ff

ecology, 13, 27
Eliade, Mircea, 21
Elwin, V., 119, 121, 124, 125, 127,
143, 145
Europe, culture of, 37, 76 n3; nomadic incursions and, 19; and the
Ottaman Empire, 19–20;
Graeco–Roman past and the
Renaissance, 37, 41 fn11, 45
fn15; significance of Mediterranean, 19–20; casting of Neo-,
152–53, 170 n49
evolutionism, 11ff, 44 n12, 47 n23

fact, and value, 12, 55–58, 77 n6; and
change, 58, 59
famine, shifting cultivation and
absence of, 90–91, 196, 198,
163–64, 173 n102
Forsyth, J., 128, 143
Fukuoka, M., 75

Gandhi, M.K., 13, 28, 71, 75, 126–27
Garha Mandala, history of the Gond
dynasty, 176; as regional centre
of power, 176–78; relationship
with Mughal Empire, 187ff;
Deogarha, 183, 187–88; San-
gram Shah, 176, 182; relation-
ship with the Marathas, 186ff
Geertz, C., 69, 71, 166, 191
Glasfurd, C.L.R., 111–14, 116, 195
Gramsci, A., 37, 43 n9
Grigson, W.V., 115, 127, 145

Habermas, J., 71
Hegel, G.W.F., 12
Hind Swaraj, 47 n22, 75
humanism, 24, 26, 88

Indus Valley Civilization,   103–5
iron (also see Agaria),   103–4,
119–27

kheti, as a statement of human presence and nature, 88–89; the
concept of, 158; as proximity
to *penda*, 162ff; and famine,
disease and epidemics, 133 n8,
90–91
Khonds, 154, 193ff
Kosambi, D.D., 87–88, 103

Levi-Strauss, C., 20, 37, 38, 52–53,
152–53; and ethnology, 68;
'Neolithic paradox', 20
limits, 52–55, 71–72, 96–97; and tribal
sensibility, 129–32
Lohia, R., 29, 47 n21, 74

Man, and nature, 22, 68–70, 86–87, 99
n23, 111ff; as primum mobile,
22–23; things as measure of,
36–42; and history, 24–25, 31,
45 n13
Marx, K., 24–25, 32
Marxist, critique of industrial society,
24; vision, 28, 32–33, 34, 61
memory, folk-memory, 63–64, 104,
201; and systematic thought,